This adorable skep, or beehive, hat will charm everyone. Make it in a few hours using knit and purl stitches. A few bee buttons add a touch of whimsy. (Knitter: Barbara Morgenroth; model: Randi Dorman)

For cold ears, this warm wool headband may be just the thing you need. Quickly knit in a wide rib, and embellish it with cute buttons like the hearts pictured. (Knitter: Barbara Morgenroth; model: Denise Butts)

Ponchos are all the rage now. You can complete this one quickly by using large needles and thick and thin bulky yarn to add texture. (Knitter: Mim Holden; model: Terrie Storm)

On a chilly night, a throw might be ideal to snuggle under. This one uses two strands of worsted weight yarn to speed the project along and requires only knit and purl stitches. (Knitter: Mim Holden)

This glamorous wrap uses three different fashion yarns for maximum eye appeal. Knit on large needles, this project can be accomplished easily over a weekend. (Knitter: Mim Holden; model: Barbara Cossentino)

How you alternate the yarn and the colors you use for the wrap are up to you. Bright and wild or understated sophistication, the yarns used will change the look entirely. (Knitter: Mim Holden)

A simple crew neck sweater can become so fashionable by interchanging stripes of luxury or fashion yarns with plain worsted weight wool. You want eye-catching? Use different stitches for unexpected bursts of texture. (Knitter: Mim Holden; model: Tonia Northrop)

Using unexpected yarns can create a truly unique project. Substitute at will—just be sure you have the same weight and yardage. (Knitter: Mim Holden)

Here's a short sleeved, sporty shrug for a brisk walk in the hills or a leisurely stroll through the park. Buttery soft merino makes this shrug a pleasure to wear. (Knitter: Barbara Morgenroth; model: Terrie Storm)

This dramatic shawl is easily knit on large needles and using ribbon yarn in garter stitch. (Knitter: Freyalynn Close-Hainsworth; model: Barbara Cossentino)

A basic child's vest can be as fanciful as your imagination allows. Use a contrasting color for the ribbing and neckline with a third color for the armholes. Clever buttons can tell a story like this escaping balloons sweater.
(Knitter: Barbara Morgenroth; model: Denise Butts)

Simple styling makes this vest a classic and a necessity for your wardrobe. Your choice of yarn can make it casual or classy.
(Knitter: Mim Holden; model: Barbara Cossentino)

Use decorative pillows to suit your needs. This Moose Pillow is perfect for a weekend retreat and is speedily completed using stockinette and duplicate stitches. (Knitter: Diana Taylor)

Mittens not only keep your hands warm, but they also can add color and creativity to your wardrobe. Use plain worsted weight yarn for the hand section, but go wild for the ribbing. Or the other way around! (Knitter: Diana Taylor, model: Lori Butta)

If your cell phone always seems to be lost in the bottom of your purse, try this handy cell phone fish cozy. Decorate it with beads or even sequins if you want scales. (Knitter: Helen Crandall)

Filled with potpourri or scented filling, this strawberry sachet is too pretty to hang in the closet. Keep the door open so you can see it and appreciate the aroma, too. (Knitter and designer: Monette Satterfield)

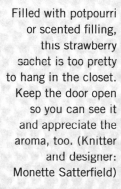

This chemo cap is made of the most luxurious silk yarns available for the softest wearing experience ever. (Knitter: Diana Taylor; model: Terrie Storm)

Ear flap hats are so popular and so easily knit. This one has a traditional tree motif you often see in Scandinavian designs. (Knitter: Diana Taylor; model: Randi Dorman)

If you need something to cover your shoulders, a capelet may be perfect. Alternate colors and textures of yarn to boost eye-appeal.
(Knitter: Barbara Morgenroth; model: Barbara Cossentino)

Everyone is wearing scarves these days, as they're so fashionable. This one is made in worsted weight yarn in the fan and feather or Old Shale stitch.
(Knitter: Barbara Morgenroth; model: Terrie Storm)

This felted trinket bag was made in a bulky merino wool. A space dyed yarn adds plenty of color to a simple design. (Knitter: Barbara Morgenroth)

A cowl can take the place of a scarf. Make it in soft yarn so it crushes softly around your neck. (Knitter: Helen Crandall; model: Barbara Cossentino)

Bulky wool makes it possible to knit these slippers up quickly. Easy enough for someone just starting out their knitting experience. (Knitter: Barbara Morgenroth; model: Barbara Cossentino)

These wristlets blooming out from the bottom of your coat can add the finishing touch to a winter outfit. They can also keep your wrists warm! (Knitter: Barbara Morgenroth; model: Terrie Storm)

This tunic is a simple design, which lets the thick and thin sport weight yarn add texture. Substitute yarn as you wish—just keep the same weight and yardage. (Knitter: Carol Moore; model: Barbara Cossentino)

Here's a sweater for warm weather. This is a simple T-shirt knit in a worsted weight cotton. Embellish to your heart's content. (Knitter: Mim Holden; model: Terrie Storm)

Once you wear hand-knit socks, you won't want to go back to commercial ones. A yarn with a little bit of elastic is forgiving if you don't get the sizing quite right the first few attempts. (Knitter: Diana Taylor; model: Terrie Storm)

When legwarmers are too much, these worsted weight wool leglets might be just enough. Knit and purl rib at the top and bottom keep them snug, but the middle section raspberry stitch supplies texture. (Knitter: Barbara Morgenroth; model: Barbara Cossentino)

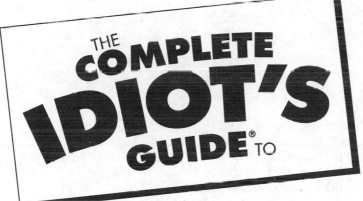

THE
COMPLETE
IDIOT'S
GUIDE® TO

Knitting Projects

Illustrated

by Barbara Morgenroth

ALPHA

A member of Penguin Group (USA) Inc.

To Malcolm and Peter, my guardian angels.

ALPHA BOOKS

Published by the Penguin Group

Penguin Group (USA) Inc., 375 Hudson Street, New York, New York 10014, U.S.A.

Penguin Group (Canada), 10 Alcorn Avenue, Toronto, Ontario, Canada M4V 3B2 (a division of Pearson Penguin Canada Inc.)

Penguin Books Ltd, 80 Strand, London WC2R 0RL, England

Penguin Ireland, 25 St Stephen's Green, Dublin 2, Ireland (a division of Penguin Books Ltd)

Penguin Group (Australia), 250 Camberwell Road, Camberwell, Victoria 3124, Australia (a division of Pearson Australia Group Pty Ltd)

Penguin Books India Pvt Ltd, 11 Community Centre, Panchsheel Park, New Delhi—10 017, India

Penguin Group (NZ), cnr Airborne and Rosedale Roads, Albany, Auckland 1310, New Zealand (a division of Pearson New Zealand Ltd)

Penguin Books (South Africa) (Pty) Ltd, 24 Sturdee Avenue, Rosebank, Johannesburg 2196, South Africa

Penguin Books Ltd, Registered Offices: 80 Strand, London WC2R 0RL, England

International Standard Book Number: 1-59257-426-2
Library of Congress Catalog Card Number: 2006925726

08   07   06   8   7   6   5   4   3   2   1

Interpretation of the printing code: The rightmost number of the first series of numbers is the year of the book's printing; the rightmost number of the second series of numbers is the number of the book's printing. For example, a printing code of 06-1 shows that the first printing occurred in 2006.

Printed in the United States of America

Note: This publication contains the opinions and ideas of its author. It is intended to provide helpful and informative material on the subject matter covered. It is sold with the understanding that the author and publisher are not engaged in rendering professional services in the book. If the reader requires personal assistance or advice, a competent professional should be consulted.

The author and publisher specifically disclaim any responsibility for any liability, loss, or risk, personal or otherwise, which is incurred as a consequence, directly or indirectly, of the use and application of any of the contents of this book.

Most Alpha books are available at special quantity discounts for bulk purchases for sales promotions, premiums, fund-raising, or educational use. Special books, or book excerpts, can also be created to fit specific needs.

For details, write: Special Markets, Alpha Books, 375 Hudson Street, New York, NY 10014.

Publisher: *Marie Butler-Knight*
Editorial Director: *Mike Sanders*
Managing Editor: *Billy Fields*
Executive Editor: *Randy Ladenheim-Gil*
Senior Development Editor: *Christy Wagner*
Production Editor: *Megan Douglass*

Copy Editor: *Krista Hansing*
Cover Designer: *Bill Thomas*
Book Designer: *Trina Wurst*
Indexer: *Angie Bess*
Layout: *Chad Dressler*
Proofreader: *Mary Hunt*

Contents at a Glance

Contents

Introduction

These days, everyone—from celebrities to the woman across from you on the bus—seems to be picking up knitting needles and yarn. It looks great but complicated. You wonder, is knitting for you?

Sure, it is! Knitting is a wonderful pastime because it can be what you want it to be. After you master a few simple techniques, you can make any number of projects. You can just relax and knit. If you have a commute to work, you can knit your way there and back. If you have to wait for an appointment, you can knit the time away.

Knitting can also afford great challenges. There are always new stitches or approaches to learn. You can cast on one way and use it for months or years and then learn a new way—along with it a feeling of accomplishment. As you progress in your skills, perhaps you'll learn colorwork such as intarsia or fair isle, and when you complete a project successfully, you'll feel a real sense of achievement. Turning the heel of a sock for the first time is a milestone.

Knitting keeps your hands and mind busy, but there's so much more to it than that. There's the delightful tactile nature of knitting. You hold smooth wooden needles in your hands as soft strands of wool slowly become a lovely garment. The colors can soothe you and please your eyes as you work. Or you may be energetically knitting stitch after stitch on shiny needles, rapidly turning fiber into wearable art.

In this book, I offer patterns for a range of knitting abilities. I've included patterns and suggestions for those who are unsure of their knitting skills and others for those who are more confident. A world of opportunity exists in these pages.

So stop fearing knitting, and pick up your needles and yarn. You'll soon master a skill that will see you through all the phases of your life—and become a most pleasant way of expressing yourself.

How to Use This Book

If you're just embarking on your knitting adventure, I suggest you start with a hat or a scarf, or any of the projects near the front of the book. Of course, some of us like to dive right in and attempt a challenge, and I'd never dream of dissuading you. Deciding to make something you really want can be a great motivator. Remember, whether you consider yourself a complete beginner or more of a novice, read the directions thoroughly before proceeding. It's amazing how many questions will be answered if you just take some time to organize your thoughts before you pick up your needles.

In each pattern, I give you a list of all the materials you need. Be sure to have everything you need at hand. Find a quiet, comfortable, and well-lighted spot where you can knit uninterrupted. Often one needs intense concentration when learning a new skill. That's true with knitting, too. After all, you're engaging not only your mind, but your fingers and hands as well. It can be quite disturbing to have the world suddenly and unexpectedly enter your private space when you're attempting to focus on the task before you.

Have patience, have confidence, and persist—you'll quickly find that knitting is for you.

Extras

Throughout each chapter of this book, I've added a few types of extra information in boxes to help you learn even more about knitting:

Knit Tips

Check these boxes for suggestions or advice to make your knitting experience easier or to learn specific techniques you may need to complete projects.

Purl Pearls

These boxes offer facts about knitting and fibers to increase your understanding.

Knots!

Be sure to read these boxes, as they offer warnings about knitting blunders to avoid.

Wild and Woolly Words

Knitting has a jargon all its own. These boxes are mini-dictionaries that define new or unfamiliar terms.

Acknowledgments

A book is often a collaborative project, and I've never worked on one that required more teamwork than this one. Truly without my technical editor, Monette Satterfield, and my illustrators, Freyalynn Close-Hainsworth and Alexandra Tiffin, this book would have been impossible. Thanks to Alexa Dawn Rose for her assistance.

Mim Holden, Diana Taylor, Helen Crandall, and Carol Moore: without my knitters and their input, the projects could never have been completed in time. I want to thank Marcos Feder for his generous contribution of Malabrigo Yarn, as well as Joan of Cascade Yarns and Iris Schreier of Artyarns. To my models, Barbara Cossentino, Terrie Storm, Lori and Denise Butts, Tonia Northrop, and Randi Dorman: thank you for making everything look so wearable!

Special thanks must go to Marilyn Allen and Coleen O'Shea. And Randy Ladenheim-Gil deserves a gold star.

Others contributed in nonknitting ways. Jerry Dupree, my Nikon mentor. John and Nancy Hegyi, gratitude and tomatoes doesn't cover it. Dr. Michael Thoesen and the team at Cornell Veterinary Hospital. Jon Kaplowitz: *Nunc Tutus Exitus Computarus*. Thank you, Rabbi Shlomo Yaffe. Thanks, Randy.

Daisy, Pippi, and Sasha, as always, my family. Will, Sparky, and Iris, you are remembered.

Trademarks

All terms mentioned in this book that are known to be or are suspected of being trademarks or service marks have been appropriately capitalized. Alpha Books and Penguin Group (USA) Inc. cannot attest to the accuracy of this information. Use of a term in this book should not be regarded as affecting the validity of any trademark or service mark.

The following manufacturers' products have been mentioned in this book:

Artyarns

Austermann Yarns

Cascade Yarns

La Mode Buttons®

Malabrigo Yarns

Noro Yarns

In This Chapter

- ◆ Learn how to begin and end knitting

- ◆ Understand how to increase and decrease or pick up dropped stitches

- ◆ Get a tutorial on reading patterns and graphs

- ◆ Read tips on selecting the right yarn

- ◆ Find out what swatching is and discover the importance of proper tension

- ◆ Properly care for your knitted items

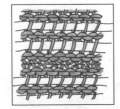
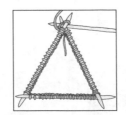

Chapter 1

Knitting Basics

Knitting has become fashionable again, although some of us didn't notice when it wasn't hip to knit! All we can say is, welcome! Years ago, I went to a famous astrologer, and she encouraged me to keep knitting because it grounds those who do it. I don't know about the Earth, Wind, and Fire aspects of knitting, but most people agree it keeps your hands busy. Knitting keeps your mind busy as well, as you challenge yourself with ever-more-difficult projects. And knitting keeps your wardrobe busy, as you constantly add new things to wear!

In this book, I assume you know a little about knitting. Before we get to the projects, though, let's go over a few basics, in case you get in the middle of a project and can't remember something important.

Beginning or Casting On

You can cast on in several ways. The method you use depends on the project—or your mood: sometimes you use one, sometimes another.

I give you instructions for beginning with the following three methods:

- Single cast on
- Basic knit stitch
- Continental cast on

Single Cast On

1. Make a loop, slip it onto the needle, and pull the yarn tight to form a slip knot.

Make a slip knot, and snug the yarn firmly.

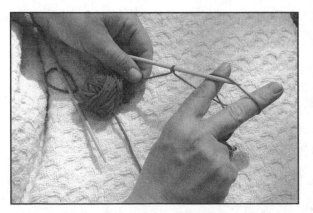

Using your right hand, make a loop, twist it, and slip it onto the left needle.

2. Using your right hand, make a loop, twist it, and slip it onto the left needle.

3. Keep going until you have enough stitches. (Your pattern will tell you how many stitches you need.)

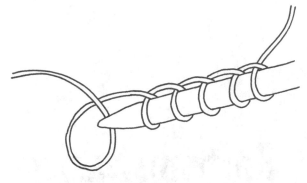

The simplest cast on method.

Basic Knit Stitch

1. Insert the right needle into a stitch on the left needle, front to back.

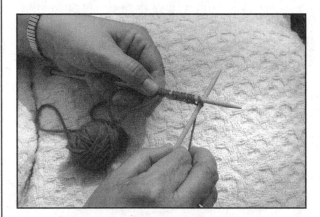

The needle tip goes through the loop.

2. Yarn over the needle and draw the loop through the stitch.

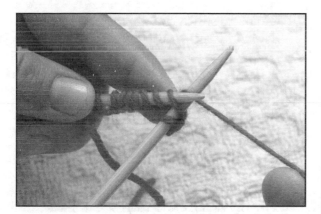

Yarn over and draw the loop through.

3. Slide the stitch from the left needle, and repeat until all the stitches are on the right needle.

Continue knitting until all the stitches are on the right needle.

Continental Cast On

1. Make a slip knot about 20" from the end of the yarn.

2. Slip it onto the needle you'll hold in your right hand.

3. Insert your left thumb and forefinger between the tail and the skein-side yarn pieces.

4. Spread your thumb and forefinger apart, and, with the needle, form a triangle.

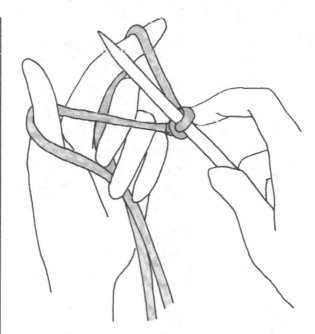

Keep *light* tension on the yarn.

5. Lower the needle so it's parallel to your palm.

6. Bring the point of the needle to the outside of your thumb, and loop it under that piece of yarn.

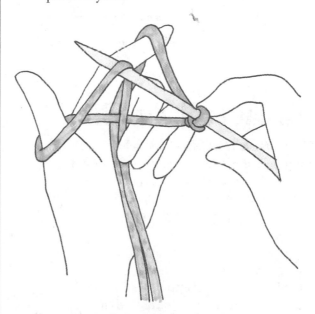

The needle begins to make a loop.

7. Bring the tip of the needle on top of the yarn being held by your forefinger. Take the needle underneath and then pull the needle toward you slightly. You should see a loop form.

8. Holding firmly to both the needle and the stitch being made, release the yarn on your thumb and then the yarn on your forefinger. Snug the stitch firmly against the needle.

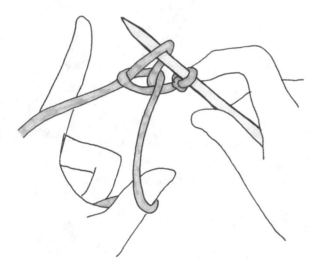

A stitch is created.

9. Repeat until you have the correct number of stitches.

Ending or Binding Off

I can remember asking my piano teacher (who attempted to teach me knitting in the same way she tried to teach me to play the piano—not with entire success; I stuck with the knitting and gave up the piano), "Mrs. Baker, how do you stop?"

Although you'd probably love to, you can't knit forever. Eventually, you have to stop, or bind off. Here's a simple method for doing just that. You'll get a nice, simple elastic edge.

1. Knit 2 together, and slip the new stitch back onto the left needle.

2. Knit 2 together, and slip the new stitch back.

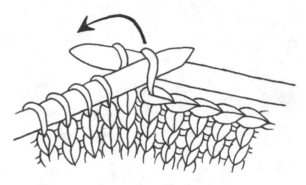

Slip one stitch over the other so one remains.

3. Repeat steps 1 and 2 until all the stitches are bound off.

4. When you get to the final stitch, *break off* the yarn.

 Wild and Woolly Words

To **break off** simply means to cut the yarn.

5. Thread the yarn tail through the last stitch, and snug it tight.

I used to tie 15 knots at the end, but I've since learned that's not necessary. One knot with normal yarn is plenty. If you're using something ultraslippery that seems to have a mind of its own, you might have to use some fabric glue if it resists holding a knot.

When you come to the end of a project or need to change yarn colors, what do you do with the ends of the yarn to keep the whole thing from unraveling? You needn't tie knots in the back of your knitting to keep the yarn from unraveling; just weave them in. This is a simple process:

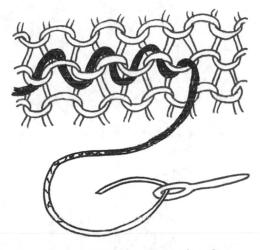

I recommend weaving in the yarn ends to keep your project looking neat. Leave a tail about 8" long, thread it into a yarn needle, and weave away.

If you're using wool, you're in luck. Wool is a bit like Velcro, and the end woven into 5 or 6 stitches will remain there for the life of the garment. If you're a bit unsure, use the tip of your yarn needle to split one of the last stitches you wove through. That will keep things in place.

Increasing

If you're knitting a square or rectangle, you needn't worry about increasing (or decreasing, which I talk about later in this chapter). But unless you're satisfied with knitting potholders and scarves, you'll want to learn these techniques so you can make other fun projects—that *aren't* square!

Yarn Over

The simplest increase is a *yarn over*, but it leaves a hole. If that doesn't matter to your garment or it sounds exciting, go ahead and yarn over.

Create a new stitch by wrapping the working yarn around the right needle, and continue to knit. Bring the yarn to the front as if to purl and then continue to knit. You have increased 1 stitch.

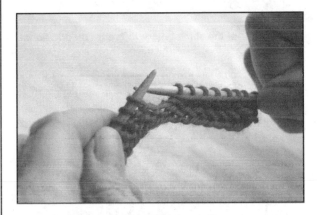

Bring the yarn to the front as if to purl.

Wild and Woolly Words

A **yarn over** is a technique to intentionally make a small hole in your knitting. Sounds crazy, but it's true. To yarn over, you simply wrap the yarn around the needle once.

Make One

With the "make one" method of increasing, you take the tip of your needle and lift the bar between the stitch you're on and the next stitch.

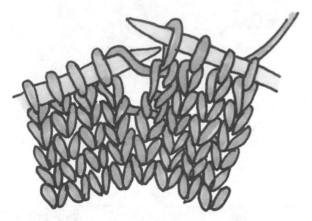

Lift the bar of the stitch below to create an additional stitch.

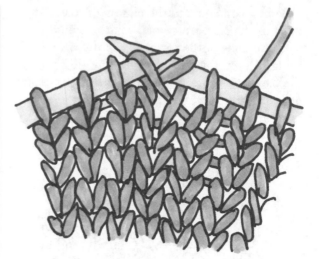

Insert the needle tip behind the next stitch.

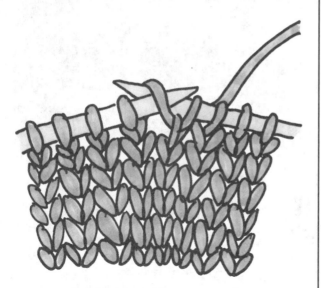

Knit the bar as if it were a stitch.

This method of increasing is the favorite of many knitters. I can't remember ever doing it this way—although I must have, right?

Lifted Increase

My default method to increase is to slip my needle tip into the stitch underneath the next stitch to be knitted.

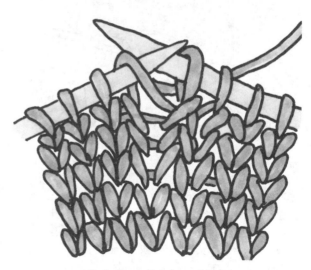

Lift the bar slightly and knit.

Some people describe this as knitting into the back of this stitch, and some say the side, but it's all the same stitch.

Knit Into the Front and Back

This increasing method, also called a bar increase, works very well at an edge. Here's how it's done:

1. Slip the right needle into the stitch, as if to knit.

2. Wrap the yarn around the needle and pull it through, as if knitting, but leave the stitch on the left needle.

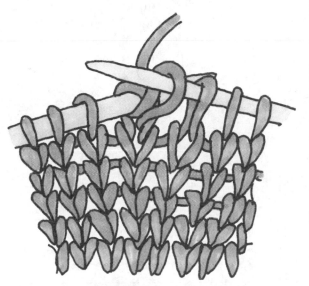

Keep the yarn on the needle.

3. Next, poke the needle into the back of that stitch and wrap the yarn around the working needle again.

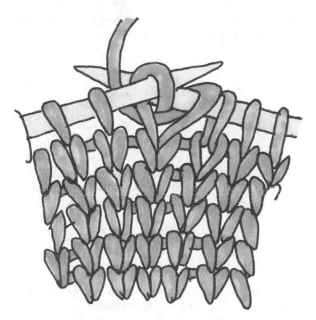

Complete the stitch and slip it off the needle.

4. Pull the yarn through, and slip the stitch off the needle.

Decreasing

Now you know how to increase. Keeping with the "what goes up must come down" line of thinking, let's go over the basics of decreasing, too.

Knit Two Together

The simplest way to decrease is knit 2 stitches together. You can also purl 2 stitches together.

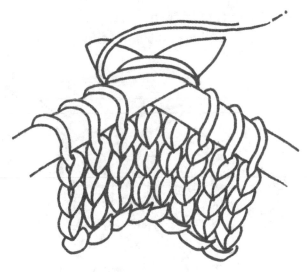

Insert the needle tip into the next two stitches and knit as one.

Slip One Knit One

This is sometimes written as *sk*, or *slip knit*. Here's how you do it.

1. Slip 1 stitch from the left needle onto the right.

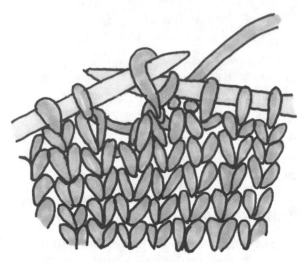

Lift the slip stitch over the knitted stitch.

2. Knit the next stitch.

3. Pass the slipped stitch over the knitted stitch.

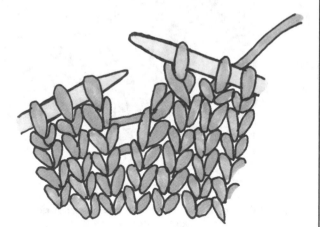

There is a decrease of one stitch.

Drawing (Picking) Up Stitches

You may need to draw up stitches along the edge of a piece for a sock gusset or to join two pieces together. I find a crochet hook very helpful with this, although some people do it with their knitting needle. You'll want to pick up stitches one vertical row from the edge, not the edge itself, as it will give you a nicer finished appearance.

Holding the right needle on top of the fabric with the yarn underneath, simply use the crochet hook to draw up a loop of yarn and place it on the needle. That's it. Draw up as many stitches as required.

Knit Tips

Stockinette is probably the most familiar of all stitches to us. On straight needles, stockinette is simply knit one row, purl the next repeated until the work is completed. On circular needles, you just knit.

Knit stitches are not square, so if you're picking up along a stockinette edge, you'll pick up 3 stitches for every 4 rows.

Picking Up Dropped Stitches

It happens. Even the best knitters do it sometimes. A dropped stitch. But it's not a reason to toss a half-completed project. Picking up a dropped stitches is easy with a crochet hook.

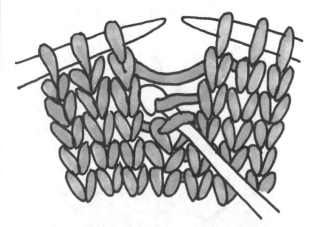

With the knit side facing you, use a crochet hook to pick up the dropped stitch.

For knit stitches:

1. Keep the knit side facing you if you're picking up a knit stitch. Use the hook to grab the dropped stitch and slide it onto the hook.

2. Pick up the bar between the two stitches on either side of the dropped stitch. Pull the bar through the picked-up stitch.

3. Repeat for as many rows as needed. Slip the stitch onto the knitting needle and proceed.

For purl stitches:

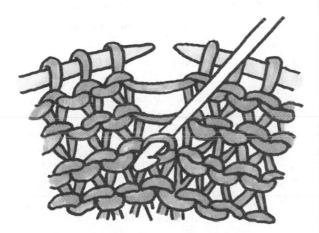

With the purl side facing you, use a crochet hook to pick up the dropped stitch.

1. Keep the purl side facing you if you're picking up a purl stitch. Use the hook to grab the dropped stitch, and slide it onto the hook.

2. Pick up the bar between the two stitches on either side of the dropped stitch. Pull the bar through the picked-up stitch.

3. Repeat for as many rows as needed. Slip the stitch onto the knitting needle and proceed.

Getting the Right Tension

If you're not relaxed, you may knit too tightly, transferring the tension you feel to your needles and yarn. The stitches won't slide easily on the needles. You'll feel it. Loosen up! Tension can also refer to how even your stitches are.

Hand-knitting is not an exercise by a knitting machine. If it were, all the stitches would be uniform. You're a human; some of your stitches are going to be a bit uneven. Yes, some knitters are better able to keep every stitch the same, but many knitters can't. If you complete your project and see all the little flaws, don't waste your time feeling discouraged. Yarn and knitting are very forgiving. Once something is washed and worn a number of times, all the unevenness disappears, as if by magic.

If you see the stitches are uneven in your work, your tension is incorrect. Relax! Your own tension or nervousness is being transmitted into your hands and fingers and causing you to pull too hard on the fiber. Practice and experience will help. Sometimes a particularly slippery yarn is more difficult to work with. If you find this bothersome, switch to a thick and thin yarn, which will disguise any unevenness in your knitting until your fingers are more sure of themselves.

Swatching Is My Pal (SIMP)

Here's the rule: always knit a sample in the stitch and yarn with the needles you're going to use for the project. This helps you determine the size of the finished garment and lets you make any necessary adjustments before you start—instead of when you've knitted half of the project! Really, swatching is your friend and will often save you headaches later.

Knots! _____

Be sure to recheck your gauge after knitting a few inches of the actual garment. Sometimes the gauge changes as you relax into the work.

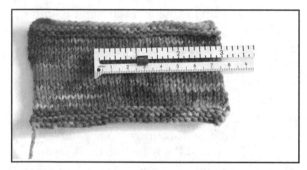

Lay the fabric flat and measure in the middle of your swatch.

A swatch for very fine yarn can be smaller, in the 4" to 5" square range. A bulky yarn might take a 10" swatch to be useful. Adjust the swatch for the weight of your yarn and the pattern. After you knit the swatch, wash it, block it, and dry it just as you would the garment.

To block your swatch, wash it using the same method as you would wash the garment, following the care label that came with the yarn. Lay the swatch out flat to dry, pressing into place with your hands. When the swatch is completely dry, measure stitches in the middle of the fabric to determine gauge, noting how many stitches there are per inch horizontally as well as how many rows are there per inch vertically.

I know this is time-consuming, but so is frogging. Only after you go through all these steps will you be able to accurately judge how many stitches you're getting per inch and per row.

Frogging

Unfortunately, we all make a mistake or decide to do things differently, and either choose to or have to start over or go back to a point before the mistake. Pulling out stitches to start over is called *frogging*.

Wild and Woolly Words _____

Frogging is ripping out your knitting. You *rip-it, rip-it.*

You can frog in two ways. One is to unknit one stitch at a time, placing the left needle into the stitch on the right needle and gently switching them as you pull the old stitch free. This is slow, but if you have to go back only a few stitches or a row, this is the best choice.

If you have to go back many rows, you can simply slide the needle out from the work and gently (try to keep it gentle, even if you're in a blind fury!) unravel the work. Wrap the used yarn into a ball, or you may be left with an unholy tangle. When you've reached the point where you would like to begin again, be sure you know you're on the correct side and slide an empty needle carefully through all the stitches. If you find you've inserted the needle in the wrong direction, be sure to untwist the stitch when you come to it.

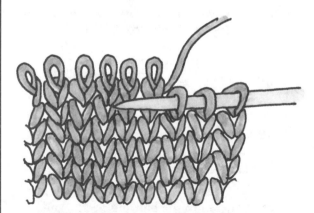

Slide the needle into a row of stitches beneath the mistake and rip back to there.

Reading Patterns and Graphs

If you're working from a pattern with many sizes in the instructions, circle the ones that apply to the size you're making. If you don't, you could get horribly confused—I always did. That's why the patterns in this book are all written out for you with sizes separate and no abbreviations. All you have to do is enjoy the knitting.

If you're working from a stitch graph, remember you'll read the graph from right to left on the first row, and the next row will be from left to right. In other words, you read in the direction you're knitting.

A Few Miscellaneous Knitting Tips

Before we get to the project chapters, I've got a few other *purls* of knitting wisdom to share. Again, I'm assuming you know a little something about knitting, so I'm not going into all the specifics and finer points of knitting instruction.

One thing I will point out, though, is this: above all, read the instructions all the way through before beginning. They might tell you something you need to know. And follow the directions, even if they don't seem to make sense. Turning the heel of a sock seems to make no sense at all unless you begin to knit it, and then it becomes clear.

The Necessary Supplies

Additionally, having everything the project requires close at hand will simplify your life. You can gather your supplies in a bin or a basket or even a tote bag—so you can carry your knitting with you!

Keep all your tools in one place.

Have a pair of sharp scissors, and reserve them for your knitting. Don't cut up dried grapevines for a wreath one week and then expect the scissors to be sharp enough to cut yarn the next.

Buy lots of yarn needles—unless you're the kind of person who really has a place for everything and puts everything back where it belongs. If you're like that, one needle will do. If you're like me, one or two in every room is a better plan. Same for the tape measure.

The Basic Purl Stitch

You might already know the basic purl stitch, but in case you don't, here's a refresher:

1. Insert the right needle into a stitch on the left needle, back to front.

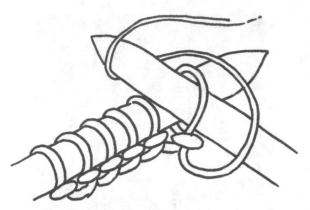

Here, the right needle is in front for a purl stitch.

2. Yarn over the needle, and draw the loop through the stitch.

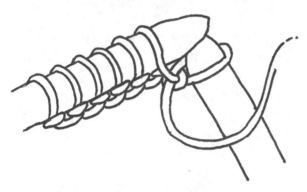

Pull the yarn through to make a stitch.

3. Slide the stitch from the left needle, and repeat until all stitches are on the right needle.

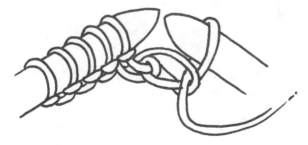

Slide stitch from the left needle.

The French Knot

Some projects in this book call for a French knot. This simple embroidery technique is useful for knitters. Here's how it's done:

1. Thread a yarn needle with a short length (not more than 8") of yarn.
2. Bring the needle up from the back of the knitting to the front where you want the knot.
3. Wrap the yarn once or twice around the point of the needle, holding the yarn firmly.

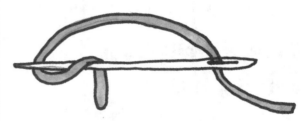

Wrap the yarn once around the needle.

4. Insert the needle near the entry spot, and push it to the back, holding the knot in place.

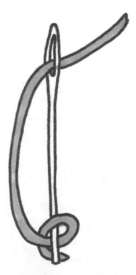

Holding the knot, push the needle through the fabric.

5. Gently pull the yarn to snug up your French knot and tie off.

A finished French knot.

Felting

I was in a yarn shop sometime ago, and a woman asked me, "Have you ever felted any-thing?" I replied, "Not on purpose." If you've been knitting for any length of time, you've probably washed some garment and it shrunk. That's called felting. The combination of hot water and then cold causes the wool fibers to contract and mat together. But you can do it on purpose as well.

There's nothing complicated about felting. You can throw your knitted item in a pillowcase, safety pin it closed, and toss it in the washing machine with your laundry. After one full wash, take a look at it to see if it needs another round in the washer. Two should be plenty.

Lay the item on a dry towel, form it into shape, and let it dry. Of course, being the impa-tient sort, I usually throw the item in the drier, too—not on full heat, but with some heat—and let it get most of the moisture out there. Then I shake the item hard a few times, lay it on a dry towel, form it into shape, and let it dry until the next morning.

You Gotta Have Yarn

After all, knitting isn't knitting without yarn! Once upon a time, people bought yarn at their local yarn shop. If you have such an establish-ment available to you, you'll probably pay retail for the yarn you purchase there, but for that investment, you'll also get advice and help with your knitting. All the needles and materials you need to complete the project will be there as well. As an added bonus, if you bought more yarn than you used, the store will most likely accept the return. All and all, yarn shops are a very good deal if you're just starting out.

If you're more sure of yourself and don't think you'll need any help in completing the project, you can go online. Many reputable businesses sell yarn and accessories online (some you will find listed in the appendix). These businesses may have a retail store, too, but they probably have a larger warehouse than your local store, so you'll have a larger selection.

Finding Discount Yarn

Some online businesses sell *past-season yarns*, which might suit your project very well. Buy enough to be sure to complete the project: once that specific yarn is sold out, you may not be able to find any more. Another way to be thrifty is to buy *mill-ends*. You can get some fabulous designer yarns this way. You also can get plain cottons and wools in myriad colors.

> **Wild and Woolly Words**
>
> A **past-season yarn** is one that has been discontinued. Because of that, you may be able to get a great deal. However, if you run out, you may not be able to find another skein or two to com-plete your project. A **mill-end** is the leftover yarn, most often wound on a cone, from a factory where garments are machine-knitted. (See the resource appendix for some sources for mill-ends.)

Businesses that sell mill-ends usually tell you the yardage and weight. And look for sport or worsted weight. (It's rare to find anything heavier than worsted.) Avoid mill-ends catered to weavers; their superfine yarns are inappropri-ate for hand-knitters.

Cone yarn is sold by the pound, so if you're working with cone yarn, you need to know how many yards there are per pound. That will give you an indication of the equivalence to hand-knitting yarn. Here are some approximates, but your mileage may vary:

Yarn	Yards per Pound
Sock yarn	1,650 to 2,100
Sport weight	1,200 to 1,650
Worsted weight	900 to 1,100
Bulky weight	500 to 900

So if you need 10 ounces for a project, you'll have 6 ounces left over for something else. If you need 20 ounces for a project, you'll have to buy 2 pounds of yarn, and you'll have quite a bit left over. I don't know many knitters who object to having a leftover yarn *stash*, though, so that's really not a problem, is it?

Wild and Woolly Words

A hoard of yarn purchased and stored simply for the joy of possessing it with no regard given to its ultimate use is called a **stash**. Many knitters have an impressive stash.

Because you're buying a mill-end and cone yarns in bulk, you're going to pay less—so much so, you'll probably get a little dizzy and want to buy lots. But be careful. Here's where I *could* caution you against such a foolhardy move, but I've done it myself and never regretted it. Why shouldn't you have lovely yarn at a great savings?

Fancy Yarns

Most of us live within some kind of budget and while we might drool over superb fibers, we can't often afford them on, for example, sweaters that require $300 worth of yarn.

Knitters, take heart! There are ways around this horrible reality, beyond picking the right lotto numbers. Splurge a little. Make something small with great fiber. A vest, a hat, a wrap, socks, or several of the projects in this book don't require a large investment, and you can still enjoy that great yarn. If you still want a whole sweater out of something fabulous, you may be able to find something similar for less.

Knit Tips

Like anything else you buy, there's probably a good reason why the expensive item is expensive. If something is priced less, just be sure the reason is something you can live with. Maybe the yarn is less because it's discontinued. Perfect! Maybe it's less because it's a mill-end. Again, perfect! Maybe you're buying from the source. Excellent! (I used such yarns for the projects in this book, but I'm not telling you which ones.)

Don't think you're going to use plastic yarn as a replacement for an extreme yarn and imagine you'll really be satisfied. You probably won't be. Few things are more sensuous in life than wearing luxurious fiber next to your skin. Save money elsewhere, and treat yourself like royalty every once in a while.

Some Yarn Basics

Again, I highly recommend that you knit swatches for any project, but the following info might give you a better idea at a glance of the yarn weight and needles that work best with it:

◆ Sock weight yarn is knit on size 1 to 3 needles and gets 7 to 8 stitches per inch.

◆ Sport weight yarn is knit on size 5 or 6 needles and gets 6 stitches per inch.

◆ Worsted weight yarn is knit on size 7 or 8 needles and gets 4½ to 5½ stitches per inch.

◆ Bulky weight yarn is knit on size 10 or 11 needles and gets 3 to 4½ stitches per inch.

Caring for Your Knitted Garment

You've spent a lot of time and energy reading the pattern, swatching, and knitting. You don't want to have that be all for naught by washing your creation and shrinking it in the dryer! Some garment-care guidelines will help you avoid this.

First, read the yarn label before you do anything. I've had cotton I could throw into the washer and dryer just as if it was a sweatshirt. It only improved because it shrunk back into shape. Other items you'll have to treat more gingerly. Wash wool in cool water and rinse in cool. Squeeze as much water as you can from the garment, but don't wring it. If you're very careful, you can put wool in the washing machine and let it spin a few revolutions to extract the water. Otherwise, put the garment on a dry towel and roll it up, pressing hard. Unroll it, lay the garment on another dry towel on a flat surface out of the sun, and press it into the shape and size it should be. Let it stay there until it's dry. If you walk past in a few hours, you can give it a firm shake or two, as that helps the wool's memory. You might also need to replace the wet towel with a dry one.

Now let's get started. Needles at the ready!

In This Chapter

◆ Learn how to make and decorate a hat

◆ Get hat variations

◆ How do you measure up? A head size chart

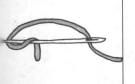 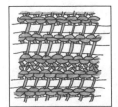 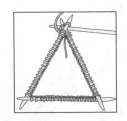   

Chapter 2

Hats

A ski hat (or a watch cap, as it's sometimes called) is a necessary part of any winter wardrobe if you're going to be outdoors in cold or inclement weather. Most of your body heat is lost from the top of your head, so putting a lid on it seems smart and very stylish to boot.

The hats in this chapter are as simple as can be. There's no shaping, almost no counting, and no ribbing. If you're just starting out your knitting adventure, you should be able to complete any of the projects in a few hours and wind up feeling very good about your growing knitting skills.

Hats make wonderful gifts, and you can make several different hats easily just by varying the color or style of yarn. Whether you're giving the hat as a gift or keeping it for yourself, you can decorate it to reflect the interests of the wearer using buttons, duplicate stitching, or different colors. A hat takes hardly any commitment in time or effort, and most can be completed in very few hours—a boon if you remember you need a birthday present the night before the party!

From fashionable to whimsical, the hats in this chapter get you started; your imagination can take you even further!

What You Need and Need to Know

Wool is a common yarn choice for hats because of its warmth and water resistance. But if you've found wool too irritating against your forehead in the past, try a merino or an alpaca blend. Many soft wools are on the market now, and your local yarn shop should carry something very appealing to the touch. A hat made of worsted weight can be crushed into a pocket and taken out when needed later. Cottons or acrylics can be substituted, provided they're of the same weight required in the pattern. But wool is so wonderful in the cold weather, and if you can commit to wearing it for a while, you might just adapt to it.

Depending on who this hat is for, you can go soft and sensuous or sturdy and bold. An alpaca blend feels delectable against the skin, and so does a merino. For someone allergic to wool, some nice acrylics would do the job. If the hat is going to get a lot of wear, you might want to use a Superwash wool so it can be thrown into the washing machine without a second thought.

You might want a very bright color yarn for your hat because winter tends to be pale and gray. Or you might want to be in sync with the subtle shades of the season and choose a winter white or a forest green. These hats are so quick to make, you can make several to fit all occasions and tastes.

Materials to complete all projects:

Yarn: Approximately 3.5 ounces worsted weight yarn in several colors

Needles: Sizes 5, 7, and 15 circular or straight, about 16" long, or to obtain specified gauge

Size H crochet hook

Bee novelty buttons

Silk flower

Small jingle bells

Green felt

Cardboard or plastic, 2" wide and 3" long, or a cardboard VHS sleeve

Yarn needle

Measuring tape

Thread or fine yarn

Scissors

Beads

Other buttons

Stitches used in this chapter:

Stockinette stitch

Purl stitch

Dropped garter stitch

Garter stitch

Duplicate stitch

Knit, purl rib

If this is your first attempt at knitting something other than a scarf, be bold. The hats in this chapter are no more difficult than a scarf and will take you less time.

Some advice that might help the new knitter: choose a lighter-color yarn rather than a darker one because it's easier to see the stitches if the yarn is lighter. If you want to count the stitches or find out whether you made a mistake, you'll be able to see the work better than if the yarn is very dark.

It's also easier to use a smoother yarn rather than a fuzzy one. It's easier to see the stitches when using a smooth yarn, and if you do have to rip back, fuzzy yarns make that process more difficult.

Using circular needles might aid you, too, because you can join the work at the first round to make tubular pieces of knitting. The important thing to remember is that the right side of the work always faces you. This means that you knit every row—that's right, every row. No purling. By knitting each row in the round, you get a stockinette stitch. Here's how:

1. Cast on, as in straight knitting.
2. Distribute the stitches evenly around the needle, being sure not to twist the cast on row.

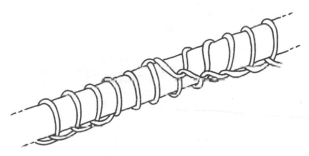

Straighten all stitches before joining the round to avoid a twist.

3. Hold the needle with the last cast on stitch in your right hand and the needle with the first stitch in your left hand.
4. Knit the first cast on stitch, pulling the yarn tight to avoid a gap or cast on an extra stitch. Knit the first stitch and the last together to join the round without a gap.

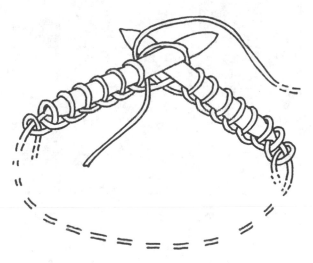

Snug the yarn firmly to avoid a gap.

5. Continue to knit, or work ribbing, around until you reach the end of the round.

Basic No-Purl, No-Rib, No-Seam Hat

This basic hat project is one that is simple yet very flexible.

Sizes: Preemie, (infant, child, small, medium, large)

Yarn: Approximately 8 ounces Cascade Yarns' Superwash 220 worsted weight

Needles: Size 8 circular, or to obtain gauge

Gauge: 5 stitches per inch and $6\frac{1}{2}$ rows per inch

Time to complete: 4 to 6 hours

Yarn needle

Measuring tape

Scissors

1. Cast on 76 (82, 92, 100, 104, 110) stitches.

Knots!

Superwash wool may be machine washable but not machine dryable. Check the label.

2. Join the round.

3. Begin knitting every round, making sure you join that first stitch with the cast-on stitch rather tightly so there isn't a big gap later. (If there is, don't worry; you can fix it with the yarn needle.)

When joining the first row when working in the round, do not twist the stitches. Be sure all stitches lay flat before you join. If you don't, you'll get a twist in the work and you'll soon have to start over.

A twist in the knitting means you have to start over.

4. Knit every round until you have approximately 6" to 9" worth of knitted fabric. A child's hat will necessarily be shorter than an adult hat. If you would like to roll the bottom more, you will need more fabric.

5. Bind off, leaving a 24" tail. You now have a knitted tube.

Continue to knit evenly until you reach the desired length.

6. Using the yarn needle, weave the tail through every 4 stitches of the last row.

Weave the end of the yarn through the bound-off stitches.

7. Draw the yarn up to close the opening at the top of the hat.

8. Fasten the yarn, and weave in all the ends. Tighten up the gap, if necessary.

Decorate That Hat!

Your hat is complete, and you can leave it at that. But if you're feeling adventurous, you can decorate your hat using one of several simple methods.

You might want a tassel or a pom-pom. If you don't want to make a pom-pom, you can buy premade pom-poms in the fabric store.

You might crochet a stem and a leaf if the hat is to be an apple (a red hat) or a pumpkin (an orange hat).

If you don't crochet, you might simply use green felt and cut a leaf shape using the leaf template. Then all you need to do is tack down the leaf with a stitch or two at the top of the hat.

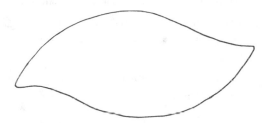

You can use this leaf template or make your own.

If you visit your local fabric store, you might well find a silk flower you can pin to the side, making this casual hat into something much more stylish.

If you used a yarn woven with gold thread and you add a sparkly ornament, this would be very appropriate for eveningwear.

Purl Pearls

Hats are an excellent way to use up the odd bit of wool or fancy yarn you have on hand. Go wild and knit a hat of many colors.

Congratulations! Now all your friends will expect hats for Christmas!

Child's Tasseled Hat

I love the whimsical nature of this next project. It reminds me of a court jester's cap, but because it requires no shaping and lacks the long points traditionally associated with a jester's hat, it takes only a few hours to make. The hat is constructed of a flat piece of knitting, so it lends itself well to duplicate stitch work, but bold stripes such as pink and purple would be wonderful as well.

Following the basic hat instructions and using a main and a contrast color …

1. Cast on for the desired size in the contrasting color.

2. Knit 6 rounds.

3. Break the yarn and attach the main color.

4. Knit every round until the hat measures approximately 5", or 1" less than the desired length.

5. Break the main color yarn, and attach the contrasting color.

6. Knit 6 rows.

7. Bind off as in the basic hat directions.

8. Turn the hat inside out and lay it flat.

9. Sew the top seam and turn the hat right-side out.

10. Make two tassels approximately 2" long, using both the main color and the contrasting color. Attach one tassel to each corner of the hat.

11. Weave in all the ends.

The Basic Tassel

Making a tassel is easy. Here's how you do it:

1. Cut a piece of cardboard or plastic 2" wide and about 3" long.

2. Wrap the yarn around the cardboard. The more wraps you make, the puffier the tassel will be.

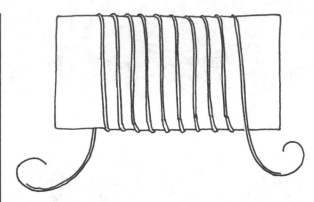

Wrap the yarn around a piece of cardboard.

3. Thread a length of yarn (it could be in the contrasting color) under the wrapped yarn at the edge of the cardboard. Pull tightly and tie firmly. You'll use this yarn to attach your tassel to your garment or item.

4. Cut the yarn at the opposite end from the tie.

5. Remove the yarn from the cardboard.

6. Approximately $\frac{1}{2}$" from the top of the tassel, firmly tie another length of yarn around the "neck" of the tassel. Again, this could be in your contrasting color.

7. Trim the bottom of the tassel to make all the ends even. Use your tassel as desired.

Knit Tips

I remind myself of two things every time I prepare to make tassels.

Because you're tying off the top section to secure all the pieces of yarn, the tassely bit always winds up being shorter than you imagine. I remember to take that into account, lest I wind up with tassels not as long as I thought they would be. I also remind myself to snug the ties firmly so that over the life of the garment, through all the washings and wearings, the tie at the neck doesn't become looser or perhaps untie itself.

Sew bells onto the corners of the hat.

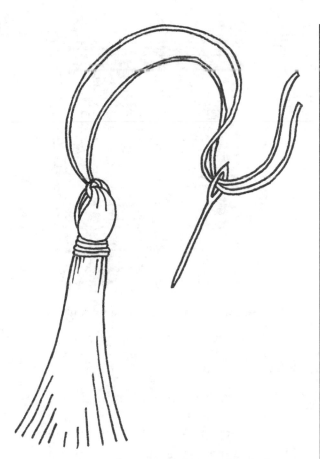

Use a yarn needle to attach the tassel to the hat.

The Long Tassel

The tassel-making procedure is the same for a longer tassel, but the template is larger. The cardboard sleeve on a VHS tape is always good. Look around, and you'll likely find something that you can put to use if you don't have cardboard. This is a great chance to recycle.

Jingle Bell Rock Hat

Here's a simple method to change the square hat in a way that will delight children of all ages. You can find bells in your local fabric store and in a lot more places at Christmastime.

Make the square hat as directed in the "Child's Tasseled Hat" section. Instead of using tassels, sew bells to the corners.

Skep or Beehive Hat

This *skep* hat is a woolen representation of a beehive, using the natural bulge of the reverse stockinette stitch to make the coils.

A beehive or skep hat.

Wild and Woolly Words

The word *skep* is from the Anglo-Saxon word *skeppa*, meaning "basket." It is a domed hive made of twisted straw.

Yarn: Cascade Yarns' Superwash 220 worsted weight 1 ball each in #282 sienna and #821 golden yellow

Needles: Sizes 5 and 7 circular, or to obtain gauge

Gauge: 5 stitches per inch and $6\frac{1}{2}$ rows per inch

Time to complete: 4 to 6 hours

La Mode bee buttons or other novelty bee-shaped buttons

Yarn needle

Measuring tape

Scissors

1. Using a smaller needle and sienna yarn, cast on for the desired size, following the instructions for the basic hat.

2. Work 8 rows in knit 2, purl 2 ribbing.

3. On a right-side row, break off the sienna and attach the yellow.

4. With a larger needle, continue in reverse stockinette stitch by purling 12 rows.

5. Break off the yellow and attach the sienna.

6. Continue in stockinette by knitting 6 rows.

7. Repeat the color pattern of 12 yellow rows and 6 sienna rows two more times. You will have three sections.

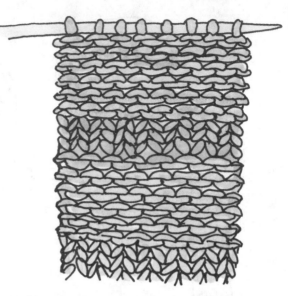

Stockinette and reverse stockinette stitch alternate.

8. Finish the hat with 6 rows of yellow.

9. Break off the yarn, leaving a tail approximately 24" long.

10. Using the yarn needle, thread the tail through the stitches. Pull tight to close, and fasten securely. Weave in the ends.

11. Attach the bee buttons randomly around the beehive.

Use a bee button to decorate the beehive.

A Labor of Love: Chemo Caps

For people undergoing chemotherapy, loss of hair is common, but the desire to keep both warm and stylish remains. That's where the idea of the chemo cap came into play.

Artyarns silk fur and silk ribbon make this cap luxurious.

Knit Tips

To keep the possibility of skin irritation to a minimum, choose a supersoft yarn such as merino wool or the softest cotton. To further decrease skin problems, this hat is done in reverse stockinette stitch.

Follow the instructions for the basic hat, or adopt the pattern for the skep hat by starting with several rows of garter stitch so the bottom edge doesn't roll, and then making stripes of a silky-soft novelty yarn, such as angora, and a merino for more visual excitement. Work 10 rows of one yarn, followed by 10 rows of another, and repeat until the hat is the desired length. That's all there is to it.

If you knit with only one color, try a space-dyed variegated yarn, or maybe pin a silk flower onto the side of the cap when it's complete.

> *Yarn:* 2 skeins Artyarns Silk Fur (25 grams per skein) and 1 skein Artyarns Silk Ribbons (25 grams per skein)
>
> *Needles:* Size 9, or to obtain gauge
>
> *Gauge:* 3 stitches per inch
>
> *Time to complete:* 4 to 6 hours
>
> Yarn needle
>
> Measuring tape
>
> Scissors

1. Cast on 64 stitches with Silk Fur.
2. Work knit 2, purl 2 ribbing for 1½".
3. Begin pattern as follows:

   Switch to Silk Ribbon and work in reverse stockinette stitch for 4 rows.

   Switch to Silk Fur and work 2 rows in dropped garter stitch.

   Repeat this sequence 3 more times.
4. Begin decrease rows as follows:

   Row 1: Working with Silk Fur, knit 2 together across.

   Row 2: Purl back (32 stitches).
5. Repeat rows 1 and 2 two more times until 8 stitches remain.
6. Break the yarn and pull through 8 remaining stitches. Sew the seam, and weave in all the ends.

This project uses the dropped garter stitch Here's how it goes:

Insert the right needle as if to knit, and wrap the yarn around the right needle once more before slipping the stitch off the left needle. On the next row, the dropped garter stitch will "unwind" and leave a long, lacy stitch.

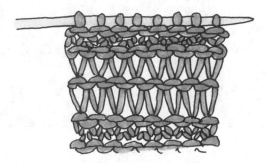

Wrapping the yarn an extra time around the needle adds length to the stitch and row.

An After-Dark Hat

For this hat, choose a novelty yarn, perhaps something that already has a bit of metallic thread running through it. You could also add a *carry along* yourself.

 Wild and Woolly Words

Carry along refers to a yarn, often a metallic or other fancy type, that's knit along with the main yarn for interest.

With this hat, the sky's the limit. You can keep it simple and sophisticated with white and gold metallic yarn, or you can go over the top and keep going with something funkier.

Basic Ski Hat

This is the perfect opportunity to create a hat to match someone's personality and preferences.

Yarn: 1 skein worsted weight yarn
Needles: Sizes 5 and 7, or to obtain gauge
Gauge: 5 stitches per inch
Time to complete: Less than 5 hours

1. On the smaller needles, cast on 112 stitches.
2. Work in knit 2, purl 2 ribbing for 3".
3. Switch to the larger needles, and begin the stockinette stitch.
4. Work until piece measures 7".
5. Begin crown shaping as follows:

   Row 1: *Knit 6, knit 2 together, repeat from * across row.

   Row 2 and all succeeding even rows: Purl.

   Row 3: *Knit 5, knit 2 together, repeat from * across row.

   Row 5: *Knit 4, knit 2 together, repeat from * across row.

   Row 7: *Knit 3, knit 2 together, repeat from * across row.

   Row 9: *Knit 2, knit 2 together, repeat from * across row.

   Row 11: *Knit 1, knit 2 together, repeat from * across row.

   Row 13: *Knit 2 together across row.

6. Cut the yarn, leaving a long tail. Weave the tail through the remaining stitches and pull tightly.
7. Sew the seam, right sides together, and weave in the ends.

Knit Tips

You can use stitch markers to mark repeats in your pattern to keep you from being confused about where you are on the row. Just a glance down at your needles tells you approximately where you left off. No stitch markers in the house? Use a small loop of contrasting yarn.

Stripe Hat

To make a stripe hat, work the ribbing in a solid color and the body of the hat in 1" stripes.

Moonlit Night Hat

For a hat resembling the night sky, sew gold star buttons onto a navy blue hat.

Apple Hat

For this fruity hat, duplicate stitch red apples on a green background.

You might also make a red hat and top it with two leafs. Refer to the leaf template earlier in this chapter if you want to make them of felt or Chapter 21 for the knit plant/leaf.

Knit Tips

You can buy a wool wash for your garments. In a pinch, though, you can use your shampoo. It's mild and won't hurt the wool.

Ear Flap Hat

You could knit this hat from the top down, but working from the bottom up seemed the simplest way to me. You start by knitting the earflaps and hold one on waste yarn while you knit the second. Without removing that one from the needle, you cast on stitches after it,

pick up the stitches from the waste yarn for the other flap, and cast on the remaining stitches. This way you have no joining or sewing to do; you just knit the hat.

Traditional ear flap hats never go out of style.

Yarn: Worsted weight yarn, 1 skein of main color, 1 skein of contrasting color
Needles: Size 7, or to obtain gauge
Gauge: 5 stitches per inch

1. Cast on 3 stitches.
2. Increase 1 stitch each side every other row to 25 stitches. Place all the stitches on waste yarn or a holder.

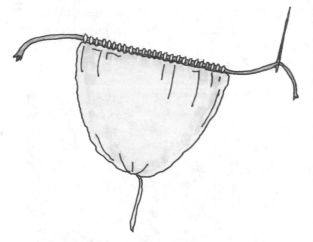

Hold the ear flap on waste yarn until needed.

3. Repeat steps 1 and 2 to make the second flap. Keep this on the working needle.

4. Cast on 31 stitches.

5. Place the remaining flap stitches on the needle, and knit across.

6. Cast on 31 stitches. You should now have a total of 112 stitches.

7. Work 6 rows in garter stitch.

8. Begin stockinette stitch, and work 2 rows in the main color.

9. Work 2 rows in the contrasting color.

10. Continue working in the main color until the piece measures 7".

11. Begin crown shaping as follows:

    Row 1: *Knit 6, knit 2 together, repeat from * across row.

    Row 2 and all succeeding even rows: Purl.

    Row 3: *Knit 5, knit 2 together, repeat from * across row.

    Row 5: *Knit 4, knit 2 together, repeat from * across row.

    Row 7: *Knit 3, knit 2 together, repeat from * across row.

    Row 9: *Knit 2, knit 2 together, repeat from * across row.

Row 11: *Knit 1, knit 2 together, repeat from * across row.

Row 13: *Knit 2 together across the row.

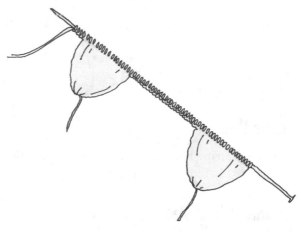

The flaps are knit first. Hat stitches are then cast on around either side of them.

12. Cut the yarn, leaving a long tail. Weave the tail through the remaining stitches and pull tightly.

13. Sew the seam, right sides together, and weave in the ends.

14. Work a fir tree or snowflake pattern in duplicate stitch.

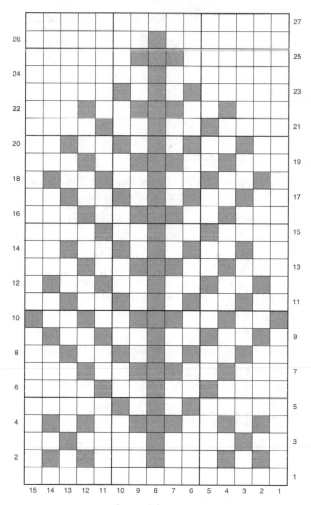

A traditional fir tree motif.

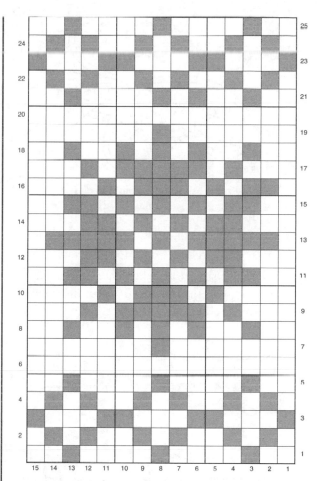

These wintry snowflakes are perfect for a ski hat.

I-Cord Ties

I-Cord is a very useful and simple-to-use trim or closure. It seems counterintuitive that you can knit flat and yet produce something that appears round, but if you follow the technique carefully, you will wind up with a very nice cord.

1. Using short double pointed needles, cast on a small number of stitches, around 3 to 6.

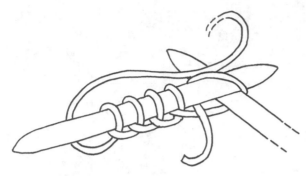

You must use double point needles.

2. Knit all the stitches.
3. Switch needles in your hands so the needle with the stitches is in your left hand again.
4. Slide the stitches to the other end of the needle, and pull the yarn across the back of the stitches. Knit the row again.

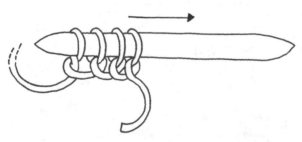

Keep the yarn in back and return to the start of the row.

5. Continue this way, sliding and knitting, until the cord is the length you want.

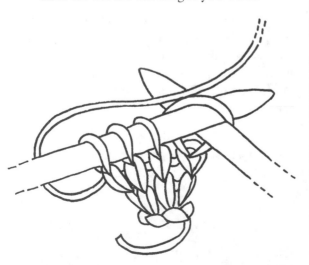

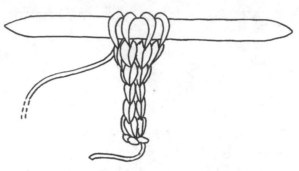

Snug the yarn firmly to create the cord. The cord will be round.

6. Although there shouldn't be much of a carry if you're knitting only 3 or 4 stitches, just in case, give the cord a tug to make the little carry across the back disappear.
7. Make 2 cords, each approximately 6" in length, and sew these to the point of the flaps.
8. Make 2 tassels approximately 3" in length, and attach them to the cords.

Braided Cord Ties

To make braided cord ties, work as if you were going to make fringe:

1. Attach 6 strands of yarn approximately 12" long to the point of the flap. Using your crochet hook, pull the lengths of yarn through the bottom of the flap.

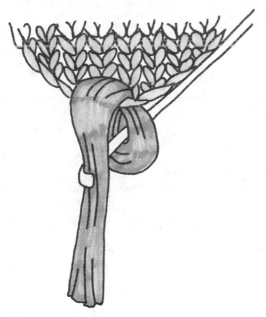

Using your crochet hook, pull the yarn through the bottom of the flap.

2. Separate the yarn into 3 equal sections and begin braiding. Continue until the braid is 6" to 8" inches long.

3. Tie a knot to secure the braid, and attach tassels, if desired.

Braid the yarn.

Determining Hat Size

The following table lists the garment industry's standard head size measurements. Keep these in mind as you're making your hats.

Even if you follow these sizes, if your finished hat is too big, all you have to do is felt it to make it smaller and warmer.

Size XS	Hat Size(s)	Circumference (Inches)
Extra small	6½, 6e	20½", 20¾"
Small	6¾, 6f	21c", 21½"
Medium	7, 7c	21f", 22¼"
Large	7¼, 7d	22e", 23"
Extra large	7½, 7e	23½", 23f"

In This Chapter

- ◆ Learn to make simple headbands and ear warmers
- ◆ Create fun variations like a Gummi Heart Headband, a Slip Stitch Ribbing Headband, a Cable Stitch Headband, and a Brocade Headband
- ◆ Warm your wrists with wristlets

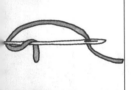
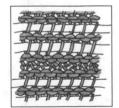

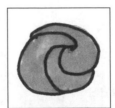

Headbands and Wrist Warmers

Sometimes you need something to cover your ears, but a hat is just too much. A headband can be the perfect solution. Plus, they're quick projects, so if you're feeling particularly impatient and want to finish something in an afternoon, a headband can do the trick. Headbands are also good if you want to perfect your skills without a big commitment of yarn or time.

Wristlets or wrist warmers are the kinds of items you can easily live without until you need them—and then you scramble to try to find them. A wristlet covers your wrist—but don't your sleeves do that, too? Not always. If you're in a cold building, wristlets can be very comforting. If you're prone to carpal tunnel syndrome and need extra warmth for your wrists, wrist warmers can save the day.

Wristlets can also be stylish and decorative. Luxury yarns, beads, colors, and stitch patterns can all lend a dash of fun and fancy if you wear the wristlet under your coat. Suddenly, a flourish is seen at your wrist, bringing color to a gray winter day!

What You Need and Need to Know

You'll probably need no more than 1 ounce yarn to create a headband, which should encourage you to splurge on your yarn choice if you're not using leftovers from another project. A mohair boucle, a fuzzy novelty yarn, or a silky fur are terrific choices for a fashionable ear-warmer-around-town. Or maybe you're thinking more along the backwoods—hiking, skating, or après skiing. In that case, a tweed, a Shetland, or an unspun wool would be outstanding.

Wool can be scratchy against your skin. But the more you wear it, the more it picks up your body oils and becomes less scratchy. To retain this quality, you'll need to refrain from washing the wool item too frequently.

Knit Tips

Even with repeated wear, some people find wool too scratchy to wear against their forehead. A soft merino could solve this problem, or look for a high-quality acrylic or a cotton. Acrylic and cotton yarns won't wear like wool, with neither the stretch nor the warmth, but these yarns can be a possible solution to the scratchy-wool problem.

Some of the projects in this chapter call for two colors of yarn. You can choose contrasting or complementary colors—the choice is up to you. If the headband you're making is for a runner or a child who needs to be noticeable, you might want to choose a bright orange or green so the person will be easily seen. If you want to make a bold fashion statement, maybe choose black and white or purple and red yarn. It's easy to make these garments as bright or as subtle and elegant as you want just by the yarn and color you choose.

Materials to complete all projects:

Yarn: 1 ounce worsted weight yarn in main color and 1 ounce contrasting color, 1 skein bulky weight yarn and 1 skein worsted weight merino yarn

Needles: Size 7 and 15 straight, or to obtain specified gauge

Gauge: 5 stitches per inch

Time to complete: Less than 4 hours

Buttons

Yarn needle

Measuring tape

Thread or fine yarn

Scissors

Stitches used in this chapter:

Knit/purl ribbing

Slip stitch ribbing

Cross stitch cable

Brocade stitch

Duplicate stitch

Lace rib stitch

Basic Headband

You can make headbands in two ways: either vertically or horizontally. You wind up with the same garment, but the ribbing is oriented either vertically or horizontally. It all depends on the look you want.

A quick project and a great gift.

For either a vertical or a horizontal headband, first measure the circumference of your head, or choose the appropriate size from the measurement table in Chapter 2. Let's assume your head is 21" in diameter at the ears, as that's the part you want to cover.

The Vertical Method

If you get 8 stitches to the inch with the yarn you're using and you'd like the headband to be 3 inches wide, you'd cast on 24 stitches to make your headband the proper width. If you use stockinette stitch, remember that it curls, so you'll need to knit 2 stitches on each long edge in garter stitch.

1. Cast on the number of stitches you calculated. Our example here is 24.
2. Knit each row, or work the pattern stitch of your choice, until the headband measures slightly longer than 21".
3. Bind off.
4. Turn the headband inside out, and sew the short edges, right sides together.
5. Weave in all the ends.

Try seed stitch for a nicely textured band that doesn't curl. It's easy to work—it's just alternating rows of knit and purl.

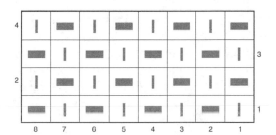

A simple stitch with texture.

The Horizontal Method

To use the horizontal method, determine how many stitches you get per inch and multiply that by the length of the headband. In this case, we will use 21". Now multiply 21 by 5 stitches per inch. The result is 105 stitches for the length of the headband.

1. Cast on the number of stitches you calculated. Our example here is 105.
2. Knit in a simple knit 1, purl 1 ribbing for 3" or the desired width of your headband.
3. Bind off loosely.

4. Turn the headband inside out, and sew the short edges, right sides together.

5. Weave in all the ends.

Purl Pearls _____

The horizontal version of the headband is very handily worked with circular needles, and results in a seamless headband. Voilà! No sewing.

Gummi Heart Headband

Here's a quick project requiring the basic skills and a raid on your stash, as it only requires about 2 ounces yarn. You can use the colors suggested or choose your favorites. It's a good idea to buy the buttons first, as you want the colors to be bold enough in contrast to be easily seen.

A quick project to please any child or the child in you.

Yarn: 1 skein Cascade Yarns Superwash #824, 1 skein #851

Needles: Size 7 straight or 16" circular, or to obtain specified gauge

Gauge: In pattern stitch, 5 stitches per inch

Time to complete: Approximately 4 hours

One package Favorite Findings Through the Heart frost heart buttons

Thread to match

Sewing needle

1. Using the contrasting color, cast on 108 stitches.

2. Work pattern stitch as follows:

   Row 1 (Right Side Rows): Purl 2, knit 4, purl 2.

   Row 2 (Wrong Side Rows): Knit 2, purl 4, knit 2.

3. Repeat Rows 1 and 2 for 4 rows.

4. Switch to the main color. In the pattern, work 14 rows.

5. Switch to the contrasting color. In the pattern, work 4 rows.

6. Bind off loosely.

7. If you did not work in the round, turn the headband inside out and sew the short edges, right sides together.

8. With thread or fine yarn and a yarn needle, sew the heart buttons randomly onto the headband on the rib knit sections.

Slip Stitch Ribbing Headband

This is a nicely stretchy rib that works well if you need a fabric that will take a lot of use: a turtleneck, a hat, or a headband.

1. Cast on a multiple of 5 stitches and then cast on 2 more stitches.

Purl Pearls _____

Some patterns use a stitch that uses a _multiple_. This means that you must be able to be divide the number you cast on by the multiple number. For example, to work a stitch pattern that calls for a multiple of 3, you will cast on 9, 12, 99, or the number needed to get the size you want. Just be sure to use a number divisible by 3.

2. Work the pattern stitch as follows:

   Row 1 (Wrong Side Row): Knit 2, *purl 3, knit 2, repeat from * across the row.

   Row 2 (Right Side Row): Purl 2, *knit 1, slip 1 with the yarn in back, knit 1, purl 2, repeat from * across the row.

3. Repeat Rows 1 and 2 until the headband is approximately 21" long or the desired length.

4. Bind off loosely.

5. Turn the headband inside out, and sew the short edges, right sides together.

Cross Stitch Cable Headband

Yes, it's true that using a *cable needle* is somewhat complicated, but here is a stitch that doesn't require the necessity of holding stitches in front of or behind the work.

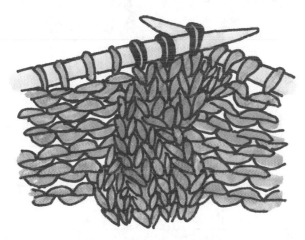

> ### Wild and Woolly Words
>
> **Cable needles** are short needles pointed at both ends, used to hold stitches while you work a cable. They can be shaped with a bend in the middle or can look like the letter U, with one arm longer than the other.

1. Cast on 9 stitches.

2. Work the pattern stitch as follows:

   Row 1: Knit 1, purl 2, knit 4, purl 2.

   Row 2: Purl 1, knit 2, purl 4, wrapping the yarn twice around the needle for each purl stitch, knit 2.

   Row 3: Knit 1, purl 2, slip 4, with the yarn in back dropping wraps from the previous row, and then, with the left needle, pick up the first 2 stitches on the right needle and pass them over the remaining 2 stitches.

Move the stitches on the right needle onto the left needle, and knit all 4 stitches in the new order, purl 2.

Cable pattern being worked.

Row 4: Purl 1, knit 2, purl 4, knit 2.

3. Repeat Rows 1 through 4 until the headband is approximately 21" long or the desired length.

4. Bind off loosely.

5. Turn the headband inside out, and sew the short edges, right sides together.

Paw Prints Brocade

I've made many hats and sweaters with a border of paw prints and have always received comments and compliments. The pattern is small, so the color combination should be easily discernible from a distance: black and white, dark green and light pink, light yellow and dark brown, for example.

Knots! _____

Don't use a novelty yarn for this pattern, as anything fuzzy will obscure the toe stitches.

1. Using the horizontal method of making a basic headband, cast on the necessary number of stitches.

2. Knit 2 rows and then purl 2 rows before beginning the brocade graph.

3. Work the brocade graph, centering it on headband and working as many repeats as desired.

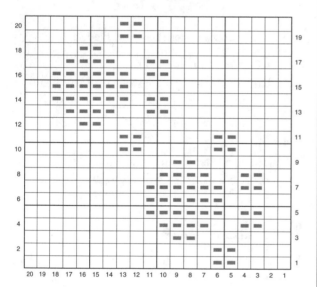

Use purl stitches against a knit background to create a motif.

4. When the graph is complete, knit 2 rows, purl 2 rows, and bind off loosely.

5. Turn the headband inside out, and sew the short edges, right sides together.

Optional method: Complete the headband as instructed, but without the brocade stitches. Then work the pattern in duplicate stitch following the graph, centering the paw prints as necessary.

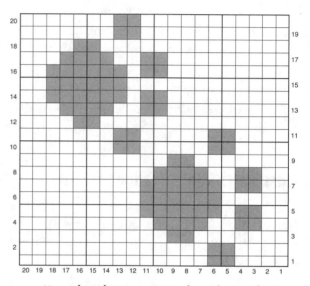

Use colors that contrast to show the motif.

Basic Wristlets

Wristlets can be as simple as cuffs from a sweater pattern, or you can put more time and effort into them. Here are several ways to make these quick and fun accessories.

Wristlet in progress.

Yarn: 1 skein bulky weight wool
Needles: Size 15 straight
Gauge: 2 stitches per inch in pattern stitch
Time to complete: Approximately 2 hours

1. Cast on 18 stitches.
2. Work in pattern stitch as follows: knit 2, purl 2 for 3".
3. Bind off loosely.
4. Turn the wristlet inside out, and sew the side edges, right sides together.
5. Make a second wristlet the same way.

Blooming Wristlets

Everyone who sees these wristlets seems to want them. These can be worn under a coat with the "petals" just peeking out. A hand-painted yarn is wonderful for this project, especially if you want to keep to the flower theme and chose a yarn with the colors of blossoms. Use a luxury and expensive yarn that you could never afford to use for an entire sweater, and you'll feel like a million dollars. Possible fiber choices might be alpaca, qiviut, cashmere, or a silk blend. I chose merino.

A completed wristlet worn under a coat.

Purl Pearls _____

An alpaca is a South American member of the camel family whose fleece, like sheep's wool, is spun into yarn. It's very soft and warm but does not have the elasticity of wool.

I used short bamboo needles for this, although you could certainly use circular needles and knit flat. If you're traveling on a bus, train, or plane, this is an excellent choice because you don't have the hassle of storing and carrying long needles with you. By the end of the trip, you'll probably be done.

Yarn: 1 skein Artyarns Ultramerino #109

Needles: Size 7 straight

Gauge: 4 $\frac{1}{2}$ stitches per inch in pattern stitch

Time to complete: Less than 4 hours

---

1. Cast on 36 stitches.
2. Work in knit 1, purl 1 ribbing for approximately 2½".
3. Continue in pattern stitch as follows:

   Row 1: Knit 1, *purl 1, make 1 purlwise, knit 1, repeat from * to end of row.

   Row 2 and all even rows: Knit 1, purl 1, keeping to pattern.

   Row 3: Knit 1, *purl 2, make 1 purlwise, knit 1, repeat from * to end of row.

   Row 5: Knit 1, *purl 3, make 1 purlwise, knit 1, repeat from * to end of row.

   Row 7: Knit 1, *purl 4, make 1 purlwise, knit 1, repeat from * to end of row.

   Row 9: Knit 1, *purl 5, make 1 purlwise, knit 1, repeat from * to end of row.

4. Bind off loosely.
5. Turn the wristlet inside out, and sew the side edges, right sides together.
6. Make a second wristlet the same way.

This is a neat pattern because it can be worn either right-side out or inside out because both sides look pretty. If you finish the bind off and weave the ends very neatly, you can wear the blooming wristlets either way.

Lace Rib Wristlets

The lace rib is a stitch that looks best in a more delicate yarn, but you can use something as heavy as worsted weight. You can guesstimate that you'll need 8 inches of width to go around your wrist, but measure your wrist to be sure.

Knit a swatch to determine the gauge, using the recommended needles for that weight yarn. Multiply the circumference of the wrist to be fit by the number of stitches per inch. This stitch pattern works with a multiple of 3 stitches plus 2 more for the selvages. Divide 3 into the total number of stitches required. It might be slightly off, so add or subtract a stitch or 2 to make the result an even multiple of 3.

1. Cast on the required stitches (a multiple of 3), plus 2.
2. Work in pattern stitch as follows:

   Row 1: Knit 1, *purl 1, knit 2 together, yarn over, repeat from * across row ending with knit 1.

   Row 2: Purl 3, *knit 1, purl 2, repeat from * across row ending with knit 1, purl 1.

   Repeat these 2 rows until the wristlet is the desired length.

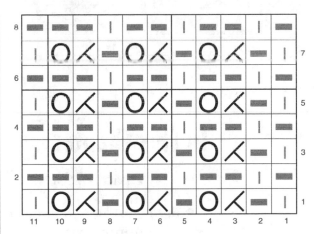

This easy openwork goes quickly.

3. Bind off loosely.
4. Turn the wristlet inside out, and sew the side edges, right sides together.
5. Make a second wristlet the same way.

In This Chapter

- ◆ Get a pattern for simple mittens

- ◆ Knit mittens for kids and adults alike with easy sizing information

- ◆ Create fun mitten projects with Fisherman's Rib Mittens, Strawberry Waffle Mittens, and more

- ◆ Learn some stitch variations

- ◆ Experiment with color and yarn variations

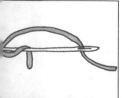
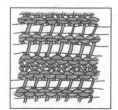

Chapter 4

Many Mittens

It's a fact: your fingers stay warmer in mittens than in gloves. So if your fingers get cold in the winter, mittens are the way to go!

Plus, mittens knit up fast and are a very portable project. They don't require a big time or money commitment, so you can make many pairs to go with all your outfits. If you spend quite a lot of time outside in the winter, sledding or having a snowball fight, you'll need at least two pairs, in case one pair gets wet. Children love mittens because they understand how playful they can be, but that doesn't mean mittens can't be very fashionable as well. In this chapter, I offer several patterns for mittens that wouldn't be out of place on the runways of Milan. Okay, maybe not Milan, but Aspen!

What You Need and Need to Know

When selecting a yarn for your mittens, be sure to choose one you can live in. A bulky yarn might look appealing at first, but very soon you'll be unable to move your fingers at all because of the thickness of the fabric.

If you're concerned about scratchiness, a wool—or a wool blended with alpaca—works the best. If the mittens are going to get quite a lot of wear, you might want to try a machine-washable wool or an acrylic, for easy care.

Purl Pearls

The lanolin in wool makes sheep waterproof. The less processed the wool, the higher the lanolin content.

If you'll be going into the woods hiking or cross-country skiing, you might want to choose a fiber that will give added protection.

Go all out with a novelty yarn if your intent is to be out about town. A fur yarn would be terrific. It's even possible to get yarn that glows in the dark, which might make you the center of attention if you're going caroling one winter's night!

Colorful and warm, these mittens brighten the longest winter day.

Materials to complete all projects:

Yarn: 8 ounces worsted weight wool in main color, 2 skeins contrasting-color wool, and 8 ounces bulky weight yarn

Needles: Sizes 4 and 6, 5 and 7, 6 and 8, or 9 and 11 double point, or to obtain specified gauge

Time to complete: Less than 10 hours

Marker

Yarn needle

Measuring tape

Thread or fine yarn

Scissors

Stitches used in this chapter:

Knit, purl rib

Fisherman's rib

Horizontal rib

Stockinette stitch

Waffle stitch

Duplicate stitch

Simple Mittens

The very first circular knitting was done on double point needles, and so are these simple mittens. If you've never used these needles, don't worry. I walk you through it.

Double point needles have points at both ends and come in sets of 4 or 5 needles. To work on double point needles …

1. Cast on the required number of stitches.
2. Divide the stitches evenly among 3 or 4 needles, reserving the last needle to knit the stitches.

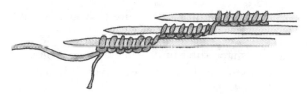

Evenly divide the stitches over 3 needles.

3. Join the work as in knitting with circular needles to form a triangle (or a square, if on 4 needles).

Form a triangle with the three needles.

4. Mark the beginning of the round, and knit around, keeping an even tension when going from one needle to the next.

5. As you knit all the stitches off one needle to the other, use the empty needle to knit off the stitches on the next needle.

That wasn't so hard, was it?

Size: Women's medium

Yarn: Approximately 8 ounces Cascade Yarns' Superwash 220 worsted weight

Needles: Sizes 5 and 7 double point, or to obtain gauge

Gauge: 5 stitches per inch

Time to complete: 8 to 10 hours

Yarn needle

Measuring tape

Scissors

1. Cast on 40 stitches on smaller needles. Divide evenly among 3 needles.

2. Work in knit 2, purl 2 ribbing for 2½".

3. Switch to larger needles, and place a marker at the beginning of the round.

4. Work in stockinette stitch for 1".

5. Continue to work in stockinette stitch, and begin to increase rounds as follows:

Round 1: Increase 1 stitch at the marker.

Round 2: Knit.

Round 3: Increase 1 stitch at the marker.

Round 4: Increase 1 stitch at the marker.

Round 5: Increase 1 stitch at the marker, knit 3, increase 1 stitch.

Round 6: Knit.

Round 7: Increase 1 stitch at the marker, knit 5, increase 1 stitch.

Round 8: Knit.

Round 9: Increase 1 stitch at the marker, knit 7, increase 1 stitch.

Round 10: Knit.

Round 11: Increase 1 stitch at the marker, knit 9, increase 1 stitch.

Round 12: Knit.

Round 13: Increase 1 stitch at the marker, knit 11, increase 1 stitch.

6. Place the 13 gusset stitches (the 11 stitches plus 2 increases) on waste yarn.

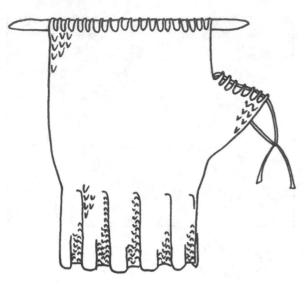

Use a yarn needle and waste yarn to thread through the gusset stitches. They will be used later.

Wild and Woolly Words

A **gusset** is a triangular insert used to add width or wearing comfort. **Waste yarn** is used to hold live stitches for later work. The waste yarn is usually in a different color, to be more easily seen, and is discarded after use.

7. You now have 40 stitches on the needles. Knit to the end of the round, placing 20 stitches on 1 needle, called Needle 1 (N1), and 20 stitches on a second needle (N2).

8. Work even for 18 rounds.

9. To begin shaping the tip:

   Row 1: On N1, knit 1; slip, slip, knit, work to last 3 stitches; knit 2 tog; knit 1. Work stitches on N2 the same.

   Row 2: Knit both needles.

   Repeat Rows 1 and 2 until 20 stitches remain.

10. Begin decreasing 4 stitches evenly spaced on every round until 4 stitches remain.

11. Cut the yarn and, using a yarn needle, thread through the remaining stitches.

Pull up tightly and secure to fasten. Weave in all the ends.

12. To shape the thumb, pick up the 13 gusset stitches from the waste yarn on larger needles.

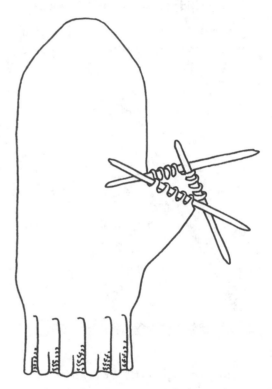

Knit the thumb the same way, with the stitches evenly divided on three needles.

13. Knit even for 7 rows.

14. To shape the tip of the thumb:

    Round 1: (Knit 2 together, knit 2) three times, knit 1. You will have 10 stitches.

    Round 2: Knit.

    Round 3: (Knit 2 together, knit 1) two times, knit 2 together two times. You should have 6 stitches remaining.

    Round 4: Knit.

15. Cut the yarn and, using a yarn needle, thread through the remaining 6 stitches. Pull up tightly and secure to fasten. Weave in all the ends.

16. Make a second mitten the same way.

Stitch Variations

Plain mittens are nice, and everyone should have at least one set in their winter wardrobe. But to show off your knitting prowess, try your hand at a pair (or two or three!) of these stitch variations.

Fuzzy Rib Mitten

You can use many novelty yarns as a contrast for the ribbing. For example, you can use 2 strands of a novelty yarn held together to work the ribbing. You can use anything, as long as it works close in gauge to worsted weight.

Fisherman's Rib Mittens

Knit the entire mitten in this very attractive rib stitch. After casting on, purl the first round. Then begin the pattern stitch:

1. *Round 1:* *Purl 1, knit the next stitch in the row below, and repeat from * around.
2. *Round 2 and following:* Repeat round 1.

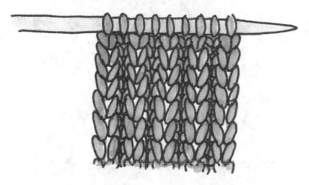

Simple but different knit purl rib.

Following the basic mittens, complete the mittens using the stitch chosen, maintaining the stitch pattern as best as you can.

Strawberry Waffle Mittens

Choose a pretty pink yarn. I'd look for a space-dyed yarn with shades of pink for the strawberries and yellow for the waffle.

After knitting the mitten's ribbing, switch to the waffle stitch and complete the mitten as directed in the "Simple Mittens" section.

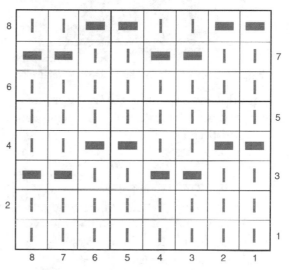

You'll love the waffle stitch in this project and find it useful for many others.

Horizontal Rib Mittens

This is just another way of saying you're going to knit some rows and then purl some rows. Make the purls really stand out by changing colors. I'd choose lime green, pink, yellow, blue, and red from my stash to make these mittens. Decide for yourself what looks right with the yarn you have.

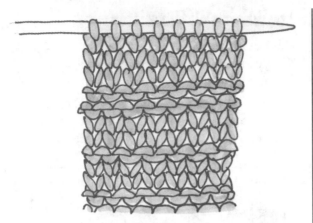

Ribbing here runs horizontally instead of vertically.

Begin the mitten as directed in the earlier pattern, and complete the ribbing. Then begin the pattern stitch as follows:

1. *Rounds 1 through 8:* Knit.
2. *Rounds 9 through 12:* Purl.

Repeat alternating rounds of knit and purl—or not! No one said your mitten had to have even spacing. Change the number of rows of knit and purl as you please.

Duplicate Stitch Variations

A duplicate stitch covers a knit stitch and looks like it was knit in instead of being added later. Use a yarn needle threaded with a contrasting or complementary color yarn similar in weight to the one used for knitting.

1. Bring the needle up below the stitch to be worked.
2. Insert the needle under both loops 1 row above and pull it through.

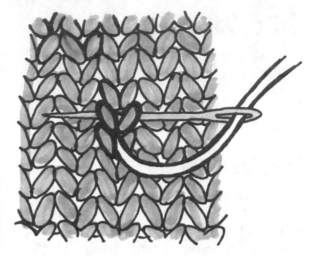

Use a yarn needle and contrasting yarn to create a design.

3. Insert the needle back into the stitch below and through the center of the next stitch.

Work the second color yarn on top of existing stitches.

Heart Mittens

Everyone seems to love hearts. Little girls do—and so do big girls! Hearts are a timeless motif and are often used in folk designs.

For adorable mittens, duplicate stitch red hearts on a white or light pink background for maximum visual impact.

Paw-Print Mittens

Do you have a friend who always refers to hands as paws? I knew a woman named Shirley who always did, and she would have loved mittens with paw prints stitched on them.

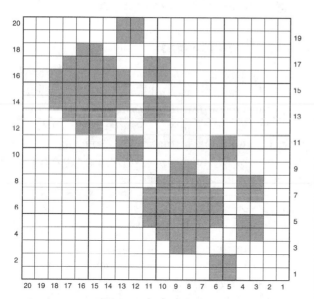

The paws motif is a real pleaser for animal lovers.

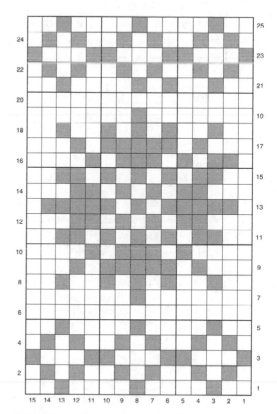

A wintry motif to be used on mittens, sweaters, or hats.

 Purl Pearls _____

Knit mittens have a history hundreds of years old. Peasants in the Middle Ages wore mittens to keep warm and dry. Intricate patterns developed in Scandinavian countries are still in use today.

Snowflake Mittens

Snowflakes are a traditional Nordic design, worn often by Scandinavian skiers. You can work the snowflake graph in either duplicate stitch or brocade across the back of the mitten. Work the colored squares in purl stitches for the brocade effect. In duplicate stitch, white stitches on green would be quite Scandinavian. You can leave off the diamond border, if you prefer.

Fir Tree Mittens

What says winter more than fir trees? Show winter your spirit in these mittens by placing a fir tree on the middle of the top side of the mitten. You could use dark green on a lighter green main color.

If you're feeling in the mood to embellish with a needle and thread, instead of placing a stitch in each one of the squares, sew a large seed bead in that spot. You can find many different colors of seed beads at most craft or fabric stores. You might also be able to find gold beads, which would make the mittens very festive.

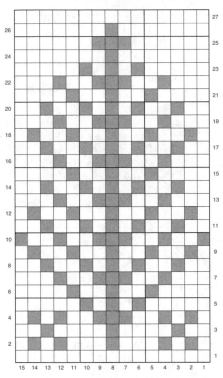

The fir tree is a traditional Nordic motif.

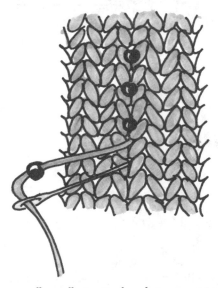

Use a small needle to sew beads to your garment.

Wild and Woolly Words

Space-dyed yarns are created by the application of dye to fiber to create colors and tones blending subtly into each other.

Color and Yarn Variations

Sometimes all you have to do to spice up a knitting project is to change the color(s) or the yarn. In this section, I offer a few suggestions to personalize your mittens. I bet you can think of lots more. Let your imagine run wild, and see if your knitting needles can keep up!

Space-Dyed Mittens

I'm a big fan of the *space-dyed* and hand-painted yarns. It's possible to find yarn in related colors but different saturations. For mittens, I'd knit the cuffs in a dark mango, switch to a lighter apricot, and move into a melon. You might do the same with blues, going from dark to light in three or four different shades.

White Wedding Mittens

Knit the mittens as in the pattern earlier, but instead of ribbing, begin immediately with several rows of garter stitch and then proceed with stockinette stitch. You can shorten the cuff to 1 inch if you like, but not less than that.

For the yarn, choose a pretty white yarn with metallic bits. Also look for trim with white seed beads to sew to the upper edge of your mittens.

Faux Leather Mittens

Leather mittens? Yep. For these, use a faux-suede yarn that knits at approximately the specified gauge. Be sure to make swatches with different needles to determine the correct size to use. If you use a light-brown yarn, you can fringe the cuff with it, too. For extra flair, sew turquoise and red beads to the back of the mitten.

Fingerless Mittens

Okay, so you like the idea of mittens, but sometimes having your fingers all snug inside the mitten isn't very efficient. It's hard to type with your fingers in mittens. It's hard to button a coat with your fingers covered. And knitting in mittens? Not so much.

But now, problem solved: fingerless mittens! They're easy.

> *Size:* Women's medium
>
> *Yarn:* Approximately 8 ounces bulky weight yarn
>
> *Needles:* Sizes 9 and 11 double point, or to obtain gauge
>
> *Gauge:* 4 stitches per inch
>
> *Time to complete:* 6 to 8 hours
>
> Yarn needle
>
> Measuring tape
>
> Scissors

1. Cast on 32 stitches on smaller needles. Divide evenly among 3 needles.

2. Work in knit 2, purl 2 ribbing for 3".

3. Switch to larger needles, and place a marker at the beginning of the round.

4. Increase 2 stitches evenly around, and continue in stockinette stitch for 1".

5. Continue to work in stockinette stitch, and begin increase rounds by increasing 1 stitch at the beginning of the next 12 rows.

6. Slip 6 stitches from each side of the marker onto waste yarn.

7. Continue in stockinette stitch on the remaining stitches until the mitten is 1" from the base of the fingers or is the desired length.

8. Continue on larger needles, and work knit 2, purl 2 ribbing for 1". Loosely bind off.

9. On the same needles, pick up the 12 stitches from the waste yarn and 2 additional stitches at the divide.

10. Knit ½" in stockinette stitch and then ½" in garter stitch. Loosely bind off.

11. Turn the mitten inside out, and weave in all the ends.

12. Make a second mitten the same way.

Changing Mitten Size

I've given you instructions for mittens in size medium to fit most women's hands, but what if you want to make your man a pair of mittens? Your infant daughter or son? By changing the weight of the yarn and the size of the needles, you can bring the size of the mitten up or down. That's all it takes. There's no necessary pattern adjustment with this method. Easy!

You may also want to experiment with different-weight yarns. A lighter-weight yarn and smaller needles produce a smaller mitten. Larger needles and a heavier yarn produce a larger mitten.

Knit Tips

If you change the size of your needle but keep the same-weight yarn, you will alter the fabric's gauge by ½ stitch per inch. Remember our motto: swatching is our friend! Going up one or two sizes by changing needles is the simplest way to change sizes. Experiment and see what you can do.

In This Chapter

- ◆ Catch the scarf fever that's been going around!

- ◆ Learn to make luxurious scarves with good-quality yarns

- ◆ Knit a scarf for those Harry Potter fans

- ◆ Create fabulous variations like a Champagne Scarf, an Old Shale Scarf, or a fancy Evening Scarf

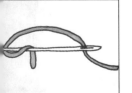 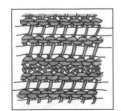 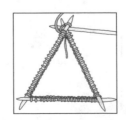   

Chapter 5

Simple Scarves

Everyone seems to be wearing and making scarves these days. They can be worn as a practical item to keep you warm, or they can be stylish when looped dramatically or jauntily around your neck. A simple item, a scarf can add flow, color, elegance, or whimsy to your wardrobe.

The design possibilities for scarves are far ranging. You can make a scarf similar to one you've seen in a store or a magazine, or you can find yarn you adore and work with that.

Scarves are knitting projects with a small investment in time or money, so why not have several at hand for many occasions? Most scarves can be made for under $20 and a few hours of work, so they can make a wonderful gift you didn't realize you needed to give or a quick addition to a wardrobe for a special occasion.

Yarn Options

The yarn choices for scarves are as extensive as your imagination. You can combine more than one yarn for a striking effect or mix colors you wouldn't normally use together.

What about novelty yarns? There are so many to choose from. Buy a skein or two of whatever yarn pleases you. Eyelash, fun fur, boa, rail ribbon, boucle, and rayon metallic yarns all lend themselves well to this kind of scarf.

Use a carry-along yarn to add visual appeal.

Knit Tips

If you're still a little shaky on your knitting skills, try a thick and thin yarn, which will cover up any inconsistencies in your stitches. A furry yarn will cover up mistakes, too, but ripping out a fuzzy or furry yarn to start over might be tricky.

Great yarn can be expensive. Go ahead and price a hank of real silk, if you don't believe me. However, it's possible to be extravagant without taking out a loan, as a skein or two of yarn will make an entire scarf.

Unlike sheep, whose coats are shorn periodically and yield a goodly amount of fiber, luxury yarns are difficult to obtain (which is reflected on the price tag):

- Cashmere is fur from the belly of a goat living in Tibet and China.
- Angora comes from rabbits.
- Camel hair is not shorn from camels; it's collected when the hair is shed.
- Alpaca is a South American member of the camel family whose fleece produces a soft and warm yarn well suited to scarves.
- Silk is the product of silkworms.
- Yak, possum, and oxen all have fur that's spun into yarn. These yarns are available if you search hard enough.

Purl Pearls

Possum yarn is similar to cashmere, in that it's both very light and very warm. The fiber is obtained from the bush tail possum, a non-native resident of New Zealand. The gathering of the fiber is strictly controlled by the New Zealand government.

What You Need and Need to Know

Here's some good news: you don't really need a pattern for a scarf. You get to decide how wide and how long you'd like the scarf.

Knit Tips

When considering the width of your scarf, remember: one skein of yarn will make a longer 3-inch-wide scarf than a 5-inch-wide scarf.

Here's more good news: you don't have to worry about gauge! All you have to do is use the recommended-size needles for the yarn you've chosen. Read the label on the skein. It will tell you the recommended needle size to use and how many stitches per inch using them will produce.

A lighter-weight yarn will go farther than a bulky weight, so you might have to buy one or two extra skeins for a yarn that works up on large needles. Worsted weight yarn is usually worked on size 7 or 8 needles. You can use straight needles or circular needles and work flat. It's all your decision.

If you'd like the scarf to be fringed, make the fringe first so you have it when the scarf is finished. If you want a long scarf and fringe, you probably need two skeins of yarn. (See Chapter 7 for a how-to on fringe.)

Knots!

Fringe first! If you don't, you may find yourself fringeless, without any leftover yarn at the end of your project.

Following the gauge given on the label, here's where you're going to do a little bit of math: if the yarn gets 3 stitches to the inch and you'd like your scarf to be approximately 4 inches wide, multiply 3 x 4 and you wind up with 12. If you cast on 12 stitches and knit to gauge, your scarf will be 4 inches wide.

If you want the scarf lacier, with a more open look, use larger needles. In this case, you'll get fewer stitches to the inch and the yarn will go farther.

Knit Tips

Always make a swatch before every knit project. This can be very helpful if you're unsure about the look you want.

Materials to complete all projects:

Yarn: 1 skein novelty yarn for novelty scarf, 1 skein Cascade 220 Superwash worsted weight wool for Old Shale Scarf; approximately 350 yards each sport weight yarn in your choice of 2 colors for a Hogwarts scarf; 200 yards luxury yarn for the luxury scarf

Needles: Size recommended on yarn label depending on what project you're doing

Time to complete: Less than 10 hours

Yarn needle

Measuring tape

Scissors

Stitches used in this chapter:

Double wrap drop stitch

Garter stitch

Stockinette stitch

Old shale stitch

Basic Pattern for a Novelty Yarn Scarf

This scarf pattern is easy and quick. Depending on how comfortable you are with knitting, it should take you only a few hours—including a chocolate break!

1. Cast on the number of stitches required to make the scarf as wide as you'd like it, be it 3", 4", 5", or whatever pleases you.
2. Knit each row until you are nearly out of yarn.
3. Bind off.

Double Wrap Drop Stitch Scarf

Instead of simply doing a garter stitch, you can give your scarf a lacier quality by using the double wrap drop stitch. This is especially effective with a ribbon tape yarn.

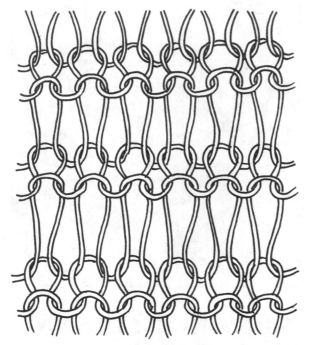

Wrapping the yarn makes the stitches longer and more open.

There are two variations on this stitch. You can knit the wrapped stitches every other row or every third row, as shown in the two graphs. It all depends on the look you prefer.

To wrap stitches every other row:

1. *Row 1:* Knit.
2. *Row 2:* Knit, wrapping the yarn around the needle twice.
3. *Row 3:* Knit, letting the extra loop drop.
4. *Row 4:* Knit, wrapping the yarn around the needle twice.

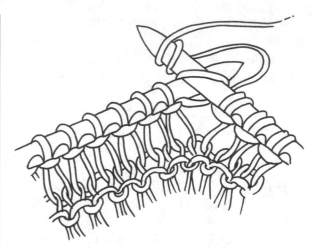

Wrap the yarn around the needle twice.

Double wrap drop stitch every other row graph.

5. Repeat Rows 1 through 4.

To wrap stitches every third row:

1. *Row 1:* Knit.
2. *Row 2:* Knit.
3. *Row 3:* Knit, wrapping the yarn around the needle twice.
4. *Row 4:* Knit, letting the extra loop drop.

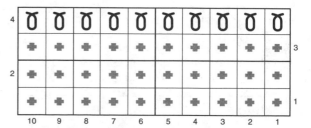

Double wrap drop stitch every third row graph.

5. Repeat Rows 1 through 4.

Champagne Scarf

It will take approximately 10 hours and 200 yards of yarn to complete this scarf. Choose a soft yarn in a pale-gold champagne color.

You'll make this scarf in stockinette stitch to see the pattern and make the scarf wide enough to fold over and seam loosely. When you finish, the purl side won't be visible and you'll have no rolling in of the edges.

1. Cast on 40 stitches, plus 4 stitches for the seam. That's 44 stitches.
2. Begin working in stockinette stitch and follow the bubbles graph, which is a simple yarn over pattern.

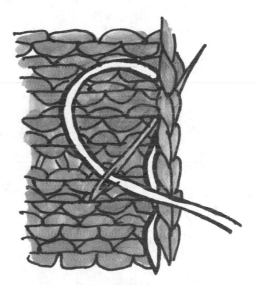

Knit Tips

The yarn over, in which you simply wrap the yarn around the needle once, is usually employed to increase a stitch. In this case, it is followed by a decrease so the fabric doesn't become wider as you knit along. A pattern can be made with the small holes, which makes this one of the easiest methods for creating a design.

3. Work in stockinette stitch until the scarf is the desired length.
4. Bind off.

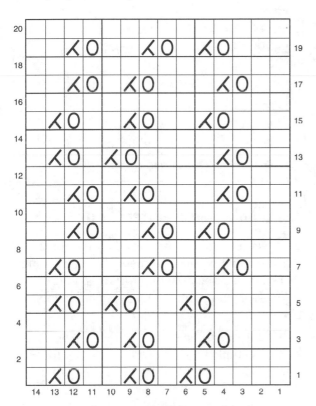

Champagne bubbles graph.

Place edges together and sew.

5. Turn the scarf inside out, and sew the long edges together firmly, making sure you do not cause the edge to contract.
6. Sew one end closed.
7. Turn the scarf right side out, and neatly sew the remaining end together.

Hogwarts' Houses Colors Scarf

Swish and flick your wands—or needles, in this case—repeating after me: *"Lanam facio!"* ("I work wool!") You don't have to be a child to inhabit the world of Harry Potter. Adults worldwide read, enjoy, and study the books with passion, and this warm and popular scarf can be for anyone.

There are several ways to approach this scarf. You can simply use a garter stitch, making color blocks following the Hogwarts graph in your choice of colors. You will need approximately 350 yards of each color of sport weight yarn to make the scarf 8" wide and 54" long. This isn't an exact duplicate of the scarf worn in the movies, though, because that's worked in stockinette stitch.

If you knit the scarf flat in stockinette stitch, the edges will curl.

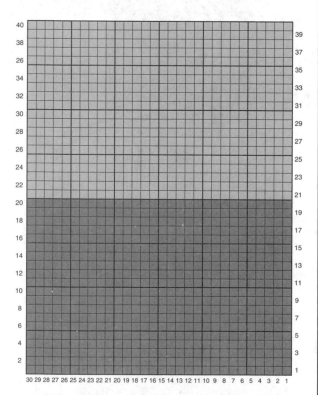

Stripes can transform a plain colored scarf.

You can either knit the scarf in the round and have no side seam, or knit it twice as wide as you would like the finished scarf to be and then sew up the side seam. After working the knitting to your liking, turn your scarf inside out to sew the seams:

1. Using a blunt yarn or tapestry needle threaded with yarn, stitch the long edges together without pulling the fabric.
2. Sew one end closed.
3. Turn the scarf right-side out.
4. Turn the edges of the last end to the inside, and carefully stitch the remaining end closed.

Purl Pearls

Although most people think of Harry and his long school-color scarf, all the houses must be represented as well:

- *Gryffindor:* scarlet and gold
- *Hufflepuff:* yellow and black
- *Ravenclaw:* blue and bronze
- *Slytherin:* green and silver

The Who's-Harry-Potter? Scarf

Not everyone gives a swish and a flick about the wizarding world, and there's no rule stating this scarf must be done in Hogwarts' houses colors—or New Milford High School colors, either.

This scarf can be knit in one solid color, perhaps to complement a winter coat or an oversize sweater. You might use this project to use the leftovers in your yarn stash, with the project consisting of different textures and colors.

Old Shale Scarf

Old Shale is a stitch pattern, also known as Fan and Feather, that lends itself particularly well to a scarf. The pattern consists simply of decreases, in the form of knit 2 together and slip slip knit, and increases, in the form of yarn overs to balance the decreases. This gives the fabric a gentle wavy ripple.

You may find the Old Shale so beautiful on its own it doesn't need fringe.

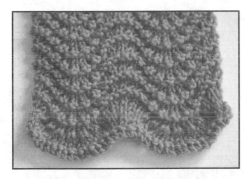

Old Shale is a simple and beautiful traditional stitch.

When considering yarn for this use, think more delicate than bulky: a fat yarn won't work up with the flow needed, nor will it let the stitch pattern take prominence. A variegated or hand-dyed yarn will complement the undulating

stitch pattern very well, but there's no reason why a solid color shouldn't work equally well.

Knit Tips _____

For lace knitting, the best yarn is light but goes a long way. Sport weight yarn is the heaviest yarn recommended for a very large scarf.

Here's how it's done:

1. *Row 1:* Knit.
2. *Row 2:* Purl.
3. *Row 3:* (knit 2 together) 3 times, *(yarn over, knit 1) 6 times, (knit 2 together) 6 times, repeat from *, ending (knit 2 together) 3 times.
4. *Row 4:* Knit.
5. When the scarf is the desired length, bind off.

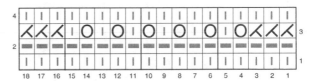

The Old Shale pattern is simply a series of yarn overs and knitting stitches together.

Evening or Country Scarf

For an evening look, try one of the many sparkly, metallic yarns available. If you can't find one, find a yarn you do like and carry along a metallic thread with the main yarn that won't change your gauge. A midnight blue with a gold thread, or a bright red with silver would be dramatic possibilities.

To go the opposite way for a country look, any handspun fiber would be outstanding in this pattern.

In This Chapter

◆ Get cozy with cowls and wimples

◆ Add some flair with the super loop technique

◆ Express your creativity with variations like the Super Simple Cowl, Old Shale Wimple, and more

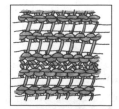

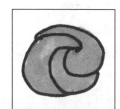

Chapter 6

Cowls

A cowl could be described as a round scarf or a turtleneck without the rest of the sweater. If you find a trailing scarf gets in your way but you'd still like something around your neck, a cowl may work for you.

The look of the cowl is dictated by the choice of yarn. A basic homespun type of yarn will look more rustic, but some yarns with dashes of metallic thread can definitely add some drama. The addition of beads or buttons can take a plain cowl into the fancy category. This is an opportunity for you to exercise your design skills and imagination.

What You Need and Need to Know

The cowl is either knit on straight needles and seamed, or knit on circular needles for a seamless finish.

Choose a yarn that is very soft and that drapes well. Mohair, alpaca, cashmere, and a fine merino all lend themselves to this project.

Knots! _____

Don't choose a yarn too thick and heavy, or you'll wind up looking like you're wearing a neck brace around your neck.

If you want a flowing, cowl or *wimple* that drapes well, use a lighter-weight yarn and perhaps a more open stitch. Then the piece will drape easily and follow the contours of your body. A heavier-weight yarn won't mold so well but will make its own, bold statement. It might be warmer, too.

Wild and Woolly Words _____

A **wimple** is a cowl that's large enough to pull over your head to double as a hat if the weather warrants.

Materials to complete all projects:

Yarn: 1 skein extra-fine merino or yarns discussed more specifically in individual patterns

Needles: Size 7 straight or circular, about 40" long for super loop technique or 24" long for standard knitting technique

Yarn needle

Measuring tape

Scissors

Stitches and techniques used in this chapter:

Knit/purl ribbing

Stockinette stitch

Old shale stitch

Lace chevrons

Moss stitch

Simple Cowl

This is a good novice project. Much like a scarf, there's no shaping, no counting of stitches, nothing you must concentrate on. You just knit and purl.

A fashionable way to keep your neck warm.

Size: 10" × 22"

Yarn: 1 skein Bollicine Dolly merino

Needles: Size 6 straight, or to obtain gauge

Gauge: 5.5 stitches per inch

Time to complete: Less than 10 hours

Yarn needle

Measuring tape

Scissors

1. Cast on 120 stitches.
2. Work knit 1, purl 1 rib for 6 rows.
3. Work in stockinette stitch until the piece measures 9".
4. Work knit 1, purl 1 rib for 6 rows.
5. Bind off loosely.
6. Using the yarn needle, sew the long edges, right sides together. Weave in the ends.

Super Simple Super Loop Cowl

This is a good opportunity to discuss the super loop technique—an old technique that's catching on again. And for good reason, as it's so simple and fast. Using one long circular needle makes knitting any diameter circular garment, including socks and sleeve cuffs, very easy.

You can abandon your double point needles and all the juggling they require. Some people feel very comfortable with all those needles, but I don't. I'm a fumble-fingers and can't manage the dexterity 3 or 4 needles demand, but I still want to make socks and mittens and hats and cowls. This method is perfect for someone like me. It's so simple, you'll get the hang of it in about 1 minute.

Here's how to make a simple cowl with the super loop technique. You'll need a long, circular needle, about 40" long (it can be longer but not shorter).

1. Cast on 110 stitches.
2. Slide the stitches to the middle of the cable.
3. Fold the entire circular needle in half, with 55 stitches on one half and 55 stitches on the other half.

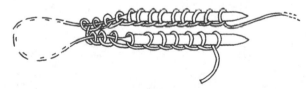

Bring the tips of the needle together, resting side by side.

4. Slide the stitches back to the tips of the needles.
5. Hold both needles parallel to each other in your left hand, with the needle with the yarn connected to the skein in back. For this technique, it will always be the needle farthest from you.

Note: At this point, I like to cast on 1 extra stitch and carefully slip it onto the front needle.

Knit Tips

When sliding stitches as you reposition them, be careful to hold the needle tips so you don't pull the stitches right off.

6. Now carefully hold the stitches on the rear needle and pull that needle out of the stitches so it's in position to begin knitting normally. The stitches that were on the needle are now on the cable.

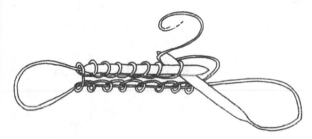

You are now ready to knit!

7. You should have a cable loop both to the left and to the right, with stitches on the left needle and an empty needle on the right, ready to knit.
8. Knit the first 2 stitches together. This minimizes any jog in the row caused by joining the stitches.
9. Knit to the end of the row.
10. The yarn connected to the skein is now in front, and the stitches in the front are on the cable. But you're thinking, *She said it must always be in back.*
11. That's right, I did. Just turn the knitting around. Now the yarn is in back.
12. Push the front needle back into the stitches. The stitches that were on the cable are now on the needle.

13. Carefully pull out the back needle again, as in step 6.

14. Knit.

15. Push.

16. Pull.

This method works for any circular knitting. You simply split the number of stitches required in half, distribute them equally on each needle tip, and go about your business. This is how I made the wristlets, socks, and cowl projects in this book.

Purl Pearls _____

Long circular needles come with brass, aluminum, bamboo, or wood tips. Aluminum is very fast, but if your yarn is slippery, you might want to use wood or bamboo. You should be able to find long circular needles at your local yarn shop or through the resources listed in the appendix at the back of the book.

Simple Wimple

Whereas a cowl is worn simply around the neck, a wimple can be worn down around the neck or pulled up over the head, should the weather dictate it. It can also be pulled up over the nose if the weather is cold and snowy enough.

A wimple is a rectangle that measures approximately 18" ×24". Knowing that, you can use whatever yarn you'd like, but bear in mind that this is supposed to be a soft and fluid garment, so heavy, chunky yarns won't work at all. The finer the yarn, the better your wimple will be. *Fingering weight* is excellent.

Wild and Woolly Words _____

Fingering weight yarn is very fine and is usually used for baby clothes, socks or lacy things shawls and such.

1. Make a swatch, and determine how many stitches to the inch your yarn makes.

2. Multiply that number by 24 because you want the wimple to be 24" around.

3. Cast on that number of stitches, and knit in the pattern for 18".

4. Loosely bind off.

Old Shale Wimple

The Old Shale stitch pattern shown in Chapter 5 works very well for this project, but remember the top and bottom edges will undulate rather than be straight. This can be a lovely feminine effect.

Lace Chevron Wimple

Here is another openwork pattern you can try. You will need a multiple of 9 stitches in your cast on stitches. You can add a few stitches at the beginning of the row or at each edge, to make it work properly.

1. *Row 1:* Knit 4, *yarn over, knit 2 together, knit 7 repeat from *, ending knit 3.
2. *Row 2 and all even rows:* Purl.
3. *Row 3:* Knit 2, *knit 2, knit 2 together, yarn over, knit 1, yarn over, knit 2 together, knit 4 repeat from *, ending knit 2.
4. *Row 5:* Knit 1, *knit 2 together, yarn over, knit 3, knit 2 together, knit 2 repeat from *, ending knit 1.
5. *Row 7:* *Knit 2 together, yarn over, knit 5, yarn over, knit 2 together, repeat from *.
6. Repeat rows 1 through 8 for the pattern.

Magic Möbius Wimple

You've probably seen a Möbius strip, a strip of paper with a twist in it. If you follow one edge, it blends and twists so there's only one side to an obviously two-sided object. The Möbius strip lends itself to a great cowl because it folds in front, thereby laying flat—nice if you have to wear a coat on top of it.

It's possible to make the cowl in a more difficult, more mathematically precise way, but for right now, we're about getting it done the easy way. You'll need to make a rectangle 18" × 25". Because both the front and back of the Möbius cowl show, choose a stitch pattern that's the same on the front as the back. That could be a plain garter stitch, moss stitch, or seed stitch. Working with needles several sizes larger than the yarn calls for automatically gives the fabric a lacier effect.

Let's make a Möbius cowl with the moss stitch. Work with an even number of stitches:

1. *Rows 1 and 2:* *Knit 1, purl 1* repeat from *.
2. *Rows 3 and 4:* *Purl 1, knit 1* repeat from *.
3. Repeat Rows 1 through 4 for the pattern.

Knit Tips _____

Before using needles a different size than the yarn calls for, make a swatch to determine how many stitches you'll get per inch. Otherwise, that little cowl could easily turn into a caftan.

In This Chapter

◆ Create your own versatile wraps and shawls

◆ Add variety to your wrap wardrobe with four fun wrap patterns

◆ Fringe it up!

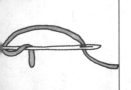 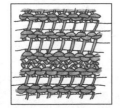    

Chapter 7

Wraps and Shawls

Wraps and shawls have been used for centuries, warming the shoulders of many people throughout the ages. What's better than curling up in front of the fire on a cool evening, a favorite book or knitting project in hand, with a shawl or wrap around your shoulders?

Shawls and wraps can be immensely practical, incredibly dramatic, or both. It all depends on your choice of yarn. You'll probably want a lightweight yarn because it will drape better. A bulky, heavy yarn won't form to you as much.

If you want something very warm, you might choose a soft merino. If you want something very light and flowing, you might choose a delicate fingering yarn. I love the look of silk because it has its own natural sheen, but I'm a pushover for ribbon yarn, with its flow and range of available colors.

Both shawls and wraps are flat pieces of fabric with minimal if any shaping, making them good projects for new knitters. They are large, but they're often knitted on large needles so they work up quickly.

You'll probably make several wraps and shawls, if not for yourself, then for others who just have to have some, too.

Purl Pearls

Knitted garments were highly prized during the Middle Ages, and craft guilds arose. Royals and the wealthy wore silk stockings and gloves mostly knitted by men. Later, as the demand grew, peasants began knitting to supplement their income.

What You Need and Need to Know

You can create a wrap or shawl for any occasion, casual or formal, conservative or explosive. Choose the fiber that suits your needs most.

Knit Tips

It might seem that a lightweight wool wouldn't be particularly warm, but check out kid mohair, which gives you not only warmth, but also the most sensuous treat of cloudlike softness against your skin.

You probably want a fairly open stitch for a mohair because it's so fuzzy that any stitch detail will be lost. A yarn less busy is perfect if you want to see the stitches—use a lace pattern, perhaps. A bulky yarn is appropriate if you want something substantial. It won't flow as well, but that might be exactly what you want.

Materials to complete all projects:

Yarn: Malizia ribbon yarn, Noro Gisha ribbon yarn, and Cascade Daytona ribbon yarn

Needles: Size 13, or appropriate to your choice of yarn

Metallic thread

Beads

Yarn needle

Measuring tape

Scissors

Stitches used in this chapter:

Double wrap drop stitch

Garter stitch

Basic Wrap

Indulge yourself in a wrap. You can pick out a luxurious yarn and literally wrap yourself in it, knowing you could never afford to make a sweater but can delight in it anyway. I love the ribbon yarns for the sleekly shiny look as well as the different textures available. If you only found 2 skeins of something in the bargain bin, this may be the ideal place to use it.

The dimensions of a basic wrap are approximately 25" × 50". Of course, you can make it longer and wider, if you choose.

Yarn: 4 skeins green Cascade Malizia (A), 2 skeins pink Noro Gisha (B) and 1 skein orange Daytona (C), or bulky yarn of your choice

Needle: Size 13 circular, long enough to hold all stitches approximately 36 inches

Time to complete: 10 hours

Scissors

Yarn needle

Knit Tips

When substituting yarn, the essential information is yardage, not weight.

1. With A, cast on 120 stitches.

2. Knit 4 rows.

3. *Row 5:* Begin double wrap drop stitch in each stitch across. (See Chapter 5 for double wrap drop stitch instructions.)

4. *Row 6:* Knit, working off wrapped stitches across row.

5. Break off A; attach B.

6. Repeat Rows 5 and 6 with B.

7. Break off B; attach A.

8. Repeat Rows 5 and 6 with A.

Double wrap stitch varies the row heights.

9. Break off A; attach C.

10. Repeat Rows 5 and 6 with C.

11. Continue this pattern until all of C has been used, ending at the end of a row.

12. Attach A.

13. Knit 4 rows.

14. Bind off loosely.

15. With A, work single crochet along the short edges.

16. Weave in all the ends.

Different colors and different textures make this wrap an exclamation point to your outfit.

Serape Wrap

Choose bright and bold earth tones, such as sienna, mustard, red, black, and green. You might even want to add a fringe in off-white or a color you didn't use in the body of the wrap. Handspun, rustic yarn would work well with this project; don't choose something delicate and soft.

Woman-on-the-Edge-of-Night Wrap

Pull out all the stops for this variation, and find the most dramatic yarn available. Look for a dark blue hand-painted yarn to represent the night sky. A fringe of a metallic gold thread would be striking, and silver beads sewn randomly over the surface can look like stars.

Knit Tips

All beads are not created equal. When you purchase beads, be sure the hole is the size you need. A yarn needle won't fit through most beads, so you'll have to use a sewing needle and thread for small seeds beads. Also be sure you know how the beads will stand up to the sort of washing and wearing you're planning on. If you're going to bead a T-shirt, it will get quite a bit more wear than a wrap would.

Hollywood and Mine Wrap

This is a retro throw a starlet would wear to a B-movie premiere. Use pink fun fur or aqua. Don't be afraid to add a few stripes in something silvery and metallic.

A Walk on the Moors Wrap

No rules state that a throw can be worn only at night, or on the town, or when you're trying to make a statement. A soft, light cashmere in floral or autumnal colors makes a lovely wrap if you're going for a walk in the country or having a weekend picnic.

Basic Shawl

You probably know what a shawl looks like. Basically, it's a big triangle. You start at the point of the shawl and knit until it's approximately 64" wide along the working edge. That's about all there is to it!

It's very difficult to judge how much yarn you'll require because it depends on what kind of yarn you choose. It'll probably be in the neighborhood of 5 or 6 skeins, unless you're using a lace-weight yarn. The pattern remains the same, no matter what yarn you choose.

Yarn: 5 skeins Colinette Giotto ribbon yarn in Florentine

Needles: Size 10 circular, about 40" long (to hold all the stitches)

Time to complete: 15 to 20 hours

Yarn needle

Measuring tape

Scissors

Knit Tips

You'll need a very long circular needle in the appropriate size for your yarn because as you increase each row, progressively more stitches will be on the needles. By the time you finish, the shawl will be about 6 feet across. Use the needle recommended for the yarn, unless you want the stitches to be more lacy and open. In that case, use larger needles.

1. Cast on 4 stitches.
2. Yarn over, and knit to the end of the row. Increase by 1 stitch at the beginning of each row.

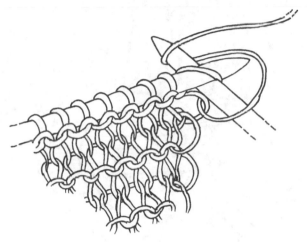

Wrap the yarn around the needle before the first stitch.

3. Repeat step 2 until you've used 4½ skeins of yarn.
4. Cast off very loosely, checking to be sure the cast off edge is as stretchy as the main fabric of the shawl—you don't want a tight, hard edge because it will keep the shawl from draping properly. It will also create a weak point where the yarn might break.
5. No need to weave in the cast on, cast off, and ball ends; they'll disappear into the fringe.

Knit Tips _____

Try to finish the row you're working on before you put down your knitting. If you're leaving it for a while, you might want to slip tip protectors on the needles so there's no chance the item will slide off if the dogs decide to play with your half-finished shawl.

Lovely and dramatic, a shawl is always in fashion.

Fringe

To finish off your shawl—or any project, for that matter, such as the ponchos in Chapter 10 or the scarves in Chapter 5—let's add some fringe:

1. Cut a piece of cardboard to serve as your fringe template. Make it the length of fringe you want, plus 1 inch (for the knot). You decide on the length of the fringe, but here are some suggestions:

   Shawl: 8" fringe (use a 9" piece of cardboard)

   Poncho: 6" fringe (use a 7" piece of cardboard)

   Scarf: 4" fringe (use a 5" piece of cardboard)

2. Wrap the yarn around the cardboard approximately 10 times. Don't wrap so much that your scissors can't cut through it.
3. Cut one end only.
4. Fold each strand in half.

5. Using a crochet hook, hold 2 strands of yarn (or however many you need to achieve the fringe fullness you want) and insert the crochet hook from back to front through the space where you want the fringe.

6. Loop the yarn over the hook, and pull it through the fabric to the wrong side.

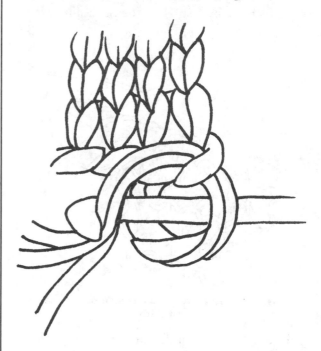

Pull the fringe through and snug it in place.

7. Carefully pull the long end of the yarn through the loop, and snug it firmly in place.

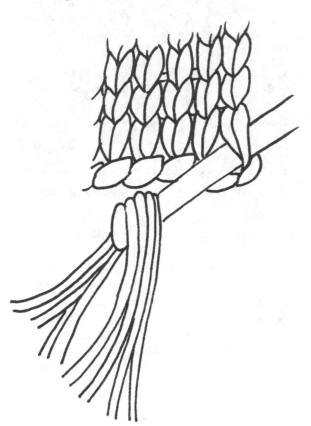

Insert the crochet hook and pull the fringe from the front to the back.

This fringe is inserted into the yarn overs.

8. Hang fringe evenly on your project. For a shawl, loop the fringe into the loops at the sides and bottom cast on stitches. For a poncho, every other row is probably good, on all the outer sides. For a scarf, you might want the fringe to be fuller, but only on the two ends.

9. When completely fringed, trim the ends of the yarn so the fringe is even.

In This Chapter

- ◆ Get cozy with shrugs
- ◆ Choose your shrug: Sporty Shrug, Evening Shrug, or Blouson Sleeve Shrug

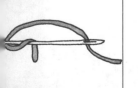
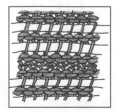
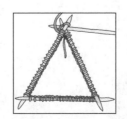
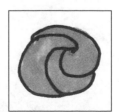

Chapter 8

Shrugs

If you like to snuggle in bed but the room is a bit cool, or if you know someone who is convalescing, a shrug is the perfect item to have or give as a gift, as it keeps the shoulders and arms warm but doesn't get tangled up in covers. This surprisingly utilitarian garment can also be quite fashionable. You choose the look you want by the weight of the fiber you use, whether it's soft and slinky or bold and substantial. Don't be afraid of using wild choices and mixing and matching colors or textures. As long as the yarn is approximately the same weight, you should be fine.

A bright red shrug over a navy blue dress would be stunning for the office. The same navy blue dress would be complemented by a lime green shrug for a completely different look. When accessorizing a dress or blouse, choose complementary colors for a subtle statement or contrasting colors for a bold statement.

Set off a solid-color shrug in a worsted weight yarn by crocheting a border of contrasting yarn along all the edges. Red with navy, pink with green, and pumpkin with brown all work. Go to the yarn shop and group together skeins of yarn to see how they look to you. You are the ultimate judge.

What You Need and Need to Know

Choose a yarn to match your needs. A marled yarn in muted tones will look sporty, so if you're wearing the shrug outside, you'll want a more rustic-appearing yarn. If you're going out in the evening, something with bangles and metallic flecks would lend itself well. For something to snuggle in, a deep and luxurious mohair, alpaca, or ultrasoft merino would be perfect.

Knit 1, purl 1 ribbing.

It seems odd that a yarn as fine as mohair would be considered worsted weight. In this case, it has nothing to do with how heavy or thick the yarn is. Mohair requires large needles so the long fibers "fluff out" and provide the warmth and comfort possible.

Purl Pearls _____

Mohair comes from angora goats; the younger the animal, the softer the fleece. Super kid mohair is the finest grade available.

If you don't want to use a mohair, you can use a worsted weight wool instead. Your intention should be to choose a yarn that will enable you to knit to the specified gauge.

Materials to complete all projects:

Yarn: Worsted weight yarns and bulky weight yarn (See individual patterns for specific amounts.)
Needles: Sizes 5 through 8 straight, or to obtain specified gauge
Yarn needle
Measuring tape
Scissors

Stitches used in this chapter:

Knit/purl ribbing
Stockinette stitch

Now on to the knitting! I give you multiple size patterns for three weights of yarn.

Knit Tips _____

Textured yarns can add visual interest to a simple or solid-colored outfit.

Evening Shrug

A shrug can take the place of a more expensive and less useful garment. If you're just transitioning from a car to a building, a shrug is all you need, especially if it's one that helps you make an eye-popping entrance!

For all sizes, you'll need the following:

Yarn: Approximately 1,200 yards worsted weight
Needles: Sizes 5 and 7 straight, or to obtain specified gauge
Gauge: $4\frac{1}{2}$ stitches per inch in pattern stitch
Time to complete: Approximately 8 hours (more if you're still learning!)
Yarn needle

Small Evening Shrug

1. With smaller needles, cast on 26 stitches.

2. Work in knit 1, purl 1 ribbing for 4 rows.

3. Change to larger needles, and begin working in stockinette stitch.

4. On the next right-side row, increase 4 stitches evenly spaced across the row.

5. Work 3 rows.

6. Beginning on the next right-side row, increase 1 stitch each side every fourth row to 58 stitches.

7. Work even in stockinette stitch until the piece measures 17 1/2". Place markers on each side.

8. Work even in stockinette stitch until the piece measures 35". Place markers on each side.

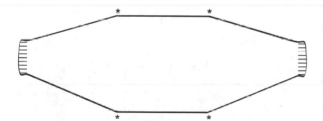

Place markers at the ends of the sleeves.

9. Beginning on the next right-side row, decrease 1 stitch each side every fourth row until the piece measures to 30 stitches.

10. Decrease 4 stitches evenly over next right-side row to 26 stitches.

11. Switch to smaller needles, and work in knit 1, purl 1 ribbing for 4 rows.

12. Bind off loosely.

13. Fold lengthways with right sides together.

14. Sew the sleeve seams from the cuff to the marker. Weave in the ends.

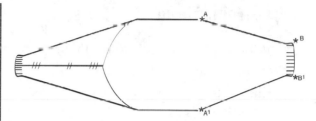

Sew the sleeve seams to the markers.

Medium Evening Shrug

1. With smaller needles, cast on 28 stitches.

2. Work in knit 1, purl 1 ribbing for 4 rows.

3. Change to larger needles, and begin working in stockinette stitch.

4. On the next right-side row, increase 4 stitches evenly spaced across the row.

5. Work 3 rows.

6. Beginning on the next right-side row, increase 1 stitch each side every fourth row to 64 stitches.

7. Work even in stockinette stitch until the piece measures 18". Place markers on each side.

8. Work even in stockinette stitch until the piece measures 36". Place markers on each side.

9. Beginning on the next right-side row, decrease 1 stitch each side every fourth row to 32 stitches.

10. Decrease 4 stitches evenly over the next right-side row to 28 stitches.

11. Switch to smaller needles, and work in knit 1, purl 1 ribbing for 4 rows.

12. Bind off loosely.

13. Fold lengthways with right sides together.

14. Sew the sleeve seams from the cuff to the marker. Weave in the ends.

Large Evening Shrug

1. With smaller needles, cast on 30 stitches.

2. Work in knit 1, purl 1 ribbing for 4 rows.

3. Change to larger needles, and begin working in stockinette stitch.

4. On the next right-side row, increase 4 stitches evenly spaced across the row.

5. Work 3 rows.

6. Beginning on the next right-side row, increase 1 stitch each side every fourth row to 66 stitches.

7. Work even in stockinette stitch until the piece measures 18 ½". Place markers on each side.

8. Work even in stockinette stitch until the piece measures 37". Place markers each side.

9. Beginning on the next right-side row, decrease 1 stitch each side every fourth row to 34 stitches.

10. Decrease 4 stitches evenly over the next right-side row to 30 stitches.

11. Switch to smaller needles, and work in knit 1, purl 1 ribbing for 4 rows.

12. Bind off loosely.

13. Fold lengthways with right sides together.

14. Sew the sleeve seams from the cuff to the marker. Weave in the ends.

Sporty Shrug

A short-sleeved shrug is great if you're like me and don't much care for long sleeves because they're always getting dragged through everything. Or maybe you just want a smaller garment but can't give up having something around your shoulders. This is the shrug for you!

For the active woman—short and warm!

The fiber options are only as endless as your imagination, but here are a few suggestions:

◆ Bulky weight merino

◆ Novelty yarn shot through with sequins

◆ Metallic thread

◆ Vermicelli yarn

◆ All of it at once!

For all sizes, you'll need the following:

> *Yarn:* 800 to 1,000 yards Malabrigo Merino worsted weight yarn
>
> *Needles:* Sizes 6 and 8 straight, or to obtain specified gauge
>
> *Gauge:* 4 stitches per inch in pattern stitch
>
> *Time to complete:* Approximately 12 hours
>
> Yarn needle

Small Sporty Shrug

1. With smaller needles, cast on 44 stitches.

2. Work in knit 1, purl 1 ribbing for 4 rows.

3. Change to larger needles, and begin working in stockinette stitch.

4. On the next right-side row, increase 4 stitches evenly spaced across the row.

5. Work 3 rows.

6. Beginning on the next right-side row, increase 1 stitch each side every fourth row to 76 stitches.

7. Work even in stockinette stitch to 7". Place markers on each side.

8. Work even in stockinette stitch until the piece measures 20 1/2". Place markers each side.

9. Beginning on the next right-side row, decrease 1 stitch each side every fourth row to 48 stitches.

10. Decrease 4 stitches evenly over the next right-side row to 44 stitches.

11. Switch to smaller needles, and work in knit 1, purl 1 ribbing for 4 rows.

12. Bind off loosely.

13. Fold lengthways with right sides together.

14. Sew the sleeve seams from the cuff to the marker. Weave in the ends.

Medium Sport Shrug

1. With smaller needles, cast on 48 stitches.

2. Work in knit 1, purl 1 ribbing for 4 rows.

3. Change to larger needles, and begin working in stockinette stitch.

4. On the next right-side row, increase 4 stitches evenly spaced across the row.

5. Work 3 rows.

6. Beginning on the next right-side row, increase 1 stitch each side every fourth row to 81 stitches.

7. Work even in stockinette stitch until the piece measures 7". Place markers on each side.

8. Work even in stockinette stitch until the piece measures 22 1/2". Place markers each side.

9. Beginning on the next right-side row, decrease 1 stitch each side every fourth row to 52 stitches.

10. Decrease 4 stitches evenly over the next right-side row to 48 stitches.

11. Switch to smaller needles, and work in knit 1, purl 1 ribbing for 4 rows.

12. Bind off loosely.

13. Fold lengthways with right sides together.

14. Sew the sleeve seams from the cuff to the marker. Weave in the ends.

Large Sporty Shrug

1. With smaller needles, cast on 50 stitches.

2. Work in knit 1, purl 1 ribbing for 4 rows.

3. Change to larger needles, and begin working in stockinette stitch.

4. On the next right-side row, increase 4 stitches evenly spaced across the row.

5. Work 3 rows.

6. Beginning on the next right-side row, increase 1 stitch each side every fourth row to 88 stitches.

7. Work even in stockinette stitch until the piece measures 7". Place markers on each side.

8. Work even in stockinette stitch until the piece measures 24 1/2". Place markers each side.

9. Beginning on the next right-side row, decrease 1 stitch each side every fourth row to 54 stitches.

10. Decrease 4 stitches evenly over the next right-side row to 50 stitches.

11. Switch to smaller needles, and work in knit 1, purl 1 ribbing for 4 rows.

12. Bind off loosely.

13. Fold lengthways with right sides together.

14. Sew the sleeve seams from the cuff to the marker. Weave in the ends.

Blouson Sleeve Shrug

This is a nicely loose shrug, but the sleeves aren't so overly large that you feel like Madame Butterfly! Use a soft and luxurious yarn for added comfort—merino is wonderful, or splurge on cashmere! You could also use a mohair, an alpaca/angora blend, or a pima cotton. For an elegant alternative, use a silk ribbon tape for the cuffs and a complementary fiber for the sleeves. Allow extra yarn for the large sleeves.

> *Yarn:* Approximately 1,200 yards worsted weight yarn
>
> *Needles:* Sizes 5 and 7 straight, or to obtain gauge
>
> *Gauge:* 5 stitches per inch in pattern stitch
>
> *Time to complete:* Approximately 15 to 20 hours
>
> Yarn needle

Small Blouson Shrug

1. With smaller needles, cast on 64 stitches.
2. Work in knit 2, purl 2 ribbing for 3".
3. Change to larger needles, and begin working in stockinette stitch.
4. On the next right-side row, increase knit 1, make 1 across the row to 96 stitches.
5. Work even in stockinette stitch until the piece measures 18". Place markers on each side.
6. Work even in stockinette stitch until the piece measures 38½". Place markers each side.
7. Work even in stockinette stitch until the piece measures 53½".
8. On the next right-side row, decrease knit 1, knit 2 together to 64 stitches.
9. Switch to smaller needles, and work in knit 2, purl 2 ribbing for 3".
10. Bind off loosely.
11. Fold lengthways with right sides together.
12. Sew the sleeve seams from the cuff to the marker. Weave in the ends.

Medium Blouson Shrug

1. With smaller needles, cast on 68 stitches.
2. Work in knit 2, purl 2 ribbing for 3".
3. Change to larger needles, and begin working in stockinette stitch.
4. On the next right-side row, increase knit 1, make 1 across the row to 102 stitches.
5. Work even in stockinette stitch until the piece measures 18". Place markers on each side.
6. Work even in stockinette stitch until the piece measures 39". Place markers each side.
7. Work even in stockinette stitch until the piece measures 54".
8. On the next right-side row, decrease knit 1, knit 2 together to 68 stitches.
9. Switch to smaller needles, and work in knit 2, purl 2 ribbing for 12 rows.
10. Bind off loosely.
11. Fold lengthways with right sides together.
12. Sew the sleeve seams from the cuff to the marker. Weave in the ends.

Large Blouson Shrug

1. With smaller needles, cast on 74 stitches.
2. Work in knit 2, purl 2 ribbing for 3".
3. Change to larger needles, and begin working in stockinette stitch.
4. On the next right-side row, increase knit 1, make 1 across the row to 111 stitches.
5. Work even in stockinette stitch until the piece measures 19". Place markers on each side.
6. Work even in stockinette stitch until the piece measures 43 1/2". Place markers each side.
7. Work even in stockinette stitch until the piece measures 59 1/2".
8. On the next right-side row, decrease knit 1, knit 2 together to 74 stitches.
9. Switch to smaller needles, and work in knit 2, purl 2 ribbing for 12 rows.
10. Bind off loosely.
11. Fold lengthways with right sides together.
12. Sew the sleeve seams from the cuff to the marker. Weave in the ends.

In This Chapter

- ◆ Meet the capelet

- ◆ Capelet variations: I Love the Nightlife Capelet, Appalachian Trail Capelet, and Light-as-Air Capelet

- ◆ Embellish your work with beads

- ◆ Learn a new stitch: 7 come 11

 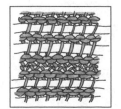    

Chapter 9

Capelets

What's a capelet? It's less than a poncho but more than a wrap, as it either has ties or slips on over the head. It's short enough so the fabric won't get in your way, but long enough to cover your shoulders where you are apt to feel the cold.

This is a good project for the novice knitter. There's no shaping but for increases. You can choose a style that's either knit flat on straight needles or in the round on circular needles, which is good if you don't like to purl. This project does require an investment in time, but you wind up with a garment more substantial than a hat or a scarf. Plus, a capelet isn't something you have to think about a great deal as you're knitting it.

What You Need and Need to Know

This project is a good opportunity for you to become a little more adventurous and experimental. I've given you instructions in this chapter that explain exactly what you need to do, and I've also provided the basic capelet instructions, which allow you plenty of room to do as you please once you understand the basics.

A capelet can be like a flowing cape, or it can be made to hug you quite closely. The basic capelet instructions allow you to make that choice.

A word about frogging: As I've mentioned, knitting is a very forgiving process, and most projects can be unraveled and begun again if you see you've had a problem or a mistake. For most yarns, this won't make a difference. Fuzzy, fluffy, or highly textured yarns might give you a problem, though.

If the process of knitting is what appeals to you, restarting a project means just more knitting. If you are goal-oriented and want the finished project, you probably won't want to be too experimental early in your knitting experience, to avoid the frustration and practice of ripping out.

Knit Tips

The capelet can be destined for the nightlife or an afternoon hiking the trails in the late autumn. It all depends on the yarn you choose.

Materials to complete all projects:

Yarn: Fingering, worsted, and bulky weight yarns in amounts and colors specified in individual patterns

Needles: Sizes 5, 7, 8, 10, 11, 13, and 15 circular, or to obtain specified gauge; one circular approximately 16″ long and another approximately 29″ long

Yarn needle

Measuring tape

Thread or fine yarn

Scissors

Stitches and techniques used in this chapter:

Knit/purl ribbing

Stockinette stitch

Seed stitch

Lace patterns

Beading

Basic Capelet

When you understand the construction of a capelet, it's a very simple pattern to work. The neckband is the same as for a sweater and is made on the smaller needle. Then you switch to the larger needle and knit approximately 4 inches. At that point, begin increasing every 6 rows. When the capelet is as wide and as long as you'd like, knit several rows of seed stitch to prevent the bottom edge from rolling.

A capelet keeps your shoulders warm while leaving your arms free. You won't sit on it, either!

For some fun, you can make the stripes random widths. For the capelet pictured above and also in the color insert, I chose the Tobago in white with pink bobbles to add contrast, sparkle, and texture.

The seed stitch adds texture to a flat fabric.

If you want your capelet not quite as wide but still long enough to reach your elbow, simply stop increasing and continue to knit until the capelet is the desired length.

Yarn: 3 skeins pink Cascade Superwash 220 and 1 skein lighter pink for the contrast color, approximately 2 skeins Austermann Tobago metallic bobble

Needles: Sizes 5 and 7 circular, or to obtain specified gauge

Yarn needle

Measuring tape

Scissors

Small Capelet

1. Cast on 92 stitches on smaller needles, and join to work in the round. Mark the beginning of the round.

Knots!

Be sure you don't twist the cast on row as you join the knitting!

2. Work knit 1, purl 1 ribbing for 1½".

3. Continue in stockinette stitch until the piece measures 5½".

4. Begin increase round: *knit 3, increase 1 stitch, repeat from * around.

5. Knit 6 rows.

6. Increase round: *knit 4, increase 1 stitch, repeat from * around.

7. Knit 6 rows.

8. Increase round: *knit 5, increase 1 stitch, repeat from * around.

9. Knit 6 rows.

10. Increase round: *knit 6, increase 1 stitch, repeat from * around.

11. Knit 6 rows.

12. Increase round: *knit 7, increase 1 stitch, repeat from * around.

13. Knit 6 rows.

14. Increase round: *knit 8, increase 1 stitch, repeat from * around.

15. Knit 6 rows.

16. Increase round: *knit 9, increase 1 stitch, repeat from * around.

17. Knit 6 rows.

18. Increase round: *knit 10, increase 1 stitch, repeat from * around.

19. Knit 6 rows.

20. Knit 4 rows seed stitch.

21. Loosely bind off, and weave in all the ends.

22. Add fringe or tassels, if desired. (Learn how to add fringe in Chapter 7. For tassel instructions, see Chapter 2.)

Medium Capelet

1. Cast on 100 stitches on smaller needles, and join to work in the round. Mark the beginning of the round.

2. Work knit 1, purl 1 ribbing for 1½".

3. Continue in stockinette stitch until the piece measures 5½".

4. Begin increase round: *knit 3, increase 1 stitch, repeat from * around.

5. Knit 6 rows.

6. Increase round: *knit 4, increase 1 stitch, repeat from * around.

7. Knit 6 rows.

8. Increase round: *knit 5, increase 1 stitch, repeat from * around.

9. Knit 6 rows.

10. Increase round: *knit 6, increase 1 stitch, repeat from * around.

11. Knit 6 rows.

12. Increase round: *knit 7, increase 1 stitch, repeat from * around.

13. Knit 6 rows.

14. Increase round: *knit 8, increase 1 stitch, repeat from * around.

15. Knit 6 rows.

16. Increase round: *knit 9, increase 1 stitch, repeat from * around.

17. Knit 6 rows.

18. Increase round: *knit 10, increase 1 stitch, repeat from * around.

19. Knit 6 rows.

20. Knit 4 rows seed stitch.

21. Loosely bind off and weave in all the ends.

22. Add fringe or tassels, if desired. (Learn how to add fringe in Chapter 7. For tassel instructions, see Chapter 2.)

Large Capelet

1. Cast on 108 stitches on smaller needles, and join to work in the round. Mark the beginning of the round.

2. Work knit 1, purl 1 ribbing for 1½".

3. Continue in stockinette stitch until the piece measures 5½".

4. Begin increase round: *knit 3, increase 1 stitch, repeat from * around.

5. Knit 6 rows.

6. Increase round: *knit 4, increase 1 stitch, repeat from * around.

7. Knit 6 rows.

8. Increase round: *knit 5, increase 1 stitch, repeat from * around.

9. Knit 6 rows.

10. Increase round: *knit 6, increase 1 stitch, repeat from * around.

11. Knit 6 rows.

12. Increase round: *knit 7, increase 1 stitch, repeat from * around.

13. Knit 6 rows.

14. Increase round: *knit 8, increase 1 stitch, repeat from * around.

15. Knit 6 rows.

16. Increase round: *knit 9, increase 1 stitch, repeat from * around.

17. Knit 6 rows.

18. Increase round: *knit 10, increase 1 stitch, repeat from * around.

19. Knit 6 rows.

20. Knit 4 rows seed stitch.

21. Loosely bind off, and weave in all the ends.

22. Add fringe or tassels, if desired. (Learn how to add fringe in Chapter 7. For tassel instructions, see Chapter 2.)

Snug the fringe firmly so it looks neat.

I Love the Nightlife Capelet

You can find a wide range of fashion or novelty yarns that knit at a chunky weight gauge but are light. This project calls for a yarn that knits at 2 stitches to the inch using size 11 and 13 circular needles. If you want to add a touch of drama, you can easily use a metallic carry along thread, which would add no bulk.

Purl Pearls _____

Carry along yarns can be used all over or limited to certain areas, such as cuffs.

Mix and match or use the yarn in the sample, Bollicine Bouton Colour, #6003. If you are off 1 stitch when you count your gauge swatch, this is because we're dealing with math and math doesn't understand you can't have half a stitch, so you have to round up or down. Don't panic—it's fine.

Knit Tips _____

What? You didn't make a swatch? Remember our motto: swatch first, smile later.

For all sizes, you'll need the following materials:

Yarn: Bollicine Bouton Colour, #6003

Needles: Sizes 11 and 13 straight or circular

Gauge: 2 stitches per inch

Time to complete: 8 to 12 hours

Ribbon for closure

Yarn needle

Measuring tape

Sewing needle and thread

Scissors

Small Capelet

1. Cast on 36 stitches on smaller needles.
2. Work in garter stitch until the piece measures 4".
3. Switch to larger needles, and work 3 rows in garter stitch.
4. Work increase row: knit 3, *knit 1, increase in the next stitch, repeat from * across, ending knit 3.
5. Work 3 rows even.
6. Work increase row: knit 3, *knit 2, increase in the next stitch, repeat from * across, ending knit 3.
7. Work 3 rows even.
8. Work increase row: knit 3, *knit 3, increase in the next stitch, repeat from * across, ending knit 3.
9. Work 3 rows even.
10. Work increase row: knit 3, *knit 4, increase in the next stitch, repeat from * across, ending knit 3.
11. Work 3 rows even.
12. Work increase row: knit 3, *knit 5, increase in the next stitch, repeat from * across, ending knit 3.
13. Work even until the piece measures 10" or the desired length.
14. Bind off loosely, and weave in the ends.

Medium Capelet

1. Cast on 40 stitches on smaller needles.
2. Work in garter stitch until the piece measures 4 1/2".
3. Switch to larger needles, and work 3 rows in garter stitch.
4. Work increase row: knit 3, *knit 1, increase in the next stitch, repeat from * across, ending knit 3.

5. Work 3 rows even.
6. Work increase row: knit 3, *knit 2, increase in the next stitch, repeat from * across, ending knit 3.
7. Work 3 rows even.
8. Work increase row: knit 3, *knit 3, increase in the next stitch, repeat from * across, ending knit 3.
9. Work 3 rows even.
10. Work increase row: knit 3, *knit 4, increase in the next stitch, repeat from * across, ending knit 3.
11. Work 3 rows even.
12. Work increase row: knit 3, *knit 5, increase in the next stitch, repeat from * across, ending knit 3.
13. Work even until the piece measures 11" or desired length.
14. Bind off loosely, and weave in the ends.

Large Capelet

1. Cast on 44 stitches on smaller needles.
2. Work in garter stitch until the piece measures 5".
3. Switch to larger needles, and work 3 rows in garter stitch.
4. Work increase row: knit 3, *knit 1, increase in the next stitch, repeat from * across, ending knit 3.
5. Work 3 rows even.
6. Work increase row: knit 3, *knit 2, increase in the next stitch, repeat from * across, ending knit 3.
7. Work 3 rows even.
8. Work increase row: knit 3, *knit 3, increase in the next stitch, repeat from * across, ending knit 3.
9. Work 3 rows even.

10. Work increase row: knit 3, *knit 4, increase in the next stitch, repeat from * across, ending knit 3.

11. Work 3 rows even.

12. Work increase row: knit 3, *knit 5, increase in the next stitch, repeat from * across, ending knit 3.

13. Work even until the piece measures 11" or desired length.

14. Bind off loosely, and weave in the ends.

Closing

You have options when it comes to a method of closure for your capelet:

◆ Ribbon

◆ I-Cord

◆ Frog

For a ribbon closure, you'll need two lengths of ribbon approximately 8" long of either a complementary or contrasting color. Thread one ribbon through each side to the wrong side of the capelet, and tack the end in place with a needle and thread. A few firm stitches is all that's necessary. Then tie the ribbon into a bow to close the capelet.

Instead of using a ribbon, you can knit two lengths of I-Cord. Cast on 4 to 6 stitches, depending on how thick you'd like the cord. Knit until the cord is approximately 8" long. Sew one cord to each side of the top front of the capelet. Tie the two cords together in a bow to close the capelet.

Use a pretty length of ribbon and tie in a bow to close.

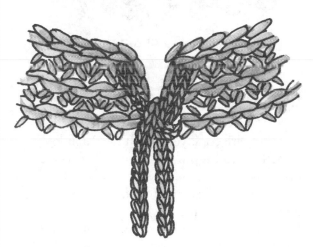

Sew two lengths of I-Cord to either side of the opening to make a good closure.

For a frog closure, you'll use an I-Cord and a button to hold your capelet together. You'll probably need a length of I-Cord approximately 8" long to go from one side of the capelet to the other and around the button.

Then proceed as follows:

1. Test the placement of the button.

2. Cut a length of yarn to see how much cord you'll need.

3. Cast on 3 stitches, and knit until you reach the desired length.

4. Hold the cord up to the garment to be sure it's the correct length, and then bind off.

5. Sew both ends to one side, forming a large loop.

6. Sew the button to the opposite side of the capelet, making sure the cord is able to loop around the button.

Loop the I-Cord around the button to close.

Appalachian Trail Capelet

If you're hiking of hill walking when the temperatures are cool, you might need a little something to keep warm until the sun comes up. This capelet might be all you need while giving you the freedom to move, break camp, pitch tent, or simple play fetch with your dog. Choose colors of nature to reflect the great outdoors.

For all sizes, you'll need the following materials:

Yarn: Approximately 600 yards bulky weight yarn

Needles: Sizes 8 and 10 straight or circular

Gauge: 3 stitches per inch

Time to complete: 8 to 10 hours

Yarn needle

Measuring tape

Scissors

Small Mountain Capelet

1. Cast on 52 stitches on smaller needles, and join.

2. Work in stockinette stitch until the piece measures 4".

3. Switch to larger needles, and work 3 rows.

4. Work increase row: knit 3, *knit 1, increase in the next stitch, repeat from * across, ending knit 3.

5. Work 3 rows even.

6. Work increase row: knit 3, *knit 2, increase in the next stitch, repeat from * across, ending knit 3.

7. Work 3 rows even.

8. Work increase row: knit 3, *knit 3, increase in the next stitch, repeat from * across, ending knit 3.

9. Work 3 rows even.

10. Work increase row: knit 3, *knit 4, increase in the next stitch, repeat from * across, ending knit 3.

11. Work 3 rows even.

12. Work increase row: knit 3, *knit 5, increase in the next stitch, repeat from * across, ending knit 3.

13. Work 3 rows even.

14. Work increase row: knit 3, *knit 6, increase in the next stitch, repeat from * across, ending knit 3.

15. Work even until the piece measures 10" or the desired length.

16. Bind off loosely, and weave in the ends.

17. Add fringe, if desired.

Medium Mountain Capelet

1. Cast on 56 stitches on smaller needles, and join.
2. Work in stockinette stitch until the piece measures 4 ½".
3. Switch to larger needles, and work 3 rows.
4. Work increase row: knit 3, *knit 1, increase in the next stitch, repeat from * across, ending knit 3.
5. Work 3 rows even.
6. Work increase row: knit 3, *knit 2, increase in the next stitch, repeat from * across, ending knit 3.
7. Work 3 rows even.
8. Work increase row: knit 3, *knit 3, increase in the next stitch, repeat from * across, ending knit 3.
9. Work 3 rows even.
10. Work increase row: knit 3, *knit 4, increase in the next stitch, repeat from * across, ending knit 3.
11. Work 3 rows even.
12. Work increase row: knit 3, *knit 5, increase in the next stitch, repeat from * across, ending knit 3.
13. Work 3 rows even.
14. Work even until the piece measures 11" or the desired length.
15. Bind off loosely, and weave in the ends.
16. Add fringe, if desired.

Large Mountain Capelet

1. Cast on 68 stitches on smaller needles, and join.
2. Work in stockinette stitch until the piece measures 5".
3. Switch to larger needles, and work 5 rows.
4. Work increase row: knit 3, *knit 1, increase in the next stitch, repeat from * across, ending knit 3.
5. Work 5 rows even.
6. Work increase row: knit 3, *knit 2, increase in the next stitch, repeat from * across, ending knit 3.
7. Work 5 rows even.
8. Work increase row: knit 3, *knit 3, increase in the next stitch, repeat from * across, ending knit 3.
9. Work 5 rows even.
10. Work increase row: knit 3, *knit 4, increase in the next stitch, repeat from * across, ending knit 3.
11. Work 8 rows even.
12. Work increase row: knit 3, *knit 5, increase in the next stitch, repeat from * across, ending knit 3.
13. Work even until the piece measures 13" or the desired length.
14. Bind off loosely, and weave in the ends.
15. Add fringe, if desired.

Light-as-Air Capelet

Bulky yarns have their place, especially when we need to make something fast. Worsted weight is very good when we know it's going to be cold. What about when we just need something to cover up a little? At such times, there's nothing quite like a fine-gauge yarn to produce a fabric that flows and moves with you.

It will take quite a bit longer to complete a garment using size 2 needles instead of size 10, but when speed and weight aren't the point, you might decide to go in the opposite direction and knit something light. There are many choices of yarn in the fingering or sock weight category—and, yes, sock yarn can be used successfully in projects other than socks.

For all sizes, you'll need the following materials:

> *Yarn:* Approximately 600 to 1,000 yards fingering or sock weight yarn
>
> *Needles:* Size 2 circular, about 40" long
>
> *Gauge:* 7 stitches per inch
>
> *Time to complete:* 30+ hours (The stitches are small, and there are lots of them!)
>
> Yarn needle
>
> Measuring tape
>
> Scissors

Small Capelet

1. Cast on 128 stitches, and join.
2. Work in stockinette stitch until the piece measures 1".
3. Work increase row: knit 3, *knit 1, increase in the next stitch, repeat from * across, ending knit 3.

4. Work 9 rows even.
5. Work increase row: knit 3, *knit 2, increase in the next stitch, repeat from * across, ending knit 3.
6. Work 9 rows even.
7. Work increase row: knit 3, *knit 3, increase in the next stitch, repeat from * across, ending knit 3.
8. Work 9 rows even.
9. Work increase row: knit 3, *knit 4, increase in the next stitch, repeat from * across, ending knit 3.
10. Work 9 rows even.
11. Work increase row: knit 3, *knit 5, increase in the next stitch, repeat from * across, ending knit 3.
12. Work 9 rows even.
13. Work increase row: knit 3, *knit 6, increase in the next stitch, repeat from * across, ending knit 3.
14. Work even until the piece measures 16" or the desired length.
15. Bind off loosely, and weave in the ends.
16. Add fringe, if desired.

Medium Capelet

1. Cast on 136 stitches, and join.
2. Work in stockinette stitch until the piece measures 1".
3. Work increase row: knit 3, *knit 1, increase in the next stitch, repeat from * across, ending knit 3.
4. Work 10 rows even.

5. Work increase row: knit 3, *knit 2, increase in the next stitch, repeat from * across, ending knit 3.

6. Work 10 rows even.

7. Work increase row: knit 3, *knit 3, increase in the next stitch, repeat from * across, ending knit 3.

8. Work 10 rows even.

9. Work increase row: knit 3, *knit 4, increase in the next stitch, repeat from * across, ending knit 3.

10. Work 10 rows even.

11. Work increase row: knit 3, *knit 5, increase in the next stitch, repeat from * across, ending knit 3.

12. Work 10 rows even.

13. Work increase row: knit 3, *knit 6, increase in the next stitch, repeat from * across, ending knit 3.

14. Work even until the piece measures 17" or the desired length.

15. Bind off loosely, and weave in the ends.

16. Add fringe, if desired.

Large Capelet

1. Cast on 156 stitches, and join.

2. Work in stockinette stitch until the piece measures 1".

3. Work increase row: knit 3, *knit 1, increase in the next stitch, repeat from * across, ending knit 3.

4. Work 11 rows even.

5. Work increase row: knit 3, *knit 2, increase in the next stitch, repeat from * across, ending knit 3.

6. Work 11 rows even.

7. Work increase row: knit 3, *knit 3, increase in the next stitch, repeat from * across, ending knit 3.

8. Work 11 rows even.

9. Work increase row: knit 3, *knit 4, increase in the next stitch, repeat from * across, ending knit 3.

10. Work 11 rows even.

11. Work increase row: knit 3, *knit 5, increase in the next stitch, repeat from * across, ending knit 3.

12. Work 10 rows even.

13. Work increase row: knit 3, *knit 6, increase in the next stitch, repeat from * across, ending knit 3.

14. Work even until the piece measures 18" or the desired length.

15. Bind off loosely, and weave in the ends.

16. Add fringe, if desired.

Knitting with Beads

This is such a great idea, and it's so easy! All you do is string beads onto the skein before you knit. Just undo every skein, thread the beads onto the yarn, and wind the yarn back into a ball.

If you don't have time for quite that much effort, there is a somewhat quicker way, although it's more random. As you're knitting along and you want a bead at that position in the garment, carefully slide that stitch off the needle and, using a sewing needle threader, slip the bead onto the stitch. Slip the stitch back onto the needle, and knit away.

Knit Tips

Be sure you select beads with a hole large enough to accommodate the diameter of your yarn.

If your beads aren't big enough to slip easily onto your yarn, the simplest way is to just use a needle and thread; when your garment is finished, go back and decorate it with all the beadwork you'd like.

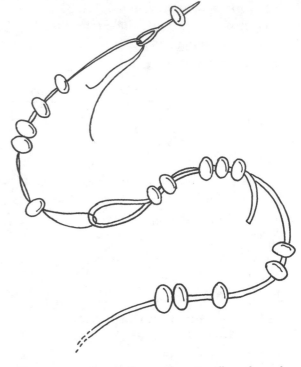

Choose a needle small enough so it will go through the beads.

7-Come-11 Stitch

Time to learn a new stitch: the 7-come-11 stitch, which is a random eyelet pattern. How do you do this stitch? Easy. Get a pair of dice and roll them. Whatever number comes up is the number of stitches you make between a set of yarn overs. Then roll again to determine the next set.

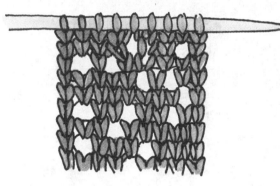

Randomly placed yarn overs create a visual design.

This method is very compatible with all the increases you must make for the capelet. Remember that each yarn over must be followed by a knit 2 together, or your garment will soon become as large as a tent!

In This Chapter

- ◆ It's back! The poncho

- ◆ Spice up the look of your poncho with variations like Asymmetrical Poncho, Mandala Poncho, and more

- ◆ Add embellishments and trim

- ◆ Ponchos for adults as well as children

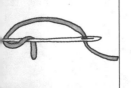 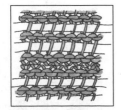    

Chapter 10

Ponchos

If you were around during the 1960s, you might know that the poncho was popular then. But look around any mall or clothing store today, and you'll see that the poncho has recently experienced a renewed popularity. And why not? The poncho is convenient, it's simple, and your arms aren't hampered by sleeves.

Everything old can be new again with intriguing yarns and attractive colors. We can reinvent, reimagine, and reconstruct using new styles of yarn unavailable in the past.

Bold blocks of colors can add a dramatic flare with no additional work on your part. Try purple and green, white and black, or light blue and dark blue. Make one panel in one color and one panel in another, if you want something more than stripes.

What You Need and Need to Know

You can construct a poncho in several ways. One of the simplest is to use a garter stitch to knit two 20" × 32" rectangles and then sew them together.

Purl Pearls

In South America, a poncho is a blanketlike cloak with a hole in the center for the head, originally hand-woven by native Indians and later commonly worn by gauchos.

But before you start to knit, spend a few minutes considering your project. Remember that a poncho will look better if made from a yarn that drapes well. Otherwise, it will be bulky and stand away from your body like a sail. Try some of the newer novelty yarns, like ribbon tapes and rail ribbons, or a smooth worsted. Reserve the bulky, chunky yarns for a rugged poncho when warmth is important.

A poncho should cover you without obscuring you completely.

Speaking of warmth, consider where you'll be wearing this poncho. If you'll mostly wear it inside as an accent to an outfit, don't choose a too-heavy yarn, or you'll overheat. You could use a furlike yarn for a great accent in cold weather, though. Or have the best of both and work a smooth, silky ribbon poncho with a fur trim.

Materials to complete all projects:

Yarns: Bulky weight yarn and assorted worsted weight yarns (See individual pattern instructions for more information.)

Needles: Sizes 9 and 11 straight, and 5 and 7 circular, or to obtain specified gauge

Novelty buttons

Yarn needle

Measuring tape

Thread or fine yarn

Scissors

Stitches and techniques used in this chapter:

Knit/purl ribbing

Garter stitch

Stockinette stitch

Single crochet

Duplicate stitch

Fringe

Basic Poncho

Some fashionistas insists ponchos cover all the right areas while being comforting and comfortable. It's true that one size fits most and it's never too tight, so these may be explanations why the poncho is so popular. I'm sure you'll find many more reasons to love your own hand-knitted poncho.

Size: One size fits most

Yarn: Bulky yarn

Needles: Size 11 or to obtain gauge

Gauge: 2 stitches per inch in pattern stitch

Time to complete: 15 to 20 hours

Yarn needle

Measuring tape

Scissors

1. Cast on 40 stitches.

2. Knit 3 rows.

3. Begin pattern stitch as follows:

   Row 4: Knit across, wrapping the yarn around the needle twice for each stitch.

   Row 5: Knit, letting the extra loop drop.

   Row 6: Knit.

   Row 7: Knit.

   Row 8: Repeat Row 4.

4. Repeat Rows 4 through 8 until the piece measures 32".

5. Knit 3 rows.

6. Bind off loosely.

7. Make a second rectangle the same way.

8. Sew the rectangles together, as indicated in the following figure.

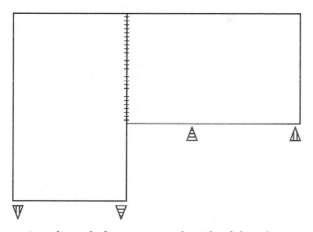

Sew the end of one piece to the side of the other.

9. Add fringe, if you want (see Chapter 7).

Knit Tips

Adding fringe on a poncho is not a given. Some ponchos and some people don't require it. For others, it's a necessity. If you want to add fringe, check out the instructions in Chapter 7.

Asymmetrical Poncho

This poncho is very easy and works up quickly. A light yarn, such as mohair, ribbon tape, or chenille, works well. This is an excellent opportunity to either use up yarns from your stash or use sale yarns that you loved but were able to buy only 1 skein of. You could even use your leftovers to make a striped poncho; just try to keep the yarns approximately the same weight.

Size: One size fits most

Yarn: Your choice, approximately 250 to 300 yards

Needles: As recommended for yarn

Gauge: As recommended for yarn

Time to complete: 6 to 10 hours

Yarn needle

Measuring tape

Scissors

You can use any of several stitches for this poncho. Garter stitch is the real workhorse for these projects. You also can use a wrapped drop or even a double wrapped drop stitch (see Chapter 5). Or try this yarn over stitch:

1. Knit a rectangle that measures approximately 14" × 40".

2. Yarn over pattern stitch, a multiple of 2 plus 1:

   Row 1: Knit.

Row 2: *Knit 1, yarn over, knit 2 together, repeat from * to end of row.

Row 3: Knit.

3. Repeat Rows 1 through 3 until the piece is the desired length.

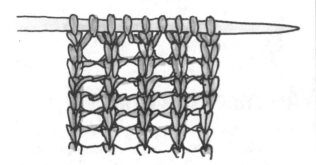

Yarn overs create an openwork, lacy appearance.

Knots! _____

Yarn overs are always followed by knitting stitches together; otherwise, you'll be increasing the number of stitches in your row.

You can stop right there and have a very nice wrap, or proceed as with the diagram and sew the rectangle together, wrong sides together. With the rectangle facing you, bring the lower right corner up to the upper left corner. This will require some positioning, and don't be afraid to use some pins or clips to help you along. The seam will be comprised of the right end of the rectangle joining with the upper left side of the rectangle. Turn right side out. Wear your poncho with the long point in front.

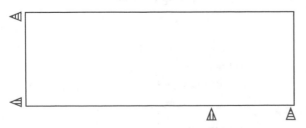

Assembling your poncho is easy!

Mandala Poncho

What goes 'round comes 'round, and this poncho is round. It's also the perfect opportunity to experiment with textures and yarns. Double or even triple yarns to create the look you want while achieving 2 stitches to the inch. Or use a chunky thick-and-thin space-dyed yarn with color tonalities. A light violet and a dark purple would work wonderfully together, and so would a mango paired with shades of brown.

Knit Tips _____

There's no rule stating you must use only two colors for this poncho. Let your imagination run wild!

You'll need 800 to 1,000 yards of yarn, depending on the length of the poncho and the amount of fringe you want. When working with a heavy yarn like this, you'll probably want to make your fringe a bit longer than what you usually would, or the fringe will look stunted.

Sizes: Women's small, medium, large

Yarn: Your choice, approximately 800 to 1,000 yards

Needles: Sizes 9 and 11, or to obtain gauge

Gauge: 2 stitches per inch in pattern stitch

Time to complete: 18 to 20 hours

Yarn needle

Measuring tape

Scissors

Small Mandala Poncho

1. On smaller needles, cast on 40 stitches, join, and place a marker at the beginning of the round.
2. Work knit 1, purl 1 ribbing for 2".
3. Begin stockinette stitch, and continue until the piece measures 4".
4. Switch to larger needles, and work 3 rounds even.
5. Increase round: knit 1, work 2 stitches in the next stitch, repeat around (60 stitches).
6. Work 3 rounds even.
7. Increase round: knit 2, work 2 stitches in the next stitch, repeat around (80 stitches).
8. Work 3 rounds even.
9. Increase round: knit 3, work 2 stitches in the next stitch, repeat around (100 stitches).
10. Work 5 rounds even.
11. Increase round: knit 4, work 2 stitches in the next stitch, repeat around (120 stitches).
12. Work 5 rounds even.
13. Increase round: knit 5, work 2 stitches in the next stitch, repeat around (140 stitches).
14. Work even until the piece measures 24" or the desired length.
15. Bind off loosely, and weave in the ends.
16. Add trim, if desired. (See the later "Braided Trim" section.)

Medium Mandala Poncho

1. On smaller needles, cast on 44 stitches, join, and place a marker at the beginning of the round.
2. Work knit 1, purl 1 ribbing for 2".
3. Begin stockinette stitch, and continue until the piece measures 5".
4. Switch to larger needles, and work 3 rounds even.
5. Increase round: knit 1, work 2 stitches in the next stitch, repeat around (66 stitches).
6. Work 3 rounds even.
7. Increase round: knit 2, work 2 stitches in the next stitch, repeat around (88 stitches).
8. Work 3 rounds even.
9. Increase round: knit 3, work 2 stitches in the next stitch, repeat around (110 stitches).
10. Work 6 rounds even.
11. Increase round: knit 4, work 2 stitches in the next stitch, repeat around (132 stitches).
12. Work 6 rounds even.
13. Increase round: knit 5, work 2 stitches in the next stitch, repeat around (154 stitches).
14. Work even until the piece measures 25" or the desired length.
15. Bind off loosely, and weave in the ends.
16. Add trim, if desired. (See the later "Braided Trim" section.)

Large Mandala Poncho

1. On smaller needles, cast on 48 stitches, join, and place a marker at the beginning of the round.
2. Work knit 1, purl 1 ribbing for 2".
3. Begin stockinette stitch, and continue until the piece measures 5 ½".
4. Switch to larger needles, and work 4 rounds even.
5. Increase round: knit 1, work 2 stitches in the next stitch, repeat around (72 stitches).
6. Work 4 rounds even.

7. Increase round: knit 2, work 2 stitches in the next stitch, repeat around (96 stitches).

8. Work 4 rounds even.

9. Increase round: knit 3, work 2 stitches in the next stitch, repeat around (120 stitches).

10. Work 6 rounds even.

11. Increase round: knit 4, work 2 stitches in the next stitch, repeat around (144 stitches).

12. Work 6 rounds even.

13. Increase round: knit 5, work 2 stitches in the next stitch, repeat around (168 stitches).

14. Work even until the piece measures 26" or the desired length.

15. Bind off loosely, and weave in the ends.

16. Add trim, if desired. (See the "Braided Trim" section.)

Braided Trim

Instead of adding fringe to your poncho, you can take three long lengths of yarn, braid them, fasten them securely, and stitch them in place along the edge of the poncho. This is particularly effective if you have a solid-color garment and use a contrasting or complementary color for the braid.

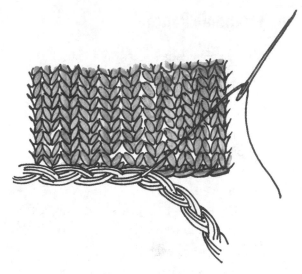

Braided trim gives a finished look to any edge.

Crocheted Stitch Edge

A single crocheted edge is an excellent way to finish off a knit garment. Here again, you can use the same yarn or contrasting yarn.

1. With the right side facing you, insert the crochet hook into the edge.

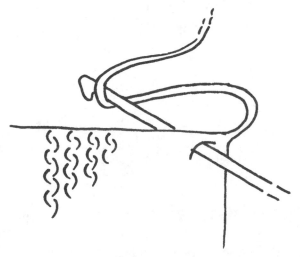

Insert the hook in the last row and catch the yarn.

2. Draw up a loop.

3. Yarn over the hook, and pull through the loop.

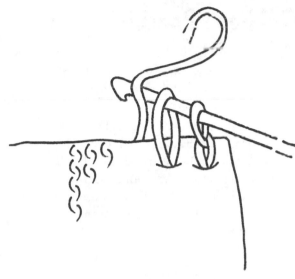

Draw up another loop as before.

6. Repeat along the entire edge.

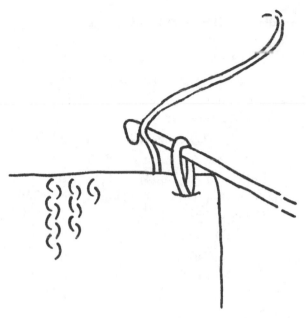

Draw the yarn through the stitch to the front, creating a loop.

4. Insert the hook into the next space.

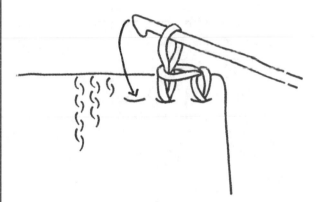

Repeat this procedure across the edge.

You'll have to judge for yourself how many stitches you need. Too few, and the edge will pull in; too many, and the edge won't be even. I wish I could say it was a 1:1 ratio, but it's not because knitting isn't square. The cast on edge is, but the row sides are not. Let your eye guide you.

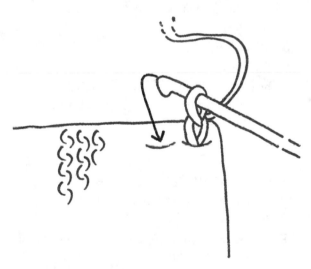

Begin the next stitch in the opening to the left of your hook.

5. Draw up a loop, yarn over, and pull through both loops.

Children's Poncho

This is an easy garment for children to wear. You feel good because they're wearing something warm, and they feel good because they're not so bundled up.

Use bright yarns, use stripes in sherbet colors, or use your stash to come up with a rainbow. You might need to buy only a little bit more to complete the poncho. If you're buying all the yarn, you'll probably need between 300 and 500 yards, depending on the size and desired fringe.

Knots!

Choose yarns that fit the size and personality of a child.

> *Sizes:* Small (22"), medium (25"), large (28")
>
> *Yarn:* Your choice, approximately 300 to 500 yards
>
> *Needles:* Size 5 circular, about 16" long; and size 7 circular, about 29" long; or to obtain gauge
>
> *Gauge:* 5 stitches per inch in pattern stitch
>
> *Time to complete:* 8 to 10 hours
>
> Yarn needle
>
> Measuring tape
>
> Scissors

Small Children's Poncho

1. On smaller needles, cast on 44 stitches.
2. Work knit 1, purl 1 ribbing for 1".
3. Work in stockinette until the piece measures approximately 2½".
4. Switch to larger needles, and work 3 rows even.
5. Increase row: *knit 1, work 2 stitches in the next stitch, repeat from * 21 times (66 stitches).
6. Work 3 rows even.
7. Increase row: knit 1, work 2 stitches in the next stitch, *knit 2, work 2 stitches in the next stitch, repeat from * 21 times (87 stitches).
8. Work 3 rows even.
9. Increase row: knit 2, work 2 stitches in the next stitch, *knit 3, work 2 stitches in the next stitch, repeat from * 21 times (109 stitches).
10. Work 5 rows even.
11. Increase row: knit 2, work 2 stitches in the next stitch, *knit 4, work 2 stitches in the next stitch, repeat from * 21 times (130 stitches).
12. Work 5 rows even.
13. Increase row: knit 3, work 2 stitches in the next stitch, *knit 5, work 2 stitches in the next stitch, repeat from * 21 times (152 stitches).
14. Work even until the piece measures 10" or the desired length.

15. Knit 2 rows.

16. Bind off loosely.

17. Decorate as desired, sew the back seam, and weave in the ends.

18. Add fringe, if desired (see Chapter 7).

Medium Children's Poncho

1. On smaller needles, cast on 48 stitches.

2. Work knit 1, purl 1 ribbing for 1".

3. Work in stockinette until the piece measures approximately 3".

4. Switch to larger needles, and work 3 rows even.

5. Increase row: *knit 1, work 2 stitches in the next stitch, repeat from * 23 times (72 stitches).

6. Work 3 rows even.

7. Increase row: knit 2, work 2 stitches in the next stitch, *knit 2, work 2 stitches in the next stitch, repeat from * 23 times (96 stitches).

8. Work 3 rows even.

9. Increase row: knit 3, work 2 stitches in the next stitch, *knit 3, work 2 stitches in the next stitch, repeat from * 23 times (120 stitches).

10. Work 5 rows even.

11. Increase row: *knit 4, work 2 stitches in the next stitch, repeat from * 24 times (144 stitches).

12. Work 5 rows even.

13. Increase row: *knit 5, work 2 stitches in the next stitch, repeat from * 24 times (168 stitches).

14. Work even until the piece measures 11" or the desired length.

15. Knit 2 rows.

16. Bind off loosely.

17. Decorate as desired, sew the back seam, and weave in the ends.

18. Add fringe, if desired (see Chapter 7).

Large Children's Poncho

1. On smaller needles, cast on 56 stitches.

2. Work knit 1, purl 1 ribbing for 1".

3. Work in stockinette until the piece measures approximately 3".

4. Switch to larger needles, and work 4 rows even.

5. Increase row: *knit 1, work 2 stitches in the next stitch, repeat from * 27 times (84 stitches).

6. Work 4 rows even.

7. Increase row: *knit 2, work 2 stitches in the next stitch, repeat from * 27 times (112 stitches).

8. Work 4 rows even.

9. Increase row: *knit 3, work 2 stitches in the next stitch, repeat from * 27 times (140 stitches).

10. Work 6 rows even.

11. Increase row: *knit 4, work 2 stitches in the next stitch, repeat from * 27 times (168 stitches).

12. Work 6 rows even.

13. Increase row: *knit 5, work 2 stitches in the next stitch, repeat from * 27 times (196 stitches).

14. Work even until the piece measures 12" or the desired length.

15. Knit 2 rows.

16. Bind off loosely.

17. Decorate as desired, sew the back seam, and weave in the ends.

18. Add fringe, if desired (see Chapter 7).

Spaced-Out Poncho

A trip to your local fabric shop or an online button emporium will offer a full range of gold and silver stars. You can sew them onto a navy blue poncho and duplicate stitch a rocket hurtling across the heavens. Small white pearl seed beads can be future worlds yet to be discovered.

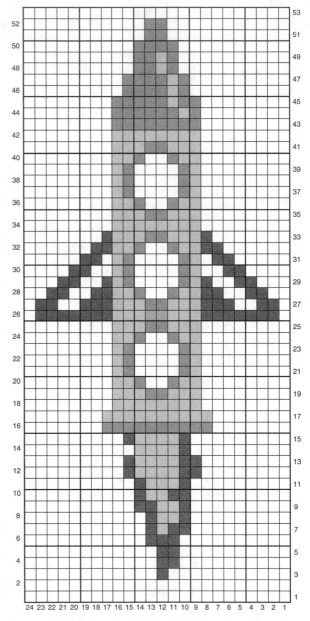

For the *Star Trek* fan or dreamer of worlds unknown, try this rocket to the outer reaches of the galaxy.

Hearts and Ribbons Poncho

You can use the small heart graph and work them in duplicate stitch along the bottom edge. You might also purchase small ribbon flowers at your local fabric store and sew them in place randomly across the poncho.

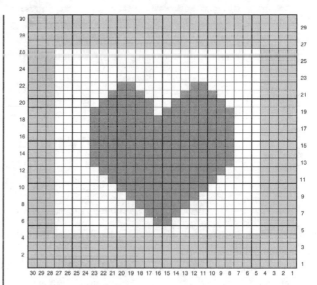

Hearts can be useful on many projects. Use them alone or in a row on the bottom of a large garment.

In This Chapter

- ◆ Knit yourself a tank top

- ◆ Add some variety to your closet with a Ribbon Tape Tank or Worsted Weight Tank

- ◆ Get creative with tank variation

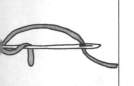
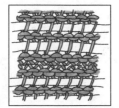

11

Tank Tops

Tank tops are perfect for the summer when it's hot and humid, and you can hardly bear to have anything on but you really must. You can purchase a plain fabric tank from most stores, but it's so much more fun to knit your own and make it exactly the way you want it.

A tank top is perfect to wear under a shirt when you leave in the morning and it's still too cool for just the tank. You can wear a bright-colored tank under a plain white shirt for very eye-catching contrast. I wore a bright pink tank under a yellow oxford shirt once when I had to be interviewed on television. I don't know what the cameraman or the audience of about three (since it was local-access cable!) thought, but I was very happy with how I looked.

An unexpected yarn choice changes a simple tank top into something exciting.

I love these small tops for summer and think they're great in a simple cotton yarn, but we're not here to be conventional. Tops are all too often boring. But not so when you can choose the yarn and pull out all the stops.

What You Need and Need to Know

These tank tops don't take a large amount of yarn, so you can choose something a little more special like a silk and cotton blend or one of the new rail ribbon yarns. Be sure to consider where you'll be wearing the top, though. If you're going to the beach and the sand bar, choose a natural-fiber yarn, such as cotton, linen, or silk, or a blend, to keep your cool.

If you're going to wear the tank under a jacket for work, you can try something a little different. Make one in a classic lightweight wool in a dark neutral for a career-perfect look. Don't forget one in a more fashion-forward yarn such as a shiny ribbon in a brighter color for a get-noticed-but-in-a-good-way bit of color and sparkle.

For an evening out, choose a yarn with sparkle and fluff. Just be sure it's soft enough to wear comfortably for the evening. Some shiny and metallic fibers can be scratchy.

Knots!

Test a skein of the yarn by rubbing the inside of your forearm vigorously with it. If even a hint of redness or itchiness develops, you'd better pass on it. If you don't, no matter how lovely the yarn is, you will be miserable by the time you get to the restaurant.

Also, when choosing your yarn, remember that man-made fibers won't shrink back into shape if they start to get shapeless. It can help to wash the top and try to pat it back into shape. Definitely make a test swatch and wash it under the same conditions you'll use for the garment. That will give you the best indication of the final gauge and how large or small you need to make your tank.

Working with two balls at once is a fast and easy way to be sure the shaping on both sides is the same. Just attach another ball of yarn to the second side and work with each ball for its respective side.

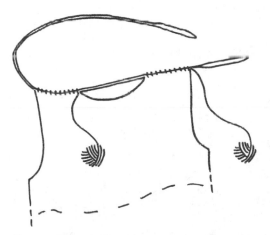

Working with two balls of yarn is easier than it looks and they won't twist themselves into knots.

Materials to complete all projects:

Yarns: Approximately 415 to 550 yards Cascade Yarns' Flurry, approximately 335 to 475 yards ribbon tape yarn, approximately 715 to 915 yards worsted weight yarn (See specific patterns for more information.)

Needles: Sizes 7 and 10 straight, or to obtain specified gauge

Beads

Buttons

Yarn needle

Measuring tape

Scissors

Stitches used in this chapter:

Knit/purl ribbing

Stockinette stitch

Seed stitch

Basic Tank

I initially thought of this yarn for a very different project, but the more I looked at it and touched it, the more I wanted to use it for something unexpected. Then I realized how great it would be worked into a simple tank top.

This cropped top works up very quickly, and because it's done with a furry yarn in garter stitch, there's no need to do armhole or neckline finishing.

◆ *Yarn:* Approximately 415 to 550 yards Cascade Yarns' Flurry

◆ *Needles:* Size 10 straight, or to obtain gauge

◆ *Gauge:* 3 stitches per inch

◆ *Time to complete:* 10 to 15 hours

◆ Yarn needle

◆ Measuring tape

◆ Scissors

Small Basic Tank

For the back of the top:

1. Cast on 60 stitches.
2. Working in garter stitch, knit every row until the piece measures 11".
3. *To shape the armhole:* bind off 4 stitches at beginning of the next 2 rows.
4. Decrease 1 stitch on each side, every other row, 3 times.
5. Work even until the piece measures 17 1/2".
6. *To shape the back of the neck:* on the next row, knit 16 stitches.
7. Attach another ball of yarn, and bind off center 30 stitches.

8. Knit to the end of the row.

9. Working both sides at the same time, on the next row, decrease 1 stitch at each neck edge (15 stitches each side).

10. Work even until the piece measures 21".

11. *To shape the shoulders:* bind off 3 stitches at the armhole edge of the next 2 rows (12 stitches each side).

12. Bind off 2 stitches at the armhole edge of the next 4 rows (8 stitches each side).

13. Bind off the remaining stitches.

For the front of the top:

1. Work as for the back, including all shaping.

2. When the piece measures 16", begin shaping the neck.

3. *To shape the front of the neck:* on the next row, knit 13 stitches.

4. Attach another ball of yarn, and bind off center 20 stitches.

5. Knit to the end of the row.

6. Working both sides at the same time, on the next row, decrease 1 stitch at each neck edge, every other row, 6 times (7 stitches each side).

7. Work even until the piece measures 19½".

8. *To shape the shoulders:* bind off 3 stitches at the armhole edge of the next 2 rows (4 stitches each side).

9. Bind off 2 stitches at the beginning of the next 2 rows (2 stitches each side).

10. Bind off the remaining stitches.

To finish the top:

1. Weave in all ends.

2. Sew the shoulder and side seams.

Knit Tips

Always refer to the yarn label before washing the garment. Follow the directions, and you will have the best results and enjoy your garment for years.

Medium Basic Tank

For the back of the top:

1. Cast on 63 stitches.

2. Working in garter stitch, knit every row until the piece measures 12".

3. *To shape the armhole:* bind off 5 stitches at the beginning of the next 2 rows.

4. Decrease 1 stitch on each armhole edge, every other row, 4 times.

5. Work even until the piece measures 19".

6. *To shape the back of the neck:* on next row, knit 7 stitches.

7. Attach another ball of yarn, and bind off center 32 stitches.

8. Knit to the end of the row.

9. Working both sides at the same time, on the next row, decrease 1 stitch at each neck edge (6 stitches each side).

10. Work even until the piece measures 21".

11. *To shape the shoulders:* bind off 2 stitches at the armhole edge of the next 6 rows.

12. Bind off.

For the front of the top:

1. Work as for the back, including all shaping.

2. When the piece measures 17", begin shaping the neck.

3. *To shape the front of the neck:* on the next row, knit 12 stitches.

4. Attach another ball of yarn, and bind off center 22 stitches.

5. Knit to the end of the row.

6. Working both sides at the same time, on the next row, decrease 1 stitch at each neck edge, every other row, 6 times (6 stitches each side).

7. Work even until the piece measures 19 ½".

8. *To shape the shoulders:* bind off 2 stitches at the armhole edge of the next 6 rows.

9. Bind off.

To finish the top:

1. Weave in all ends.

2. Sew the shoulder and side seams.

Large Basic Tank

For the back of the top:

1. Cast on 69 stitches.

2. Working in garter stitch, knit every row until the piece measures 12 ½".

3. *To shape the armhole:* bind off 5 stitches at the beginning of the next 2 rows.

4. Decrease 1 stitch on each side, every other row, 5 times.

5. Work even until the piece measures 20".

6. *To shape the back of the neck:* on the next row, knit 16 stitches.

7. Attach another ball of yarn, and bind off center 33 stitches.

8. Knit to the end of the row.

9. Working both sides at same time, on the next row, decrease 1 stitch at each neck edge (15 stitches each side).

10. Work even until the piece measures 22".

11. *To shape the shoulders:* bind off 3 stitches at the armhole edge of the next 4 rows (9 stitches each side).

12. Bind off 2 stitches at the beginning of the next 4 rows (5 stitches each side).

13. Bind off the remaining stitches.

For the front of the top:

1. Work as for the back, including all shaping.

2. When the piece measures 18", begin shaping the neck.

3. *To shape the front of the neck:* on the next row, knit 13 stitches.

4. Attach another ball of yarn, and bind off center 23 stitches.

5. Knit to the end of the row.

6. Working both sides at the same time, on the next row, decrease 1 stitch at each neck edge, every other row, 6 times (7 stitches each side).

7. Work even until the piece measures 22".

8. *To shape the shoulders:* bind off 3 stitches at the armhole edge of the next 2 rows (4 stitches each side).

9. Bind off 2 stitches at the beginning of the next 2 rows (7 stitches each side).

10. Bind off.

To finish the top:

1. Weave in all ends.

2. Sew the shoulder and side seams.

Ribbon Tape Tank

So many lovely and exciting ribbon tapes are available; I love to use them whenever possible. This is a small top with a small yardage requirement, so you can indulge yourself here without taking out a loan for the yarn.

Ribbon tape is flat. The wider it is, the larger the needle you'll use.

Ribbon tape yarns are often made of nylon, cotton blends, and wool blends. Some are fanciful; some elegant; some summery; some wintry. Choose your yarn to suit your needs and your budget.

> *Yarn:* Approximately 335 to 475 yards ribbon type yarn
> *Needles:* Size 10 straight, or to obtain gauge
> *Gauge:* $2\frac{3}{4}$ stitches per inch
> *Time to complete:* 10 to 15 hours
> Yarn needle
> Measuring tape
> Scissors

Small Ribbon Tape Tank

For the back of the top:

1. Cast on 58 stitches.

2. Working in garter stitch, knit every row until the piece measures 10".

3. *To shape the armhole:* bind off 4 stitches at the beginning of the next 2 rows.

4. Decrease 1 stitch on each armhole edge, every other row, 3 times.

5. Work even until the piece measures $15\frac{1}{2}$".

6. *To shape the back of the neck:* on the next row, knit 8 stitches.

7. Attach another ball of yarn, and bind off center 28 stitches.

8. Knit to the end of the row.

9. Working both sides at same time, on the next row, decrease 1 stitch at each neck edge (7 stitches each side).

10. Work even until the piece measures $18\frac{1}{2}$".

11. *To shape the shoulders:* bind off 3 stitches at the armhole edge of the next 2 rows (4 stitches each side).

12. Bind off 2 stitches at the beginning of the next 2 rows (2 stitches each side).
13. Bind off the remaining stitches.

For the front of the top:

1. Work as for the back, including all shaping.
2. When the piece measures 14", begin shaping the neck.
3. *To shape the front of the neck:* on the next row, knit 15 stitches.
4. Attach another ball of yarn, and bind off center 14 stitches.
5. Knit to the end of the row.
6. Working both sides at the same time, on the next row, decrease 1 stitch at each neck edge, every other row, 8 times (7 stitches each side).
7. Work even until the piece measures 18 ½".
8. *To shape the shoulders:* bind off 3 stitches at the armhole edge of the next 2 rows (4 stitches each side).
9. Bind off 2 stitches at the beginning of the next 2 rows (2 stitches each side).
10. Bind off the remaining stitches.

To finish the top:

1. Weave in all ends.
2. Sew the shoulder and side seams.
3. Work single crochet around the armholes and necklines.

Medium Ribbon Tape Tank

For the back of the top:

1. Cast on 65 stitches.
2. Working in garter stitch, knit every row until the piece measures 11".
3. *To shape the armhole:* bind off 4 stitches at the beginning of the next 2 rows.
4. Decrease 1 stitch on each armhole edge, every other row, 4 times.
5. Work even until the piece measures 17".
6. *To shape the back of the neck:* on the next row, knit 9 stitches.
7. Attach another ball of yarn, and bind off center 31 stitches.
8. Knit to the end of the row.
9. Working both sides at the same time, on the next row, decrease 1 stitch at each neck edge (8 stitches each side).
10. Work even until the piece measures 20".
11. *To shape the shoulders:* bind off 3 stitches at the armhole edge of the next 4 rows (2 stitches each side).
12. Bind off the remaining stitches.

For the front of the top:

1. Work as for the back, including all shaping.
2. When the piece measures 15 ½", begin shaping the neck.
3. *To shape the front of the neck:* on the next row, knit 16 stitches.
4. Attach another ball of yarn, and bind off center 17 stitches.
5. Knit to the end of the row.
6. Working both sides at the same time, on the next row, decrease 1 stitch at each neck edge, every other row, 8 times (8 stitches each side).

7. Work even until the piece measures 20".

8. *To shape the shoulders:* bind off 3 stitches at the armhole edge of the next 4 rows (2 stitches each side).

9. Bind off the remaining stitches.

To finish the top:

1. Weave in all ends.

2. Sew the shoulder and side seams.

3. Work single crochet around the armholes and necklines.

Large Ribbon Tape Tank

For the back of the top:

1. Cast on 70 stitches.

2. Working in garter stitch, knit every row until the piece measures 12".

3. *To shape the armhole:* bind off 5 stitches at the beginning of the next 2 rows.

4. Decrease 1 stitch on each armhole edge, every other row, 4 times.

5. Work even until the piece measures 18½".

6. *To shape the back of the neck:* on the next row, knit 10 stitches.

7. Attach another ball of yarn, and bind off center 32 stitches.

8. Knit to the end of the row.

9. Working both sides at the same time, on the next row, decrease 1 stitch at each neck edge (9 stitches each side).

10. Work even until the piece measures 21½".

11. *To shape the shoulders:* bind off 3 stitches at the armhole edge of the next 4 rows (3 stitches each side).

12. Bind off the remaining stitches.

For the front of the top:

1. Work as for the back, including all shaping.

2. When the piece measures 16½", begin shaping the neck.

3. *To shape the front of the neck:* on the next row, knit 18 stitches.

4. Attach another ball of yarn, and bind off center 16 stitches.

5. Knit to the end of the row.

6. Working both sides at the same time, on the next row, decrease 1 stitch at each neck edge, every other row, 9 times (9 stitches each side).

7. Work even until the piece measures 21½".

8. *To shape the shoulders:* bind off 3 stitches at the armhole edge of the next 4 rows (3 stitches each side).

9. Bind off the remaining stitches.

To finish the top:

1. Weave in all ends.

2. Sew the shoulder and side seams.

3. Work single crochet around the armholes and necklines.

Worsted Weight Tank

You probably don't want to make a tank top in wool, but you'd probably be delighted to have one in an interesting slub or multicolored variegated thick and thin cotton. You'll find Tencel as well as silk and rayon in worsted weight. This is a slightly larger design than the other two.

Yarn: Approximately 715 to 915 yards worsted weight yarn

Needles: Size 7 straight, or to obtain gauge

Gauge: 5 stitches per inch

Time to complete: 15 to 25 hours

Yarn needle

Measuring tape

Scissors

Small Worsted Weight Tank

For the back of the top:

1. Cast on 102 stitches.
2. Work in knit 1, purl 1 ribbing for 1".
3. Switch to stockinette stitch, and work even until the piece measures 15".
4. *To shape the armhole:* bind off 8 stitches at the beginning of the next 2 rows.
5. Decrease 1 stitch on each armhole edge, every other row, 8 times.
6. Work even until the piece measures 20".
7. *To shape the back of the neck:* on the next row, knit 16 stitches.

8. Attach another ball of yarn, and bind off center 54 stitches.
9. Knit to the end of the row.
10. Working both sides at the same time, on the next row, decrease 1 stitch at each neck edge (15 stitches each side).
11. Work even until the piece measures 23½".
12. *To shape the shoulders:* bind off 3 stitches at the armhole edge of the next 2 rows (12 stitches each side).
13. Bind off 2 stitches at the armhole edge of the next 4 rows (8 stitches each side).
14. Bind off the remaining stitches.

For the front of the top:

1. Work as for the back, including all shaping.
2. When the piece measures 20½", begin shaping the neck.
3. *To shape the front of the neck:* on the next row, knit 17 stitches.
4. Attach another ball of yarn, and bind off center 36 stitches.
5. Knit to the end of the row.
6. Working both sides at the same time, on the next row, decrease 1 stitch at each neck edge, every other row, 10 times (7 stitches each side).
7. Work even until the piece measures 23½".
8. *To shape the shoulders:* bind off 3 stitches at the armhole edge of the next 2 rows (4 stitches each side).
9. Bind off the remaining stitches.

To edge the armhole and neck:

1. Pick up 101 stitches around the armhole edge.
2. Work in knit 1, purl 1 ribbing for 1".
3. Bind off loosely.
4. Using circular needles, pick up 140 stitches around the neck edge.
5. Work in knit 1, purl 1 ribbing for 1".
6. Bind off loosely.

To finish the top:

1. Weave in all ends.
2. Sew the shoulder and side seams.

Medium Worsted Weight Tank

For the back of the top:

1. Cast on 112 stitches.
2. Work in knit 1, purl 1 ribbing for 1".
3. Switch to stockinette stitch, and work even until the piece measures 15 $\frac{1}{2}$".
4. *To shape the armhole:* bind off 9 stitches at the beginning of the next 2 rows.
5. Decrease 1 stitch on each armhole edge, every other row, 9 times.
6. Work even until the piece measures 22 $\frac{1}{2}$".
7. *To shape the back of the neck:* on the next row, knit 10 stitches.
8. Attach another ball of yarn, and bind off center 56 stitches.
9. Knit to the end of the row.

10. Working both sides at the same time, on the next row, decrease 1 stitch at each neck edge (9 stitches each side).
11. Work even until the piece measures 24 $\frac{1}{2}$".
12. *To shape the shoulders:* bind off 3 stitches at the armhole edge of the next 4 rows (3 stitches each side).
13. Bind off the remaining stitches.

For the front of the top:

1. Work as for the back, including all shaping.
2. When the piece measures 21 $\frac{1}{2}$", begin shaping the neck.
3. *To shape the front of the neck:* on the next row, knit 19 stitches.
4. Attach another ball of yarn, and bind off center 38 stitches.
5. Knit to the end of the row.
6. Working both sides at the same time, on the next row, decrease 1 stitch at each neck edge, every other row, 10 times (9 stitches each side).
7. Work even until the piece measures 24 $\frac{1}{2}$".
8. *To shape the shoulders:* bind off 3 stitches at the armhole edge of the next 4 rows (3 stitches each side).
9. Bind off the remaining stitches.

To edge the armhole and neck:

1. Pick up 108 stitches around the armhole edge.
2. Work in knit 1, purl 1 ribbing for 1".

3. Bind off loosely.

4. Using circular needles, pick up 144 stitches around the neck edge.

5. Work in knit 1, purl 1 ribbing for 1".

6. Bind off loosely.

To finish the top:

1. Weave in all ends.

2. Sew the shoulder and side seams.

Large Worsted Weight Tank

For the back of the top:

1. Cast on 123 stitches.

2. Work in knit 1, purl 1 ribbing for 1".

3. Switch to stockinette stitch, and work even until the piece measures 16".

4. *To shape the armhole:* bind off 11 stitches at the beginning of the next 2 rows.

5. Decrease 1 stitch on each armhole edge, every other row, 10 times.

6. Work even until the piece measures 23 ½".

7. *To shape the back of the neck:* on the next row, knit 22 stitches.

8. Attach another ball of yarn, and bind off center 58 stitches.

9. Knit to the end of the row.

10 Working both sides at the same time, on the next row, decrease 1 stitch at each neck edge (21 stitches each side).

11. Work even until the piece measures 25 ½".

12. *To shape the shoulders:* bind off 4 stitches at the armhole edge of the next 2 rows (17 stitches each side).

13. Bind off 3 stitches at the armhole edge of the next 4 rows (11 stitches each side).

14. Bind off the remaining stitches.

For the front of the top:

1. Work as for the back, including all shaping.

2. When the piece measures 22 ½", begin shaping the neck.

3. *To shape the front of the neck:* on the next row, knit 31 stitches.

4. Attach another ball of yarn, and bind off center 40 stitches.

5. Knit to the end of the row.

6 Working both sides at the same time, on the next row, decrease 1 stitch at each neck edge, every other row, 10 times (21 stitches each side).

7. Work even until the piece measures 25 ½".

8. *To shape the shoulders:* bind off 4 stitches at the armhole edge of the next 2 rows (17 stitches each side).

9. Bind off 3 stitches at the armhole edge of the next 4 rows (11 stitches each side).

10. Bind off the remaining stitches.

To edge the armhole and neck:

1. Pick up 117 stitches around the armhole edge.
2. Work in knit 1, purl 1 ribbing for 1".
3. Bind off loosely.
4. Using circular needles, pick up 148 stitches around the neck edge.
5. Work in knit 1, purl 1 ribbing for 1".
6. Bind off loosely.

To finish the top:

1. Weave in all ends.
2. Sew the shoulder and side seams.

Variations on a Theme

A tank top can be quite plain, but there's no reason why you can't express your creative side to take them off the beach and into the office or nightclub. Stay with plain yarn and choose your own decorations. A motif in duplicate stitch or intarsia can work very well. A plain yarn with a design in metallic yarn would be very eye-catching, especially for evening wear. Here are a few more suggestions to spur your imagination.

Beads

When you don't want just a simple tank, sew contrasting or complementary-colored glass beads randomly around the neck and armholes.

Tons of Buttons

Find the prettiest, most outlandish buttons you can, and sew them randomly around the tank.

Stripes

Knit in sherbet colors, watermelon stripes, or whatever you please for the summer. Combine a metallic yarn with a solid. Combine plain and textured yarns.

Crocheted Edging

Instead of knitting a rib around the edge, finish with a crocheted edge in an unexpected yarn like a fur or eyelash or bobbles.

Fringe

Make a short fringe all the way around the bottom of your top. This is very cute, especially on beachwear. (See Chapter 7 for fringe instructions.)

Stitch Star

No one said you had to stick to stockinette stitch. With a plain solid yarn, you might want a textured stitch. Try seed stitch, for example. (See Chapter 3 for seed stitch instructions.)

In This Chapter

◆ Knit your favorite kid a vest

◆ Create cool vests with such patterns as Stripes Vest, Escaping Balloons Vest, Voyage to Saturn Vest, and more

◆ Add whimsical embellishments to personalize the vest

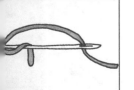 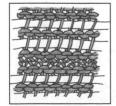    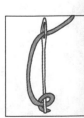

Chapter 12

Children's Vests

A child's vest is a terrific project, as it involves very little shaping and can be knit quite quickly. If you need a present for a child, you should have no trouble completing this project in your spare time in under a week because there's no neck shaping. You simply work the back and front sections the same and sew them together. The ribbing at the top adds visual interest.

I've provided several motifs in this chapter. You can work them in either duplicate stitch or intarsia. Use complementary or contrasting colors, whatever suits your tastes or those of the child. Children like bright colors, so let your imagination run wild with combinations. Crayon colors always work well. Primary colors are eye-catching and uncomplicated.

Let the threads dangle from the balloons as they seek their freedom.

What You Need and Need to Know

Because this project is for a child, be certain to choose yarns that can be laundered and will stand up to hard wear. This is not the project for those expensive hand-washable wools and cashmeres. The novelty yarns probably won't work well either, with their little eyelashes and furries to snag on things. And be sure the yarn is comfortable, because no amount of cajoling will convince a youngster to wear something that itches or pokes.

These considerations generally leave you in the territory of acrylic, cotton, Superwash wool, and blends of these. Fortunately, you have a huge choice of colors and styles, as most yarn manufacturers make yarns in this category. Many times you can find yarns designed especially for children.

Do keep your little recipients' preferences in mind. Children have their own ideas of what they like, and once they like something, it often becomes their favorite and they want to wear it every day—another reason to choose a sturdy yarn. If your nephew is crazy about space, make him an outer-space vest. For your neighbors' very sweet daughter, how about the balloon sweater in pinks with lavender, green, and yellow balloons?

Materials to complete all projects:

Yarns: Approximately 250 to 350 yards Cascade Yarns' Superwash in main and contrasting colors, small amounts of assorted colors of scrap yarns

Needles: Size 5 and 7 straight, or to obtain specified gauge

Beads

Novelty buttons

Yarn needle

Measuring tape

Thread or fine yarn to attach beads and buttons

Scissors

Stitches and techniques used in this chapter:

Knit/purl ribbing

Stockinette stitch

Duplicate stitch

Working color stripes

Basic Child's Vest

This is a project you can complete in a relatively short amount of time, even if you are a beginning knitter. There are no intricate stitches, and the only shaping is at the armhole. The use of different colors or decorations will garner you many compliments and boost your knitting self-confidence!

> *Yarn:* Approximately 250 to 350 yards Cascade Yarns' Superwash in main and contrasting colors
>
> *Needles:* Size 5 and 7 straight, or to obtain gauge
>
> *Gauge:* 5 stitches per inch
>
> *Time to complete:* 15 to 20 hours
>
> Yarn needle
>
> Measuring tape
>
> Scissors

Chest Size 23 Inches

For the back of the vest:

1. On smaller needles with contrasting yarn, cast on 58 stitches.
2. Work in knit 2, purl 2 ribbing for 1".
3. Change to larger needles and main color, and begin stockinette stitch.
4. On the first right-side row, increase 6 stitches evenly across.
5. Work even in stockinette stitch until the piece measures 7½".

6. To shape the underarm: bind off 2 stitches at the beginning of the next 2 rows.
7. Work even in stockinette stitch until the piece measures 12".
8. Continuing on larger needles, work in knit 2, purl 2 ribbing for 1".
9. Bind off loosely.

For the front of the vest: Work as for the back.

To finish the vest:

1. Weave in all ends.
2. With right sides together, sew the front to the back. Left and right shoulder seams are 3¾", and the neck opening is 4½" long.

Knit Tips

If possible, try on the vest to see if it's the correct fit. You might need to adjust the opening for a specific individual.

3. With right sides together, sew the side seams, leaving 5½" opening for the armholes.

To edge the armholes:

1. With smaller needles and contrasting yarn, pick up 59 stitches around the armhole edge.
2. Work in knit 2, purl 2 ribbing for 1".

Single crochet makes a quick and easy armhole finishing.

3. Bind off loosely, and weave in all ends.

You may also single crochet around the armhole.

Chest Size 25 Inches

For the back of the vest:

1. On smaller needles and with contrasting yarn, cast on 64 stitches.
2. Work in knit 2, purl 2 ribbing for 2".
3. Change to larger needles and main color, and begin stockinette stitch.
4. On the first right-side row, increase 4 stitches evenly across.

5. Work even in stockinette stitch until the piece measures 8 1/2".
6. *To shape the underarm:* bind off 4 stitches at the beginning of the next 2 rows.
7. Work even in stockinette stitch until the piece measures 13".
8. Continuing on larger needles, work in knit 2, purl 2 ribbing for 1 1/2".
9. Bind off loosely.

For the front of the vest: Work as for the back.

To finish the vest:

1. Weave in all ends.
2. With right sides together, sew the front to the back. Left and right shoulder seams are 3 1/4" long, and the neck opening is 5 1/2" long.
3. With right sides together, sew the side seams, leaving 6 1/2" opening for the armholes.

To edge the armholes:

1. With smaller needles and contrasting yarn, pick up 75 stitches around the armhole edge.
2. Work in knit 2, purl 2 ribbing for 1".
3. Bind off loosely, and weave in all ends.

You may also single crochet around the armhole.

Chest Size 28 Inches

For the back of the vest:

1. On smaller needles with contrasting color, cast on 68 stitches.

2. Work in knit 2, purl 2 ribbing for 2".

3. Change to larger needles and main color, and begin stockinette stitch.

4. On the first right-side row, increase 8 stitches evenly across.

5. Work even in stockinette stitch until the piece measures 9".

6. *To shape the underarm:* bind off 5 stitches at the beginning of the next 2 rows.

7. Continuing on larger needles, work in knit 2, purl 2 ribbing for 1".

8. Bind off loosely.

For the front of the vest: Work as for the back.

To finish the vest:

1. Weave in all ends.

2. With right sides together, sew the front to the back. Left and right shoulder seams are 3 ½" long, and the neck opening is 6 ½" long.

3. With right sides together, sew the side seams, leaving 7" opening for the armholes.

To edge the armholes:

1. With smaller needles and contrasting yarn, pick up 80 stitches around the armhole edge.

2. Work in knit 2, purl 2 ribbing for 1".

3. Bind off loosely, and weave in all ends.

You may also single crochet around the armhole.

Stripes

I'm a fan of stripes. You can use contrasting colors or complementary colors—the choice depends on how bold or subtle you'd like to be. A nautical or Fourth of July sweater could be done with a red ribbing and navy and white stripes on the body. An Easter sweater might be pale yellow and pale green. A Halloween sweater would be orange and black.

I wouldn't like the stripes smaller than 1", but you could change every 2 rows and make it possible to not break off the yarn. Just let the unused color run up the edge of the knitting until you need to pick it up again.

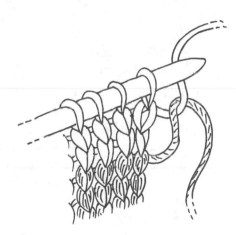

The yarn you're not knitting with can be carried along the edge so you don't have to cut and rejoin.

Escaping Balloons

For this vest, you need at least one different color of scrap yarn. It doesn't need to be the same weight as the sweater, but use the needle suggested for it. The balloon will be larger or smaller, depending on the weight of the yarn.

1. Cast on 4 stitches.

2. Knit 2 rows.

3. At the beginning of each of the next 4 rows, increase 1 stitch by knitting into the front and back of the stitch.

4. Knit 4 rows even.

5. At the beginning of each of the next 4 rows, decrease 1 stitch by knitting 2 stitches together.

6. When 4 stitches are left on the needles, knit each set of 2 stitches together.

7. On the next row, knit the last 2 stitches together.

8. Break the yarn and fasten off. This will be the more pointy end of the balloon and should be sewn pointing toward the bottom edge. (*Note:* I used buttons on the following photo, but these knitted balloons are so much cuter!)

9. Make as many balloons as you'd like, in as many colors as you'd like, and position them randomly on the sweater.

10. Sew the balloons in place.

11. Cut 2" of decorative thread or heavy yarn. Sew one end in place directly under the balloon. Let the other end dangle as the balloon "escapes."

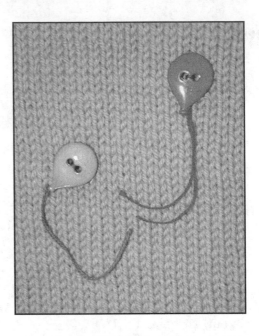

You can also attach fun balloon-shaped buttons.

Voyage to Saturn

Make a dark blue vest, and duplicate stitch the rocket ship and Saturn from the graphs. Use a color scheme that inspires you to reach for the heavens. Sew metallic star buttons randomly on the sweater star field. Sew small pearly seed beads as stars in distant galaxies. (You can find the rocket ship graph in Chapter 10.)

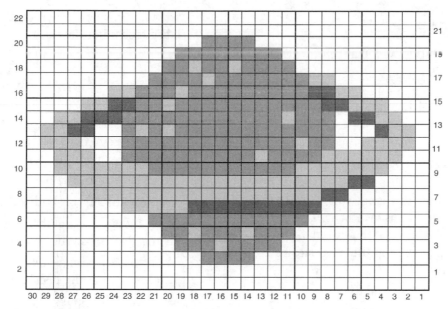

Saturn's rings give you the opportunity to use a truly extreme yarn in duplicate stitch.

Good Things Come in Small Packages

This makes an adorable Christmas present. Knit the vest entirely of red, white, or green. Then use a contrasting yarn, or perhaps one with metallic thread or flecks.

1. Cast on 6 to 10 stitches, depending on how wide you want the ribbon to be.

2. Knit a long strip in garter stitch that reaches vertically from the top of the ribbing to the top of the sweater at the shoulder.

3. Sew the ribbon strip in place.

4. Knit another strip the same width that runs either entirely around the sweater or just from one side seam to the other.

5. Sew the second ribbon strip in place.

6. Knit a third strip the same width approximately 8" long, and sew the ends together. This will be the loops of the bow.

7. Cast on approximately 10 stitches, and work 2 rows. Bind off. This will wrap around the bow.

8. Fold the loop in half, and sew the wrap in place.

9. Sew the bow onto the vest where the vertical and horizontal ribbons meet.

Snail's Pace

You can easily make a woodland scene using brown and green yarns, worked in stripes, to make the vest. Then duplicate stitch the snail and the sun face from the graphs around the bottom of the sweater.

Crew Neck

It's a simple matter to change the vest into a crew neck, if you prefer. Work the back as written for all sizes to the length desired, but do not knit the ribbing at the top. Bind off all stitches loosely.

For the front, work as written, but shape the neck as indicated in the following sections.

For chest size 23 inches: When the front measures 10½", begin shaping the neck:

1. Work to center 12 stitches.
2. Attach another ball of yarn, bind off center 12 stitches, and complete row.
3. Working both sides at the same time, decrease 1 stitch at each neck edge, every other row, 5 times.
4. Work even until the piece measures 13".
5. Bind off stitches on both sides.
6. With right sides together, sew the front to the back at the shoulders.
7. With smaller circular needles, pick up 64 stitches around the neck edge.
8. Work in knit 2, purl 2 ribbing for 1".
9. Bind off loosely.
10. Finish as written.

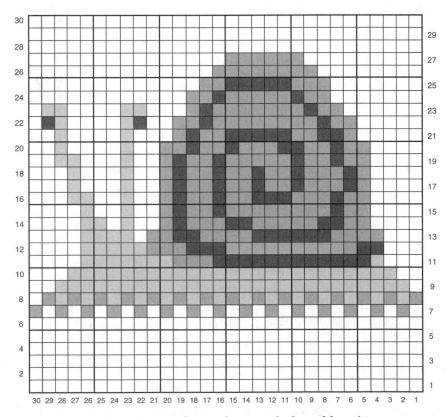

Snakes and snails and puppy dog's tails ... an ideal motif for a boy's vest.

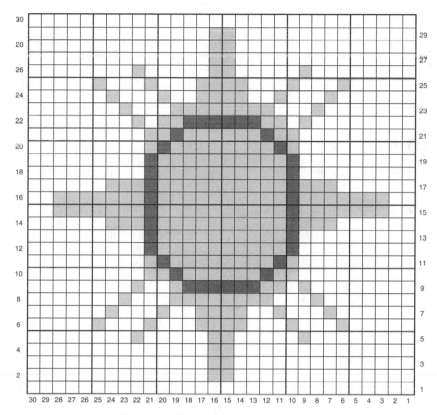

This sun motif can brighten anyone's day!

For chest size 25 inches: When the front measures 12", begin shaping the neck:

1. Work to center 15 stitches.
2. Attach another ball of yarn, bind off center 15 stitches, and complete row.
3. Working both sides at the same time, decrease 1 stitch at each neck edge, every other row, 7 times.
4. Work even until the piece measures 14½".
5. Bind off stitches on both sides.
6. With right sides together, sew the front to the back at the shoulders.
7. With smaller circular needles, pick up 68 stitches around the neck edge.
8. Work in knit 2, purl 2 ribbing for 1".
9. Bind off loosely.
10. Finish as written.

For chest size 28 inches: When the front measures 14½", begin shaping the neck:

1. Work to center 17 stitches.
2. Attach another ball of yarn, bind off center 17 stitches, and complete row.
3. Working both sides at the same time, decrease 1 stitch at each neck edge, every other row, 7 times.
4. Work even until the piece measures 17½".
5. Bind off stitches on both sides.
6. With right sides together, sew the front to the back at the shoulders.
7. With smaller circular needles, pick up 64 stitches around the neck edge.
8. Work in knit 2, purl 2 ribbing for 1".
9. Bind off loosely.
10. Finish as written.

In This Chapter

◆ Make a Mix-and-Match Sweater

◆ Personalize your sweater with a rolled neckline, a scoop neckline, or short sleeves

◆ Get creative with a Sampler Sweater

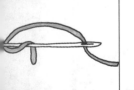
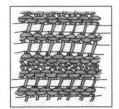

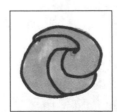

Chapter 13

Women's Sweaters

I can't think of anyplace you couldn't wear a sweater. As utilitarian as sweaters are, they don't have a long history, dating back only into the 1600s. What we call the sweater and the English call a jersey or jumper has evolved from an undergarment to something we wear everywhere. The style and the fiber sets the tone, making it formal, playful, elegant, or casual.

A sweater might seem a complicated item to knit, but you'll find that the ones in this chapter aren't very difficult. They require minimal shaping. In this pattern, that means decreasing the number of stitches under the arm so you don't have extra fabric to bunch up. You shape the neckline slightly by decreasing a few stitches there as well.

If you read the directions and it seems confusing, try knitting very slowly while following the steps as presented. Read them out loud, if that helps. Sit upright in the chair. Have plenty of light so you can see the stitches. Press forward. Sometimes it's very difficult to imagine what the instructions mean if you've never seen the procedure done before. When you reach that part in your sweater, you may find it much easier to see what needs to be done.

You can always rip out any mistakes. Everyone has moments when things aren't going as they should, and that's one thing that makes knitting so wonderful. You can always have a do-over!

What You Need and Need to Know

You're going to need patience and determination if this is the first fill-size sweater you've made. Keep plugging away, and it really will be done in a surprisingly short amount of time. You might want to keep a notebook nearby so you can remind yourself of where you are or what you may discovered. Choose a fiber you love to touch, and you'll find working with it will be a pleasure.

Materials to complete all projects:

Yarn: worsted weight wool

Needles: Sizes 5 and 7 straight or circular or to obtain gauge and double point or circular in the smaller size for neck band.

Time to complete: 20 to 40 hours

Crochet hook for picking up stitches (optional)

Marker

Yarn needle

Measuring tape

Scissors

Stitches used in this chapter:

Knit, purl rib

Stockinette stitch

Waffle stitch

Duplicate stitch

Mix-and-Match Sweater

With this pattern, I give you the basic sweater instructions and then give you a few options for different necklines and sleeves so you can mix and match to get the sweater you want. Be sure to consider duplicate stitch and other embellishments to personalize your sweater.

You can make a simple and unique sweater with very little effort.

Yarn: Approximately 1,215 to 1,250 yards worsted weight yarn

Needles: Sizes 5 and 7 straight, or to obtain gauge, plus smaller size double point or circular for neck band

Gauge: 5 stitches per inch

Time to complete: 20 to 40 hours

Yarn needle

Measuring tape

Scissors

Small Mix-and-Match Sweater

For the back of the sweater:

1. With smaller needles, cast on 91 stitches.

2. Work in knit 1, purl 1 ribbing for $1\frac{1}{2}$".

3. Change to larger needles and increase 11 stitches evenly over the row to 102 stitches.

4. Work in stockinette stitch until the piece measures 15".

5. _To shape the underarms:_ Bind off 5 stitches beginning on the next 2 rows.

6. Work even in stockinette stitch until the piece measures $24\frac{1}{2}$".

7. Bind off all stitches.

For the front of the sweater:

1. Work as for the back, including all shaping.

2. When the piece measures $21\frac{1}{2}$", begin shaping the neck.

3. _To shape the front of the neck:_ Work to center 18 stitches, and attach another ball of yarn.

4. Bind off center 18 stitches, and work to the end of the row.

5. Working both sides at the same time, on the next row, decrease 1 stitch at each neck edge, every other row, 7 times (30 stitches each side).

6. Work even until the piece measures $24\frac{1}{2}$".

7. Bind off the shoulders.

For the sleeves:

1. With smaller needles, cast on 41 stitches.

2. Work knit 1, purl 1 ribbing for $1\frac{1}{2}$".

3. Change to larger needles, and increase 5 stitches evenly over the row to 46 stitches.

4. On the next right-side row, begin shaping the sleeve.

5. Work in stockinette stitch, and increase 1 stitch on each side, every fourth row, 25 times.

6. Work even until the piece measures 18".

7. Bind off all stitches.

To finish the crew neck:

1. With smaller short circular needles or double point needles, pick up 84 stitches around the neck edge.

2. Work in knit 1, purl 1 ribbing for 2".

3. Bind off loosely.

4. Fold the neck ribbing in half so the bound-off edge is on the inside.

5. Tack to the inside.

To finish the sweater:

1. With right sides together, sew 30 shoulder stitches on each side for the shoulder seams.

2. Center the sleeve top on the shoulder seams, and sew the right sides together.

3. Sew the side and under-sleeve seams, right sides together.

4. Weave in all ends.

Rolled Neckline

1. Instead of ribbing for the neck edging, knit approximately 1½".
2. Bind off loosely.

Scoop Neckline

1. Work the front as written to 20½".
2. Work to center 10 stitches, and attach another ball of yarn.
3. Bind off center 10 stitches.
4. Working both sides at the same time, bind off 2 stitches at the neck edge 2 times.
5. Decrease 1 stitch at each neck edge every other row, 7 times.
6. Work even until the piece measures 24½".
7. Finish sewing 30" shoulder stitches on each side.
8. Using a circular needle or double point needles, pick up 90 stitches around the neck edge, and rib or roll as desired. Or simply single crochet around the edge.

Short Sleeves

1. Work the front and back as written.
2. For the sleeves, with smaller needles, cast on 53 stitches.
3. Work knit 1, purl 1 ribbing for 1½".
4. Change to larger needles, and increase 7 stitches evenly over row to 60 stitches.
5. On the next right-side row, begin shaping the sleeve.
6. Work in stockinette stitch, and increase 1 stitch on each side every second row 16 times and then every fourth row 2 times (96 stitches).
7. Work even until the piece measures 8".
8. Bind off all stitches.

Knit Tips

To get rid of those fuzzy bumps on your sweater, try some packing tape. Make a loop of it around your hand, sticky side out, and gently but firmly place against the pilling. You'll be surprised at how many come off.

Medium Mix-and-Match Sweater

For the back of the sweater:

1. With smaller needles, cast on 109 stitches.
2. Work in knit 1, purl 1 ribbing for 1½".
3. Change to larger needles, and increase 13 stitches evenly over row to 122 stitches.
4. Work in stockinette stitch until the piece measures 15½".
5. *To shape the underarm:* Bind off 7 stitches at the beginning of the next 2 rows.
6. Work even in stockinette stitch until the piece measures 26".
7. Bind off all stitches.

For the front of the sweater:

1. Work as for the back, including all shaping.
2. When the piece measures 23", begin shaping the neck.
3. *To shape the front of the neck:* Work to center 22 stitches, and attach another ball of yarn.
4. Bind off center 22 stitches, and work to the end of the row.
5. Working both sides at the same time, on the next row, decrease 1 stitch at each neck edge, every other row, 7 times (36 stitches each side).
6. Work even until the piece measures 26".
7. Bind off the shoulders.

For the sleeves:

1. With smaller needles, cast on 43 stitches.
2. Work knit 1, purl 1 ribbing for 1 ½".
3. Change to larger needles, and increase 5 stitches evenly over the row to 48 stitches.
4. On the next right-side row, begin shaping the sleeve.
5. Work in stockinette stitch, and increase 1 stitch on each side every second row 5 times, and then every fourth row 5 times.
6. Work even until the piece measures 18".
7. Bind off all stitches.

To finish the crew neck:

1. With smaller short circular needles or double point needles, pick up 96 stitches around the neck edge.
2. Work in knit 1, purl 1 ribbing for 2".
3. Bind off loosely.
4. Fold the neck ribbing in half so the bound-off edge is on the inside.
5. Tack to the inside.

To finish the sweater:

1. With right sides together, sew 36 shoulder stitches on each side for the shoulder seams.
2. Center the sleeve top on the shoulder seams, and sew the right sides together.
3. Sew the side and under-sleeve seams, right sides together.
4. Weave in all ends.

Rolled Neckline

1. Instead of ribbing for the neck edging, knit approximately 1 ½".
2. Bind off loosely.

Scoop Neckline

1. Work front as written to 23".
2. Work to center 12 stitches, and attach another ball of yarn.
3. Bind off center 12 stitches.
4. Working both sides at the same time, bind off 2 stitches at the neck edge 3 times.
5. Decrease 1 stitch at each neck edge, every other row, 6 times.
6. Work even until the piece measures 26".
7. Finish sewing 36 shoulder stitches on each side.
8. Using circular needle or double point needles, pick up 92 stitches around the neck edge, and rib or roll as desired. Or simply single crochet around the edge.

Short Sleeves

1. Work the front and back as written.
2. For the sleeves, with smaller needles, cast on 57 stitches.
3. Work knit 1, purl 1 ribbing for 1 ½".
4. Change to larger needles, and increase 7 stitches evenly over the row to 64 stitches.
5. On the next right-side row, begin shaping the sleeve.
6. Work in stockinette stitch, and increase 1 stitch on each side, every second row, 21 times (106 stitches).
7. Work even until the piece measures 8".
8. Bind off all stitches.

Knit Tips

If you find a knot as sometimes happens in the manufacturing process in the middle of your row, go back, break off the yarn, and start over again. You really don't want that bump in your sweater.

Large Mix-and-Match Sweater

For the back of the sweater:

1. With smaller needles, cast on 109 stitches.
2. Work in knit 1, purl 1 ribbing for 1½".
3. Change to larger needles, and increase 13 stitches evenly over the row to 122 stitches.
4. Work in stockinette stitch until the piece measures 16".
5. *To shape the underarms:* Bind off 7 stitches at the beginning of the next 2 rows.
6. Work even in stockinette stitch until the piece measures 27".
7. Bind off all stitches.

For the front of the sweater:

1. Work as for the back, including all shaping.
2. When the piece measures 23½", begin shaping the neck.
3. *To shape the front of the neck:* Work to center 23 stitches, and attach another ball of yarn.
4. Bind off center 23 stitches, and work to the end of the row.
5. Working both sides at same time, on the next row, decrease 1 stitch at each neck edge, every other row, 10 times (33 stitches each side).
6. Work even until the piece measures 27".
7. Bind off the shoulders.

For the sleeves:

1. With smaller needles, cast on 47 stitches.
2. Work knit 1, purl 1 ribbing for 1½".
3. Change to larger needles, and increase 5 stitches evenly over the row to 52 stitches.
4. On the next right-side row, begin shaping the sleeve.
5. Work in stockinette stitch, and increase 1 stitch on each side, every second row, 8 times, and then every fourth row 21 times.
6. Work even until the piece measures 19".
7. Bind off all stitches.

To finish the crew neck:

1. With smaller short circular needles or double point needles, pick up 107 stitches around the neck edge.
2. Work in knit 1, purl 1 ribbing for 2".
3. Bind off loosely.
4. Fold the neck ribbing in half so the bound-off edge is on the inside.
5. Tack to the inside.

To finish the sweater:

1. With the right sides together, sew 33 shoulder stitches on each side for the shoulder seams.
2. Center the sleeve top on the shoulder seams, and sew the right sides together.
3. Sew the side and under-sleeve seams, right sides together.
4. Weave in all ends.

Rolled Neckline

1. Instead of ribbing for the neck edging, knit approximately 1½".
2. Bind off loosely.

Scoop Neckline

1. Work the front as written to 23½".
2. Work to center 14 stitches, and attach another ball of yarn.
3. Bind off center 14 stitches.
4. Working both sides at the same time, bind off 2 stitches at the neck edge 3 times.
5. Decrease 1 stitch at each neck edge, every other row, 8 times.
6. Work even until the piece measures 27".
7. Finish sewing 33 shoulder stitches on each side.
8. Pick up 102 stitches around the neck edge, and rib or roll as desired. Or simply single crochet around the edge.

Short Sleeves

1. Work the front and back as written.
2. For the sleeves, with smaller needles, cast on 61 stitches.
3. Work knit 1, purl 1 ribbing for 1½".
4. Change to larger needles, and increase 7 stitches evenly over the row to 68 stitches.
5. On the next right-side row, begin shaping the sleeve.
6. Work in stockinette stitch, and increase 1 stitch on each side, every second row, 21 times (110 stitches).
7. Work even until the piece measures 9".
8. Bind off all stitches.

Sampler Sweater

This is how we did it, but feel free to use other colors, patterns, and stripes to please yourself. Use a main color and contrasting colors A, B, C, D, E, and F. You can use as many yarns as you want, and the stripes don't have to be uniform—this is a great chance to use up your stash.

Following the pattern of your choice, work the color patterning on front and back:

1. Cast on in the main color, and work the ribbing to 2½".

2. Work 4 rows of stockinette stitch.

3. Change to yarn B, and work 2 rows of stockinette stitch.

4. Work 1 row of wrap stitch. (See Chapter 5 for more on wrap stitch.)

5. Knit 1 row.

6. Switch to the main color, and work waffle stitch for 2 pattern repeats. (See Chapter 4 for more on waffle stitch.)

7. Switch to yarn C, and work 2 rows.

8. Work 1 row of wrap stitch.

9. Knit 1 row.

10. Switch to the main color, and work 8 rows of raspberry stitch. (See Chapter 16 for more on raspberry stitch.)

The raspberry stitch offers great texture to your sweater.

Rows 1 and 3: Purl.

Row 2: Knit 1, *(knit 1, purl 1, knit 1) into the next stitch, purl 3 together, repeat from * to end of row.

Row 4: Knit 1, *purl 3 together (knit 1, purl 1, knit 1) into the next stitch, repeat from * to end of row.

Repeat Rows 1 through 4 for desired length.

11. Switch to yarn C, and work 2 rows.

12. Work 1 row of wrap stitch.

13. Knit 1 row.

14. Switch to the main color, and work 8 rows of basket weave stitch:

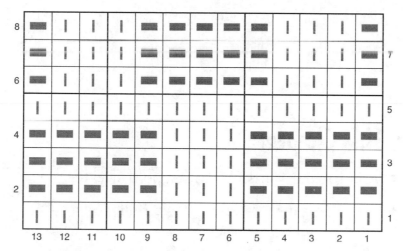

The basket weave is a simple knit purl stitch with great utility.

15. Switch to yarn D, and work 2 rows.

16. Work 1 row of wrap stitch.

17. Knit 1 row.

18. Switch to the main color, and work 8 rows of waffle stitch.

19. Switch to yarn E, and work 2 rows.

20. Work 1 row of wrap stitch.

21. Knit 1 row.

22. Switch to the main color, and work 8 rows of raspberry stitch.

23. Switch to yarn D, and work 2 rows.

24. Work 1 row of wrap stitch.

25. Knit 1 row.

26. Switch to the main color, and work 8 rows of basket weave stitch.

27. Switch to yarn F, and work 2 rows.

28. Work 1 row of wrap stitch.

29. Knit 1 row.

30. Switch to the main color, and finish as per the directions for the back and for the front, working all neckline and underarm shaping.

For the sleeves: Work sleeves in stockinette stitch in the main color.

Knit Tips _____

When knitting a sleeve, leaving quite a long tail when you cast on can be very helpful when you return to sew the seam. That way, you only have one piece of yarn to hide in the sleeve body instead of two.

In This Chapter

- ◆ Add to your wardrobe with a polo sweater
- ◆ Too warm for a sweater? Try a Bulky Vest

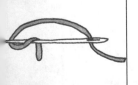
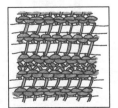

Chapter 14

Casual and Classy Polos and Vests

You're probably familiar with the polo shirt—they're classics and always look stylish. You can also knit a polo-style sweater. This is typically known as an Italian sweater. If you need a little warmth but not a full sweater, you can easily leave off the sleeves for a vest.

Polo sweaters and vests can be worn over a blouse or alone. Knit one in cashmere, and you'll want to wear it next to your skin, as it's the ultimate in luxury.

A vest is perfect for spring and fall or if you need a little something to wear around the house or office.

What You Need and Need to Know

Sometimes you want to be fashionable, and sometimes you want to be stylish. This polo sweater has wide-ranging versatility. It's especially good in the summer when you're planning on being away for hours and you're not sure what the day may bring weather-wise.

You can use so many cottons or cotton blends, and most would serve you well, but you can take this casual and sporty top into another realm by going to shimmery-soft silk.

Materials to complete all projects:

Yarn: Worsted weight and bulky yarn of your choice (See individual patterns for specific amounts.)

Needles: Sizes 5, 7, and 11; size 5 16" circular needle; or to obtain specified gauge

Markers

Yarn needle

Measuring tape

Scissors

Stitches used in this chapter:

Knit, purl rib

Stockinette stitch

Garter stitch

Polo Sweater

These very stylish sweaters are also known as Italian shirts and are easy to wear because of the placket front. The collar construction is far simpler than you may think; it's just a matter of picking up stitches and working in ribbing like any collar.

A soft Egyptian cotton would make a sleek sweater for the cool nights of summer. A cashmere would make a luxurious sweater for the winter. Search for sophisticated buttons to finish the look. You can hardly go wrong with this sweater if you want a present for a loved one.

Knit Tips

This pattern specifies stockinette stitch for the body of the sweater, but that doesn't mean you have to stick to it. Try using another stitch, say seed stitch, for those sections. Just be very sure to work a gauge swatch, to make sure your chosen stitch works to the same gauge. You'll probably have to try different needle sizes.

Small Polo Sweater

Yarn: Approximately 965 yards worsted weight yarn

Needles: Sizes 5 and 7, or to obtain gauge

Gauge: 5 stitches per inch

Time to complete: Approximately 20 to 25 hours

For the back of the sweater:

1. With smaller needles, cast on 91 stitches.
2. Work knit 1, purl 1 rib for 2".
3. Switch to larger needles, and begin stockinette stitch.
4. Increase 11 stitches evenly over the next right-side row.
5. Work even until the piece measures 15".
6. *To shape the underarm:* bind off 5 stitches at the beginning of the next 2 rows.
7. Work even until the piece measures 24½".
8. Loosely bind off all stitches.

For the front of the sweater:

1. Work as for the back, including all shaping, until the piece measures 18".

2. To shape the placket, work to center 12 stitches, and attach another ball of yarn.
3. Bind off center 12 stitches, and work across the row.
4. Working both sides at the same time, work even until the piece measures 23".
5. *To shape the neck:* continue to work both sides at the same time. Bind off 4 stitches at each neck edge.
6. Decrease 1 stitch at each neck edge, every other row, 4 times.
7. Work even until the piece measures 24½".
8. Bind off all shoulder stitches.

For the sleeves:

1. With smaller needles, cast on 61 stitches.
2. Work knit 1, purl 1 rib for 1".
3. Switch to larger needles, and begin stockinette stitch.
4. Increase 7 stitches evenly across the next right-side row.
5. Increase 1 stitch each side every third row to 96 stitches.
6. Work even until the piece measures approximately 8" or the desired length.
7. Loosely bind off all stitches.

To finish the neck:

1. Using the smaller needle, sew the front to the back at the shoulder seams.
2. With right sides facing, and starting at the placket edge, pick up 4 bound-off stitches, pick up 10 side neck stitches, pick up 32 back neck stitches, pick up 10 side neck stitches, and pick up 4 bound-off stitches.
3. Work knit 1, purl 1 rib for 1".
4. Bind off loosely.

To finish the placket:

1. Using the smaller needle, with right sides facing and starting at the neck edge of the placket opening, pick up stitches from the side of the neck band, and pick up 29 stitches along the placket edge. Work in knit 1, purl 1 rib for 1½".

2. Bind off loosely.

3. On the opposite side of the placket opening, pick up and work the overlap in the same way, working the buttonholes at regular intervals.

4. Stitch the bottom of the overlap to the garment.

To finish the collar:

1. With the smaller short circular needle, and with the right side facing, start at the neck edge and pick up 4 bound-off front neck stitches, 10 side neck stitches, 32 back neck stitches, 10 side neck stitches, and 4 bound-off front neck stitches.

2. Work knit 1, purl 1 rib for approximately 4".

3. Bind off loosely in pattern.

To finish the sweater:

1. Weave in all ends.

2. Sew the side seams, sew the sleeve seams, and sew the sleeves to the armhole openings.

3. Sew on the buttons.

4. Weave in all ends.

Knit Tips

Use a bright Post-it note to help you keep your place in a pattern. These usually can be stuck to a book or pattern and peeled off again with no damage.

Medium Polo Sweater

Yarn: Approximately 1,110 yards worsted weight yarn

Needles: Sizes 5 and 7, or to obtain gauge

Gauge: 5 stitches per inch

Time to complete: Approximately 20 to 25 hours

For the back of the sweater:

1. With smaller needles, cast on 101 stitches.

2. Work knit 1, purl 1 rib for 2".

3. Switch to larger needles, and begin stockinette stitch.

4. Increase 12 stitches evenly over the next right-side row.

5. Work even until the piece measures 15½".

6. *To shape the underarm:* bind off 7 stitches at the beginning of the next 2 rows.

7. Work even until the piece measures 26".

8. Loosely bind off all stitches.

For the front of the sweater:

1. Work as for the back, including all shaping, until the piece measures 19".

2. To shape the placket, work to center 14 stitches, and attach another ball of yarn.

3. Bind off center 14 stitches, and work across the row.

4. Working both sides at the same time, work even until the piece measures 24½".

5. *To shape the neck:* continue to work both sides at the same time. Bind off 4 stitches at each neck edge.

6. Decrease 1 stitch at each neck edge, every other row, 4 times.

7. Work even until the piece measures 26".

8. Bind off all shoulder stitches.

For the sleeves:

1. With smaller needles, cast on 65 stitches.

2. Work knit 1, purl 1 rib for 1".

3. Switch to larger needles, and begin stockinette stitch.

4. Increase 7 stitches evenly across the next right-side row.

5. Increase 1 stitch each side every third row to 106 stitches.

6. Work even until the piece measures approximately 8" or the desired length.

7. Loosely bind off all stitches.

To finish the neck:

1. Using the smaller needle, sew the front to the back at the shoulder seams.

2. With right sides facing and starting at the placket edge, pick up 4 bound-off stitches, 9 side neck stitches, 36 back neck stitches, 9 side neck stitches, and 4 bound-off stitches.

3. Work knit 1, purl 1 rib for 1".

4. Bind off loosely.

To finish the placket:

1. Using the smaller needle, with right sides facing and starting at the neck edge of the placket opening, pick up stitches from the side of the neck band, and pick up 32 stitches along the placket edge. Work in knit 1, purl 1 rib for 1½".

2. Bind off loosely.

3. On the opposite side of the placket opening, pick up and work the overlap in the same way, working the buttonholes at regular intervals.

4. Stitch the bottom of the overlap to the garment.

For the collar:

1. With smaller short circular needles and right sides facing, start at the neck edge and pick up 4 bound-off front neck stitches, 9 side neck stitches, 36 back neck stitches, 9 side neck stitches, and 4 bound-off front neck stitches.

2. Work knit 1, purl 1 rib for approximately 4".

3. Bind off loosely in pattern.

To finish the sweater:

1. Weave in all ends.

2. Sew the side seams, sew the sleeve seams, and sew the sleeves to the armhole opening.

3. Sew on the buttons.

4. Weave in all ends.

 Purl Pearls

In England, a pullover sweater is called a *jersey* or a *jumper*. Much earlier, it was known as a *knitted frock*.

Large Polo Sweater

> *Yarn:* Approximately 1,250 yards worsted weight yarn
>
> *Needles:* Sizes 5 and 7, or to obtain gauge
>
> *Gauge:* 5 stitches per inch
>
> *Time to complete:* Approximately 20 to 25 hours

For the back of the sweater:

1. With smaller needles, cast on 109 stitches.
2. Work knit 1, purl 1 rib for 2".
3. Switch to larger needles, and begin stockinette stitch.
4. Increase 13 stitches evenly over the next right-side row.
5. Work even until the piece measures 16".
6. *To shape the underarm:* bind off 7 stitches at the beginning of the next 2 rows.
7. Work even until the piece measures 27".
8. Loosely bind off all stitches.

For the front of the sweater:

1. Work as for the back, including all shaping, until the piece measures 19½".
2. *To shape the placket:* work to center 14 stitches, and attach another ball of yarn.
3. Bind off center 14 stitches, and work across the row.
4. Working both sides at the same time, work even until the piece measures 25".
5. *To shape the neck:* continue to work both sides at the same time. Bind off 5 stitches at each neck edge.
6. Decrease 1 stitch at each neck edge, every other row, 5 times.

7. Work even until the piece measures 27".
8. Bind off all shoulder stitches.

For the sleeves:

1. With smaller needles, cast on 67 stitches.
2. Work knit 1, purl 1 rib for 1".
3. Switch to larger needles, and begin stockinette stitch.
4. Increase 8 stitches evenly across the next right-side row.
5. Increase 1 stitch each side every second row to 110 stitches.
6. Work even until the piece measures approximately 8" or the desired length.
7. Loosely bind off all stitches.

To finish the neck:

1. Using the smaller needle, sew the front to the back at the shoulder seams.
2. With right sides facing and starting at the placket edge, pick up 5 bound-off stitches, 10 side neck stitches, 38 back neck stitches, 10 side neck stitches, and 5 bound-off stitches.
3. Work knit 1, purl 1 rib for 1".
4. Bind off loosely.

To finish the placket:

1. Using the smaller needle, with right sides facing and starting at the neck edge of the placket opening, pick up stitches from the side of the neck band, and pick up 33 stitches along the placket edge. Work in knit 1, purl 1 rib for 1½".
2. Bind off loosely.
3. On the opposite side of the placket opening, pick up and work the overlap in the same way, working the buttonholes at regular intervals.

4. Stitch the bottom of the overlap to the garment.

For the collar:

1. With smaller short circular needles and right sides facing, start at the neck edge and pick up 5 bound-off front neck stitches, 10 side neck stitches, 38 back neck stitches, 10 side neck stitches, and 5 bound-off front neck stitches.

2. Work knit 1, purl 1 rib for approximately 4".

3. Bind off loosely in pattern.

To finish the sweater:

1. Weave in all ends.

2. Sew the side seams, sew the sleeve seams, and sew the sleeves to the armhole opening.

3. Sew on the buttons.

4. Weave in all ends.

Bulky Vest

Vests can be very practical in the "Oh, I feel a little chilly and need to wear something but not a lot" sort of way, or they can fill in when you're in an "I want to wear something different" mood.

For more versatility, you can use different-weight yarns. For example, you might use a bulky merino in worsted weight. A very light ribbon tape knits at a bulky weight, too. You could make this vest in one yarn for the winter, and use something entirely opposite for the summer.

With bulky yarn, this is a project that will go quickly!

Purl Pearls

The tighter a yarn is spun, the more durable it is. A loosely twisted yarn has more loft. Think of a down comforter. It's thick but not heavy due to all the air between the feathers. Yarn that has loft may be thick but it's not heavy due to its inherent lightness.

Small Bulky Vest

Yarn: Approximately 495 yards bulky weight yarn

Needles: Size 11, or to obtain gauge

Gauge: 11 stitches per 4 inches

Time to complete: Approximately 15 hours

For the back of the sweater:

1. Cast on 66 stitches.

2. Work 8 rows of garter stitch.

3. Switch to stockinette stitch, and work even until the piece measures 14".

4. *To shape the underarm:* bind off 3 stitches at the beginning of the next 2 rows.

5. Work even until the piece measures 23½".

6. Loosely bind off all stitches.

For the front of the sweater:

1. Work as for the back, including all shaping, until the piece measures 15½".

2. *To shape the neck:* work to center 6 stitches, and attach another ball of yarn.

3. Bind off center 6 stitches, and work across the row.

4. Working both sides at the same time, decrease 2 stitches at each neck edge, every other row, 3 times. Then decrease 1 stitch at neck edge, every other row, 6 times.

5. Work even until the piece measures 23½".

To finish the sweater:

1. Sew the front to the back at the shoulders.

2. Work single crochet edging around the neck edges.

3. Work a continuous band of single crochet approximately 1½" around the entire bottom, side, and sleeve edges.

4. Sew buttons on the back, evenly spaced along the side.

5. Using a large knitting needle, make an opening in the front single crochet edging, and push a button through to close the sides.

Knit Tips

It's always wise to buy a little extra yarn to have on hand as you work on your project. If you don't need it, you can return it. If you don't have it, you might not be able to find the same dye lot later, and you'll have to scramble to complete the garment.

Medium Bulky Vest

Yarn: Approximately 585 yards bulky weight yarn

Needles: Size 11, or to obtain gauge

Gauge: 11 stitches per 4 inches

Time to complete: Approximately 15 hours

For the back of the sweater:

1. Cast on 72 stitches.

2. Work 8 rows of garter stitch.

3. Switch to stockinette stitch, and work even until the piece measures 15".

4. *To shape the underarm:* bind off 5 stitches at the beginning of the next 2 rows.

5. Work even until the piece measures 25½".

6. Loosely bind off all stitches.

For the front of the sweater:

1. Work as for the back, including all shaping, until the piece measures 17½".

2. *To shape the neck*: work to center 8 stitches, and attach another ball of yarn.

3. Bind off center 8 stitches, and work across the row.

4. Working both sides at the same time, decrease 2 stitches at each neck edge, every other row, 3 times. Then decrease 1 stitch at the neck edge, every other row, 6 times.

5. Work even until the piece measures 25½".

To finish the sweater:

1. Sew the front to the back at the shoulders.

2. Work single crochet edging around the neck edges.

3. Work a continuous band of single crochet approximately 1½" around the entire bottom, side, and sleeve edges.

4. Sew the buttons on the back, evenly spaced along the side.

5. Using a large knitting needle, make an opening in the front single crochet edging, and push a button through to close the sides.

Purl Pearls

Worsted is a term describing the spinning of the fiber, rather than the weight or content. All ends are tightly twisted into the yarn.

Large Bulky Vest

- *Yarn:* Approximately 675 yards bulky weight yarn
- *Needles:* Size 11, or to obtain gauge
- *Gauge:* 11 stitches per 4 inches
- *Time to complete:* Approximately 15 hours

For the back of the vest:

1. Cast on 78 stitches.
2. Work 8 rows of garter stitch.
3. Switch to stockinette stitch, and work even until the piece measures 16".
4. *To shape the underarm:* bind off 4 stitches at the beginning of the next 2 rows.
5. Work even until the piece measures 27".
6. Loosely bind off all stitches.

For the front of the vest:

1. Work as for the back, including all shaping, until the piece measures 18½".
2. *To shape the neck:* work to center 7 stitches, and attach another ball of yarn.
3. Bind off center 7 stitches, and work across the row.

4. Working both sides at the same time, decrease 2 stitches at each neck edge, every other row, 3 times. Then, decrease 1 stitch at each neck edge, every other row, 8 times.
5. Work even until the piece measures 27".

To finish the vest:

1. Sew the front to the back at the shoulders.
2. Work single crochet edging around the neck edges.
3. Work a continuous band of single crochet approximately 1½" around the entire bottom, side, and sleeve edges.
4. Sew the buttons on the back, evenly spaced along the side.
5. Using a large knitting needle, make an opening in the front single crochet edging and push a button through to close the sides.

In This Chapter

◆ Cover up with a Basic Tunic

◆ Go out on the town—or stay at home—with tunic variations to suit your wardrobe

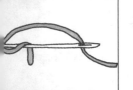 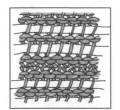    

Chapter 15

Cardigan Tunics

Sometimes you just want to pull on something that's uncomplicated. The tunic in this chapter is a simple sweater with lots of utility. You could take it on a weekend of leaf peeping or, done in a metallic fashion yarn, wear it for an evening rendezvous.

You can make the sweater any length you want. If you want something hip length, it's easy enough to measure to your hip and make any adjustments. Perhaps you want a tunic longer than the one in the pattern. That's another simple adjustment. Just remember, the longer the sweater, the more yarn you'll need to complete the project, so purchase plenty in the same dye lot before beginning.

What You Need and Need to Know

Don't let buttons and buttonholes hold you back. You can skip buttons entirely or place buttons evenly spaced on one side and simply do what so many knitters do: gently push the button through a stitch on the other side. Do that enough times, and you'll create a permanent opening.

This graceful sweater has great utility.

Materials to complete all projects:

Yarn: Worsted weight of your choice (See individual patterns for specific amounts.)

Needles: Size 7, or to obtain specified gauge

Time to complete: 20 to 25 hours

Markers

Yarn needle

Measuring tape

Scissors

Stitches used in this chapter:

Garter stitch

Stockinette stitch

> **Knots!**
>
> When you store your sweater, don't hang it on a hanger. Its own weight will pull it out of shape. Instead, fold it flat and put it in a drawer or a lidded plastic storage bin. You can also store it in a large, heavy plastic bag.

Basic Tunic

This sweater is so easy to wear you'll find it indispensable in your wardrobe. The added length makes it possible for this sweater to replace a light jacket, too. You can easily adjust the length making this as long or as short as you please, none of the shaping instructions change. The front bands may change, but if you pick up stitches based on the length of the knitting in front of you, you'll have no trouble at all.

Small Tunic

> *Yarn:* Approximately 1,315 yards worsted weight
>
> *Gauge:* 5 stitches per inch

For the back of the tunic:

1. Cast on 91 stitches.
2. Work garter stitch for 1".
3. Begin stockinette stitch.
4. Increase 11 stitches evenly over the next right-side row.
5. Work even until the piece measures 19", and place a marker for the underarm.
6. Work even until the piece measures 28½".
7. Loosely bind off all stitches.

For the front of the tunic:

1. Make two, reversing the shaping.
2. Cast on 45 stitches.
3. Work garter stitch for 1".
4. Begin stockinette stitch.
5. Increase 6 stitches evenly over the next right-side row.
6. Work even until the piece measures 19", and place a marker for the underarm.
7. When the piece measures 24", begin shaping the neck.
8. At the neck edge, bind off 8 stitches. Then decrease 1 stitch at the neck edge, every other row, 8 times.
9. Work even until the piece measures 28½".
10. Loosely bind off all stitches.

For the sleeves:

1. Cast on 41 stitches.
2. Work garter stitch for 1".
3. Begin stockinette stitch.
4. Increase 5 stitches evenly over the next right-side row. Work another row.
5. Increase 1 stitch each side every fourth row 25 times to 96 stitches.
6. Work even until the piece measures approximately 17½" or the desired length.
7. Loosely bind off all stitches.

To finish the neck:

1. Sew the front to the back at the shoulder seams.
2. With right sides facing and starting at the neck edge, pick up 8 bound-off stitches, 21 side neck stitches, 32 back neck stitches, 21 side neck stitches, and 8 bound-off stitches.

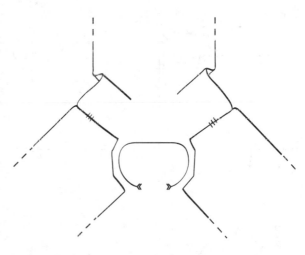

Sew the front to the back at shoulder seams first.

3. Work garter stitch for 1".
4. Bind off loosely.

Knit Tips

To make a turtleneck sweater, simply extend the crewneck for as many inches as you'd like, probably about 6 to 8 inches.

To finish the front band:

1. Work the band on both front pieces.
2. With right sides facing, pick up 1 stitch for every row of garter stitch and approximately 3 stitches for every 4 rows of stockinette.
3. Work 1 row of garter stitch.
4. Bind off loosely.

To finish the tunic:

1. Weave in all ends.
2. Sew the side seams, sew the tops of the sleeves to the body, and sew the underarm seams.

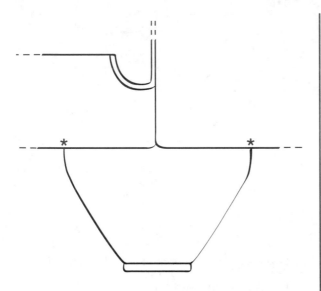

Sew the sleeves to the body.

Medium Tunic

> *Yarn:* Approximately 1,505 yards worsted weight
> *Gauge:* 5 stitches per inch
> *Needles:* Size 7, or to obtain specified gauge

For the back of the tunic:

1. Cast on 101 stitches.
2. Work garter stitch for 1".
3. Begin stockinette stitch.
4. Increase 11 stitches evenly over the next right-side row.
5. Work even until the piece measures 20", and place a marker for the underarm.
6. Work even until the piece measures 29".
7. Loosely bind off all stitches.

For the front of the tunic:

1. Make two, reversing the shaping.
2. Cast on 50 stitches.
3. Work garter stitch for 1".
4. Begin stockinette stitch.
5. Increase 7 stitches evenly over the next right-side row.
6. Work even until the piece measures 19½", and place a marker for the underarm.
7. When the piece measures 24", begin shaping the neck.
8. At the neck edge, bind off 9 stitches and then decrease 1 stitch at the neck edge, every other row, 9 times.
9. Work even until the piece measures 29".
10. Loosely bind off all stitches.

For the sleeves:

1. Cast on 43 stitches.
2. Work garter stitch for 1".
3. Begin stockinette stitch.
4. Increase 5 stitches evenly over the next right-side row. Work another row.
5. Increase 1 stitch each side every second row 7 times and then every fourth row 22 times to 106 stitches.
6. Work even until the piece measures approximately 18" or the desired length.
7. Loosely bind off all stitches.

To finish the neck:

1. Sew the front to the back at the shoulder seams.
2. With right sides facing and starting at the neck edge, pick up 9 bound-off stitches, 21 side neck stitches, 36 back neck stitches, 21 side neck stitches, and 9 bound-off stitches.

3. Work garter stitch for 1".

4. Bind off loosely.

To finish the front band:

1. Work the band on both front pieces.

2. With right sides facing, pick up 1 stitch for every row of garter stitch and approximately 3 stitches for every 4 rows of stockinette.

3. Work 2 rows of garter stitch.

4. Bind off loosely.

To finish the tunic:

1. Weave in all ends.

2. Sew the side seams, sew the tops of the sleeves to the body, and sew the underarm seams.

Large Tunic

Yarn: Approximately 1,818 yards worsted weight

Gauge: 5 stitches per inch

For the back of the tunic:

1. Cast on 109 stitches.

2. Work garter stitch for 1".

3. Begin stockinette stitch.

4. Increase 13 stitches evenly over the next right-side row.

5. Work even until the piece measures 18½", and place a marker for the underarm.

6. Work even until the piece measures 29½".

7. Loosely bind off all stitches.

For the front of the tunic:

1. Make two, reversing the shaping.

2. Cast on 54 stitches.

3. Work garter stitch for 1".

4. Begin stockinette stitch.

5. Increase 7 stitches evenly over the next right-side row.

6. Work even until the piece measures 18½", and place a marker for the underarm.

7. When the piece measures 26", begin shaping the neck.

8. At the neck edge, bind off 10 stitches and then decrease 1 stitch at the neck edge, every other row, 9 times.

9. Work even until the piece measures 29½".

10. Loosely bind off all stitches.

For the sleeves:

1. Cast on 47 stitches.

2. Work garter stitch for 1".

3. Begin stockinette stitch.

4. Increase 5 stitches evenly over the next right-side row. Work one row.

5. Increase 1 stitch each side, every second row, 5 times, and then every fourth row 24 times to 112 stitches.

6. Work even until the piece measures approximately 17½" or the desired length.

7. Loosely bind off all stitches.

To finish the neck:

1. Sew the front to the back at the shoulder seams.

2. With right sides facing and starting at the neck edge, pick up 10 bound-off stitches, 23 side neck stitches, 38 back neck stitches, 23 side neck stitches, and 10 bound-off stitches.

3. Work garter stitch for 1".

4. Bind off loosely.

To finish the front band:

1. Work the band on both front pieces.

2. With right sides facing, pick up 1 stitch for every row of garter stitch and approximately 3 stitches for every 4 rows of stockinette.

3. Work 2 rows of garter stitch.

4. Bind off loosely.

To finish the tunic:

1. Weave in all ends.

2. Sew the side seams, sew the tops of the sleeves to the body, and sew the underarm seams.

Knit Tips

Use the same yarn you knitted the garment with to sew it together. If the yarn is particularly textured and sewing with it is difficult, switch to a plain yarn in the same color to sew the seams. The plain yarn will probably be less bulky, too, and give the finished garment a smoother appearance.

A Sweater That's Got Glitz

Use the wildest yarn you can find. If you can't find one over-the-top enough, use a lightweight metallic yarn as a carry along. Then, decorate with metallic trims or metallic buttons. If you really want to make a dramatic statement, make this sweater floor length!

Country Sampler

Use homespun yarns in muted colors. Work in stripes, each in a different stitch pattern. Find suitable buttons like ducks, apples, or pieces of wood for a touch of country.

Walk, Don't Run Sweater

Some wonderful cotton chenilles are available now. Use this soft and absorbent yarn to make a terrific warm-up sweater.

Home Is Where the Heart Is Sweater

If you want a challenge and a stunning sweater, you can chart a diagram of your town on the sweater. It doesn't have to be an exact architectural representation, but if you choose the prominent buildings, your friends and family will certainly recognize the location. Use duplicate stitch and as many colors of yarn as it takes to portray your very own Hometown, USA.

In This Chapter

◆ Keep warm with leglets

◆ Add some fun with zigzag ribbing and other yarn and stitch variations

◆ Make some leglets for the kids in your life

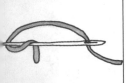
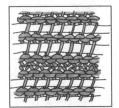

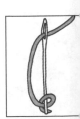

Chapter **16**

Leg Warmers

Whether you're a dancer or a skater—or have an inner dancer trying to get out—these leglets are for you. When the weather turns cool or downright cold, you'll appreciate these for the extra warmth. Even if it isn't cold, the slouchy casual look always is appealing.

These leglets don't take much yarn, so you have a small investment in time and money. I say splurge when you choose your yarn. A hand-painted merino would be delicious against your skin and add that flash of color on your legs. A silk and merino blend would be stunning with its natural sheen. A solid yarn can always be embellished with beads and buttons or even rhinestones.

But you don't have to choose a plain yarn. Get a bouclé if you're feeling particularly adventurous. Chenille is soft and warm, and comes in many shades as well as weights. A kid mohair would be like wearing a cloud on your leg.

When you start to knit, let these luxury yarns do your work for you. A plain stockinette is all you need. No fancy stitches are required; most of the time, they would just be lost.

What You Need and Need to Know

One size should fit most. If you knit one, try it on, and find it's too big or too small, you can either switch your needle size or add or subtract a few stitches.

Decide how long you want your leg warmer to be. Measuring your leg will give you a good indication. And don't forget to allow for as much slouch as you'd like. Measure your ankle, and write down that number. Then, measure your calf and write that down, too.

If you're like most people, your calf is larger than your ankle. That means you'll have to increase as you knit. Think of a leg warmer as a sleeve. With a sleeve, you start with the cuff and increase 1 stitch each side every 4 or 6 rows. Do the same with your leg warmer. On smaller needles, cast on the number of stitches required to form a cuff around your ankle. Then, switch to larger needles, and increase 2 stitches each side every 4 or 6 rows.

Why 4 or 6? If you need to make quite a few increases to get the right calf diameter, you'll need to increase quickly over the length. If you don't need to make many increases, you can spread them out a bit more. It will be undetectable when you're wearing the leg warmer.

Knit Tips

At some point in your knitting experience, you'll want to customize a garment. These leglets are a great simple place to begin.

Wool is more forgiving than acrylic; it stretches and bounces back into shape. Alpaca hardly stretches at all and will probably not retain its shape once worn. Cotton doesn't stretch much, but it shrinks back into shape after making a trip through the washer and dryer. A lighter-weight yarn will drape better than a bulky weight. If you want slouch, a bulky weight yarn probably won't work for this project.

When you're shopping for leg warmer yarn, rub the skein against your inner arm, if possible. How does it feel? You might be wearing this against your bare skin, so you want it to be comfy. If you're wearing the leg warmers over tights, you can probably choose almost anything.

Materials to complete all projects:

Yarn: Worsted weight yarn, bulky weight yarn (See individual patterns for specific amounts.)

Needles: Sizes 5, 6, 7, 8, 9, and 10, or to obtain specified gauge

Time to complete: 2 to 4 hours

Yarn needle

Measuring tape

Scissors

Stitches used in this chapter:

Knit, purl ribbing

Stockinette stitch

Zigzag ribbing

Duplicate stitch

Basic Leglets

Maybe you'd like a little warmth around your leg but don't want something that goes up almost to your knee. A leglet is the perfect solution.

Yarn: 1 skein worsted weight wool

Needles: Size 7 or to obtain gauge

Gauge: 5 stitches per inch

---

1. Cast on 50 stitches.
2. Work in knit 1, purl 1 rib for approximately 10" or desired length to allow for slouching.
3. Bind off loosely.

4. Weave in the ends.

5. Sew the long edges together.

6. Make 2.

Knit Tips

If your ribbing becomes too loose through wear, run a piece of fine, round elastic thread into the stitches. (This is available at most fabric stores.) Do this for about 3 rows. It will be almost invisible.

Raspberry Leglets

> *Yarn:* 1 skein each Cascade 220 Superwash worsted weight wool, light pink and dark pink
>
> *Needles:* Size 5, 6, or 7 for small, medium, or large

These fun leglets cover an adult's lower leg perfectly but can be used as an older child's legwarmer, too.

1. Cast on 48 stitches with light pink yarn.

2. Work in knit 2, purl 2 rib pattern for approximately 3".

3. Switch to dark pink yarn and raspberry stitch, increasing 1 stitch each side of the first row:

   Rows 1 and 3: Purl.

   Row 2: Knit 1, *knit 1, yarn over, knit 1 into the next stitch, purl 3 together, repeat from * to end of row, ending with knit 1.

   Row 4: Knit 1, *purl 3 together, knit 1, yarn over, knit 1 into the next stitch, repeat from * to end of row, ending with knit 1.

4. Work for 4".

5. Switch to the light pink yarn, and knit 2, purl 2 rib.

6. Work for 3".

7. Bind off loosely.

8. Weave in the ends.

9. Repeat for the desired length.

Bulky Yarn Leglets

> ◆ *Yarn:* 1 or 2 skeins bulky weight wool
> ◆ *Needles:* Size 8 or 9

1. Cast on 24 stitches.

2. Work in knit 1, purl 1 rib for approximately 10" or desired length to allow for slouching.

3. Bind off loosely.

4. Weave in ends.

5. Sew the long edges together.

6. Make 2.

Basic Child's Leg Warmers

You might want to look at a light and fluffy yarn that works to a bulky weight gauge for these children's leg warmers instead of something that's really heavy.

Sizes: Small (medium, large)

Yarn: 1 skein bulky weight yarn

Needles: Size 8 and 10 circular

Gauge: 3 stitches per inch on size 10 needles

1. Cast on 20 (22, 24) stitches.
2. Work in knit 1, purl 1 rib for 2".
3. Begin stockinette stitch, and work until the piece is approximately 14" long or the desired length to allow for slouching.
4. Begin knit 1, purl 1 rib, and continue for 2" more.
5. Bind off loosely.
6. Weave in ends.
7. Sew the long edges together.
8. Make 2.

Strawberry Waffle Warmers

Merino is soft, warm, and comforting—just what you might need on a blustery day. Hold the syrup on these waffle warmers, though! Make these as long as you want in case you like slouchy warmers like I do.

Yarn: 1 or 2 skeins worsted weight merino wool

Needles: Size 5 and 7

1. Cast on 50 stitches.
2. Work knit 1, purl 1 rib for 4".
3. Switch to larger needles and waffle stitch:

    Row 1: Knit.

    Row 2: Knit.

    Row 3: Knit 2, purl 2.

    Row 4: Knit 2, purl 2.
4. Keeping to the pattern, increase 1 stitch each side, every fourth row, to 78 stitches, incorporating increases into the pattern.
5. When the piece measures 18" or desired length, switch to smaller needles and begin ribbing.
6. Work knit 1, purl 1 rib for 4".
7. Bind off loosely.
8. Weave in ends.
9. Sew the long edges together.
10. Make 2.

Purl Pearls

When hand-washing your garment, do not agitate. Simply push the soapy water through the fabric and then rinse well. Squeeze out the water, do not wring. And always lay your garment flat to dry.

Zigzag Rib Leg Warmers

It you'd like your leg warmer to fit more closely, you can rib the entire piece.

Yarn: 1 or 2 skeins worsted weight wool
Needles: Size 5 or 6

1. Cast on 52 stitches (multiple of 5 stitches plus 2).

2. Begin zigzag rib:

   Rows 1, 3, 5, 7, and 9 (right-side rows): Knit 1, *purl 2 together, make 1, knit 2, repeat from * across, end knit 1.

   Row 2 and all wrong-side rows: Purl.

   Rows 11, 13, 15, 17, and 19 (right-side rows): Knit 1, *make 1, purl 2 together, purl 1, knit 2, repeat from * across, end knit 1.

   Row 20: Purl.

3. Repeat Rows 1 through 10 for desired length.

4. Bind off loosely.

5. Weave in ends.

6. Sew the long edges together.

7. Make 2.

Knit Tips

If you have a favorite pattern, laminate it to preserve it.

Novelty Yarn Leg Warmers

These leg warmers are fun. Go wild with a fun fur, or carry along an eyelash yarn or metallic thread.

Fluffy, Furry Cuffs

Make the cuffs in a contrasting fluffy or fur-type yarn and then duplicate stitch or embroider snowflakes on the solid leg section.

Winter Scene

Using a light blue space-dyed yarn, duplicate stitch the fir tree pattern on top. Embroider small snowflakes randomly spaced in a fuzzy yarn. (See Chapter 2 for both the fir tree and snowflake patterns.)

In This Chapter

◆ Warm your feet with hand-knit socks

◆ Learn to make kitchener toes

◆ Knit some tube socks for your favorite little one(s)

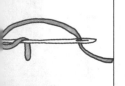
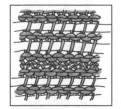
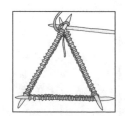
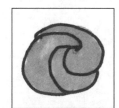

Socks

Knitting socks can be addictive, and it's certainly an art form—but luckily, not a very difficult one! I love to knit socks because they're something I actually wear every day, and it's a project that goes quickly. For the person who doesn't want to do much purling, except for the ribbing, you'll be doing all stockinette for the basic socks. Soon that won't be enough and you'll be using other stitches.

You don't know what comfort is until you wear hand-knit socks.

You'll be hooked once you wear luscious merino socks. You won't want to go back to store-bought socks!

Purl Pearls

The earliest examples of knitting—patterned cottons socks were from Egypt—date back to 1100 C.E.

What You Need and Need to Know

Most sock yarn—that is, yarn intended for socks—has some nylon it, to make the fabric more sturdy at the points where the sock wears most. Other times, the manufacturer includes a small spool of reinforcing thread to be used at the heel and toe. If the yarn you've chosen doesn't have nylon already and no extra thread is hidden in the skein, go to your local fabric store and buy a spool of Woolly Nylon serger thread. It will work very well to reinforce the heel and won't cut the yarn. To use it, or the little spool that comes with your skein, just carry the nylon along with the main yarn as you knit the heels and toes. There's no need to use it for the whole sock.

The yarn for the women's sock project is cotton with a small amount of elastic, which makes it very nice to knit and even better to wear because if your foot is a little wider or longer, the yarn stretches to accommodate your foot.

Socks are most often made with size 4 or 5 double point needles. Some people get overwhelmed by all those needles and prefer to knit on two circular needles or one very long circular needle.

Be sure to read the pattern all the way through before you begin knitting.

Knit Tips

Make a copy of your pattern and put it someplace safe. In fact, make a couple copies. You never know what can happen to a piece of paper!

Materials to complete all projects:

Yarn: Approximately 2 skeins sock weight yarn, per pair

Needles: Size 4, 5, 6, or 7 double point needles, or to obtain specified gauge

Markers

Yarn needle

Measuring tape

Scissors

Stitches used in this chapter:

Knit, purl rib

Stockinette stitch

Kitchener stitch

Basic Socks

These basic socks are worked from cuff to toe. All socks are worked in the round.

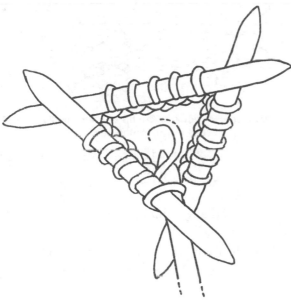

A triangle is formed when you knit on three needles.

Small Socks

Yarn: Approximately 240 yards Cascade Fixation

Needles: Size 4 double point

Gauge: 6 stitches per inch, 7 rows per inch

1. Cast on 46 stitches loosely.
2. Divide the stitches on 3 needles as follows:

   Needle 1 (N1): 11 heel stitches

   Needle 2 (N2): 23 instep stitches

   Needle 3 (N3): 12 heel stitches

3. Join the stitches to begin working in rounds.
4. For the leg, work in knit 1, purl 1 rib for 56 rounds or until the piece measures 8".
5. Work to end of N2.
6. Begin stockinette stitch.
7. For the heel, slip stitches from N3 onto N1 (23 stitches). Note: the heel is worked back and forth in rows.

Slip stitches reinforce the heel flap and give added wear.

8. On the first row only, work 2 stitches in the pattern stitch. Make 1 complete row (24 stitches).
9. Continue the heel in rows as follows:

   Row 1: *Slip 1 purl wise, knit 1. Repeat from * to the end.

   Row 2: Slip 1 purl wise, purl to the end.

Knit Tips

Here, *slip 1* means to slip purl wise. Insert the needle into the stitch from the right to the left as if to purl and then slip off the needle without working that stitch.

10. Repeat these 2 rows until 24 rows are complete or the heel measures $3\frac{1}{2}$".

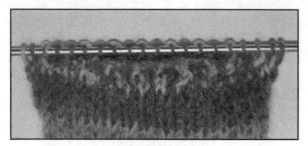

Working the heel.

11. Turn the heel as follows (Row 1 and all odd-numbered rows are right-side rows):

    Row 1: Knit 14, slip slip knit, knit 1. Turn.

    Row 2: Slip 1, purl 5, purl 2 together, purl 1. Turn.

    Row 3: Slip 1, knit 6, slip slip knit, knit 1. Turn.

    Row 4: Slip 1, purl 7, purl 2 together, purl 1. Turn.

    Row 5: Slip 1, knit 8, slip slip knit, knit 1. Turn.

    Row 6: Slip 1, purl 9, purl 2 together, purl 1. Turn.

    Row 7: Slip 1, knit 10, slip slip knit, knit 1. Turn.

    Row 8: Slip 1, purl 11, purl 2 together, purl 1. Turn.

    Row 9: Slip 1, knit 12, slip slip knit. Turn.

    Row 10: Slip 1, purl 12, purl 2 together. Turn.

    Row 11: Knit across. All the heel stitches are on N1.

12. For the heel gusset, with N1, pick up and knit 12 stitches along the side of the heel (N1: 28 stitches total).

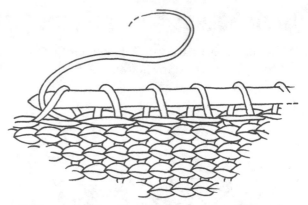

With a crochet hook or the tip of your needle, pick up stitches evenly at the heel gusset.

13. Work across the 23 instep stitches (N2).

14. With N3, pick up and knit 12 stitches along the other side of the heel, and work across the remaining heel stitches. (N3: 12 stitches total).

15. Redistribute the stitches so N1 and N3 both have 20 stitches each. Begin working in rounds.

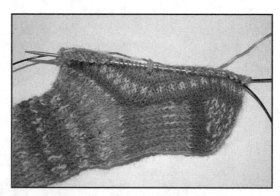

If the stitches are picked up evenly along the gusset, there will be no gaps.

16. To shape the gusset, decrease round:

    N1: Work to 3 stitches from the end, knit 2 together, knit 1.

    N2: Work even.

    N3: Knit 1, slip slip knit, work to the end.

    Next round: Work even.

17. Repeat these 2 rounds until 47 stitches remain.

18. Decrease 1 stitch in the heel section on the last even round for 46 stitches.

19. For the foot, continue working even in rounds until the foot measures 7¾".

20. Work to the end of N3.

21. Shape the toe:

    Round 1:

    N1: Work to the last 3 stitches, knit 2 together, knit 1.

    N2: Knit 1, slip slip knit, work to the last 3 stitches, knit 2 together, knit 1.

    N3: Knit 1, slip slip knit, complete the round.

    Round 2: Work even.

22. Repeat these 2 rounds until 26 stitches remain.

23. To finish the sock, work Round 1 only until 14 stitches remain.

24. Cut the yarn, leaving several inches to work with.

25. Using a yarn needle, thread the yarn through the remaining stitches. Pull firmly and fasten off.

26. Weave in the ends on the inside of the sock.

27. Make 2.

Knots!

Never assume that because you're using the same size needles the pattern calls for with the same yarn, you will obtain the same gauge. Always make a swatch. You knit in your own particular way, as did the pattern designer. Check your gauge to be sure the garment will wind up being the size you need.

Medium Socks

> *Yarn:* Approximately 245 yards Cascade Fixation
>
> *Needles:* Size 4, 5, 6, or 7 double point
>
> *Gauge:* 6 stitches per inch, 7 rows per inch

1. Cast on 48 stitches loosely.

2. Divide the stitches on 3 needles as follows:

    Needle 1 (N1): 16 heel stitches

    Needle 2 (N2): 16 instep stitches

    Needle 3 (N3): 16 heel stitches

3. Join the stitches to begin working in rounds.

4. For the leg, work in knit 1, purl 1 rib for 56 rounds or until the piece measures 8".

5. Work to the end of N2.

6. Begin stockinette stitch.

7. For the heel, slip stitches from N3 onto N1 (24 stitches). Note that the heel is worked back and forth in rows.

8. On the first row only, work 2 stitches in the pattern stitch. Make 1 complete row (24 stitches).

9. Continue the heel in rows as follows:

    Row 1: *Slip 1 purl wise, knit 1. Repeat from * to the end.

    Row 2: Slip 1 purl wise, purl to the end.

Knit Tips

Here, *slip 1* means to slip purl wise.

10. Repeat these 2 rows until 24 rows are complete or the heel measures 3½".

11. Turn the heel as follows (Row 1 and all odd-numbered rows are right-side rows):

    Row 1: Knit 14, slip slip knit, knit 1. Turn.

    Row 2: Slip 1, purl 5, purl 2 together, purl 1. Turn.

    Row 3: Slip 1, knit 6, slip slip knit, knit 1. Turn.

    Row 4: Slip 1, purl 7, purl 2 together, purl 1. Turn.

    Row 5: Slip 1, knit 8, slip slip knit, knit 1. Turn.

    Row 6: Slip 1, purl 9, purl 2 together, purl 1. Turn.

    Row 7: Slip 1, knit 10, slip slip knit, knit 1. Turn.

    Row 8: Slip 1, purl 11, purl 2 together, purl 1. Turn.

    Row 9: Slip 1, knit 12, slip slip knit. Turn.

    Row 10: Slip 1, purl 12, purl 2 together. Turn.

    Row 11: Knit across. All the heel stitches are on N1.

12. For the heel gusset, with N1, pick up and knit 12 stitches along the side of the heel (N1: 28 stitches total).

13. Work across the 24 instep stitches (N2).

14. With N3, pick up and knit 12 stitches along the other side of the heel, and work across the remaining heel stitches. (N3: 12 stitches total).

15. Redistribute the stitches so N1 and N3 both have 20 stitches each. Begin working in rounds.

16. To shape the gusset, decrease round:

    N1: Work to 3 stitches from the end, knit 2 together, knit 1.

    N2: Work even.

    N3: Knit 1, slip slip knit, work to the end.

    Next round: Work even.

17. Repeat these 2 rounds until 48 stitches remain.

18. For the foot, continue working even in rounds until the foot measures 8".

19. Work to the end of N3.

20. Shape the toe:

    Round 1:

    N1: Work to the last 3 stitches, knit 2 together, knit 1.

    N2: Knit 1, slip slip knit, work to the last 3 stitches, knit 2 together, knit 1.

    N3: Knit 1, slip slip knit, complete the round.

    Round 2: Work even.

21. Repeat these 2 rounds until 24 stitches remain.

22. To finish the sock, work Round 1 only until 12 stitches remain.

23. Cut the yarn, leaving several inches to work with.

24. Using a yarn needle, thread the yarn through the remaining stitches. Pull firmly and fasten off.

25. Weave in the ends on the inside of the sock.

26. Make 2.

Purl Pearls

During almost every war in modern time, women have knit garments for the soldiers. Socks were desperately needed in World War I. The November 24, 1941, *LIFE* magazine featured instructions on how to knit, as well as a pattern for a simple vest. Eleanor Roosevelt was often photographed knitting for the war effort and carried around a huge bag full of her materials. Women knit bandages for the wounded. Today the American Red Cross continues to supply needed patterns, as it did in the past.

Large Socks

> *Yarn:* Approximately 270 yards Cascade Fixation
>
> *Needles:* Size 4, 5, 6, or 7 double point
>
> *Gauge:* 6 stitches per inch, 7 rows per inch

1. Cast on 50 stitches loosely.

2. Divide the stitches on 3 needles as follows:

   Needle 1 (N1): 12 heel stitches

   Needle 2 (N2): 25 instep stitches

   Needle 3 (N3): 13 heel stitches

3. Join the stitches to begin working in rounds.

4. For the leg, work in knit 1, purl 1 rib for 56 rounds or until the piece measures 8".

5. Work to the end of N2.

6. Begin stockinette stitch.

7. For the heel, slip stitches from N3 onto N1 (25 stitches). Note: the heel is worked back and forth in rows.

8. On the first row only, work 2 stitches in the pattern stitch. Make 1 complete row (26 stitches).

9. Continue the heel in rows as follows:

   Row 1: *Slip 1 purl wise, knit 1. Repeat from * to the end.

   Row 2: Slip 1 purl wise, purl to the end.

Knit Tips

Note: here, *slip 1* means to slip purl wise.

10. Repeat these 2 rows until 24 rows are complete or the heel measures 3¾".

11. Turn the heel as follows (Row 1 and all odd-numbered rows are right-side rows):

    Row 1: Knit 15, slip slip knit, knit 1. Turn.

    Row 2: Slip 1, purl 5, purl 2 together, purl 1. Turn.

    Row 3: Slip 1, knit 6, slip slip knit, knit 1. Turn.

    Row 4: Slip 1, purl 7, purl 2 together, purl 1. Turn.

    Row 5: Slip 1, knit 8, slip slip knit, knit 1. Turn.

    Row 6: Slip 1, purl 9, purl 2 together, purl 1. Turn.

    Row 7: Slip 1, knit 10, slip slip knit, knit 1. Turn.

    Row 8: Slip 1, purl 11, purl 2 together, purl 1. Turn.

    Row 9: Slip 1, knit 12, slip slip knit. Turn.

    Row 10: Slip 1, purl 13, purl 2 together. Turn.

    Row 11: Knit across. All heel stitches are on N1.

12. For the heel gusset, with N1, pick up and knit 13 stitches along the side of the heel (N1: 22 stitches total).

13. Work across the 25 instep stitches (N2).

14. With N3, pick up and knit 12 stitches along the other side of the heel, and work across the remaining heel stitches (N3: 12 stitches total).

15. Redistribute the stitches so N1 and N3 both have 22 stitches each. Begin working in rounds.

16. To shape the gusset, decrease round:

    N1: Work to 3 stitches from the end, knit 2 together, knit 1.

    N2: Work even.

    N3: Knit 1, slip slip knit, work to the end.

    Next round: Work even.

17. Repeat these 2 rounds until 51 stitches remain.

18. Decrease 1 stitch in the heel section on the last even round for 50 stitches.

19. For the foot, continue working even in rounds until the foot measures 8½".

20. Work to the end of N3.

21. Shape the toe:

    Round 1:

    N1: Work to the last 3 stitches, knit 2 together, knit 1.

    N2: Knit 1, slip slip knit, work to the last 3 stitches, knit 2 together, knit 1.

    N3: Knit 1, slip slip knit, complete the round.

    Round 2: Work even.

22. Repeat these 2 rounds until 26 stitches remain.

23. To finish the sock, work Round 1 only until 14 stitches remain.

24. Cut the yarn, leaving several inches to work with.

25. Using a yarn needle, thread the yarn through the remaining stitches. Pull firmly and fasten off.

26. Weave in the ends on the inside of the sock.

27. Make 2.

Kitchener Stitch Toe Finish

Some people prefer to graft the toe stitches together. Here's how it's done:

1. Slip the remaining stitches onto one needle so half are from the top of the sock and half are from the bottom.

2. Cut approximately 10" yarn, and thread the yarn needle.

3. Hold the knitting needles together with right sides out. The needle closest to you is designated "lower," and the one farthest from you is the "upper."

4. Thread the yarn through the first lower stitch from the back.

5. Thread the yarn into the first stitch on the upper needle front to back.

6. Insert the yarn needle into the first stitch on the lower needle as if to knit and then slip the stitch off.

7. Insert the yarn needle into the next-lower needle stitch, as if to purl; leave on the needle.

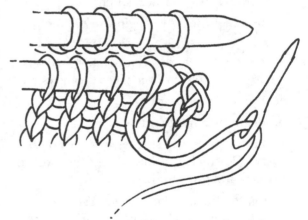

Insert the yarn needle purlwise, right to left, into the stitch.

8. Thread the yarn needle into the first upper needle stitch, as if to purl and then slip the stitch off the knitting needle.

9. Insert the yarn into the next-upper needle stitch, as if to knit; leave on the needle.

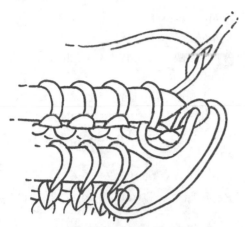

Insert the needle knitwise, left to right, into the next stitch.

10. Repeat steps 6 through 9 until all stitches are woven.

11. Adjust the tension of the woven stitches.

12. Weave in the ends.

Children's Easy Socks

Here's a simple and quick pattern that wears well for children. The sock isn't shaped, so the wear is distributed around the sock. The pattern works well if you're just starting out and are concerned about your ability to work the heel gusset (You can put off that lesson until another time.)

Children's Shoe Size 1

> *Yarn:* 195 yards sock weight
> *Needles:* Size 2, or to obtain gauge
> *Gauge:* 8 stitches per inch
> *Time to complete:* 10 hours

1. Cast on 56 stitches.

2. Divide the stitches on 3 double point needles:

   Needle 1 (N1): 18 stitches

   Needle 2 (N2): 19 stitches

   Needle 3 (N3): 19 stitches

3. Join the stitches to begin working in rounds. Mark the beginning of a round.

4. Work in knit 1, purl 1 rib for approximately 9" or the desired length to within 2" of the end.

5. Shape the toe:

   Round 1:

   N1: Work to the last 3 stitches, knit 2 together, knit 1.

   N2: Knit 1, slip slip knit, work to the last 3 stitches, knit 2 together, knit 1.

   N3: Knit 1, slip slip knit, complete the round.

   Round 2: Work even.

6. Repeat these 2 rounds until 28 stitches remain.

7. Work Round 1 only until 16 stitches remain.

8. Cut the yarn, leaving a 6" tail.

9. With the yarn needle, draw the end through the remaining stitches.

10. Pull firmly, and fasten off.

11. Make 2.

Children's Shoe Size 3

> *Yarn:* 245 yards sock weight
> *Needles:* Size 2, or to obtain gauge
> *Gauge:* 8 stitches per inch
> *Time to complete:* 10 hours

1. Cast on 62 stitches.
2. Divide the stitches on 3 double point needles:

   Needle 1 (N1): 20 stitches.

   Needle 2 (N2): 21 stitches.

   Needle 3 (N3): 21 stitches.
3. Join the stitches to begin working in rounds. Mark the beginning of a round.
4. Work in knit 1, purl 1 rib for approximately 10" or the desired length to within 2" of the end.

5. Shape the toe:

   Round 1:

   N1: Work to the last 3 stitches, knit 2 together, knit 1.

   N2: Knit 1, slip slip knit, work to the last 3 stitches, knit 2 together, knit 1.

   N3: Knit 1, slip slip knit, complete the round.

   Round 2: Work even.
6. Repeat these 2 rounds until 34 stitches remain.
7. Work Round 1 only until 18 stitches remain.
8. Cut the yarn, leaving a 6" tail.
9. With the yarn needle, draw the end through the remaining stitches.
10. Pull firmly, and fasten off.
11. Make 2.

Children's Shoe Size 5

> *Yarn:* 275 yards sock weight
> *Needles:* Size 2, or to obtain gauge
> *Gauge:* 8 stitches per inch
> *Time to complete:* 10 hours

1. Cast on 64 stitches.
2. Divide the stitches on 3 double point needles:
   Needle 1 (N1): 16 stitches.
   Needle 2 (N2): 32 stitches.
   Needle 3 (N3): 16 stitches.
3. Join the stitches to begin working in rounds. Mark the beginning of a round.
4. Work in knit 1, purl 1 rib for approximately 10½" or the desired length to within 2" of the end.

5. Shape the toe:
   Round 1:
   N1: Work to the last 3 stitches, knit 2 together, knit 1.
   N2: Knit 1, slip slip knit, work to the last 3 stitches, knit 2 together, knit 1.
   N3: Knit 1, slip slip knit, complete the round.
   Round 2: Work even.
6. Repeat these 2 rounds until 32 stitches remain.
7. Work Round 1 only until 16 stitches remain.
8. Cut the yarn, leaving a 6" tail.
9. With the yarn needle, draw the end through the remaining stitches.
10. Pull firmly, and fasten off.
11. Make 2.

In This Chapter

◆ Treat your feet with cozy slippers

◆ Add some fun with Fluffy Cuff Slippers

◆ Warm your man's feet with his own slippers

◆ Learn common foot sizes

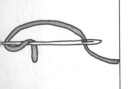 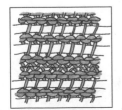  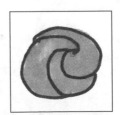  

Chapter 18

Simple Slippers

There's nothing more luxurious than curling up on a cold winter's night while wearing soft and warm slippers. Slippers are excellent for padding around on cold floors or transitioning from the shower to the bedroom. These are always good to have handy, and they make a thoughtful present. For the person confined in bed, slippers can be a wonderful solution to cold feet.

What You Need and Need to Know

A bulky chenille or a merino wool would be first-rate choices; anything soft and fluffy is appropriate for women. Want something really unusual? Try yak yarn. Men might appreciate something a bit more rugged, such as a marled or handspun wool in a navy or forest green.

In this chapter, I give you a basic slipper pattern. You can make it exactly as it is, with the yarn suggested, or you can make it in the yarn of your choice in any number of sizes—I also give you a chart of common foot sizes at the end of the chapter.

Nothing says relaxation like warm slippers.

Materials to complete all projects:

Yarn: Bulky weight yarn (See individual patterns for specific amounts.)

Needles: Size 10.5 and 11 straight needles, or to obtain specified gauge and size

Yarn needle

Measuring tape

Thread or fine yarn

Scissors

Stitches and techniques used in this chapter:

Knit/purl ribbing

Garter stitch

Single crochet edging

Purl Pearls _____

If you love to knit and want to do something for someone else, consider knitting for charity. Cancer patients, homeless shelters, and other charities are always in need of donations. Hats, gloves, scarves, sweaters, throws, and even slippers are among the items needed. Even if you're a beginning knitter, you can make a garment someone needs.

Basic Slippers

This is a very simple project and an excellent one for a beginning knitter. There is no shaping, the only stitches used are knit and purl, and there is very little sewing to make the flat fabric into a slipper. Once you knit the basic shape, you can decorate the slippers to suit your tastes.

Size: Women's medium

Yarn: 2 skeins Bollicine Victor bulky merino wool blend

Needles: Size 10.5

Time: Approximately 5 hours

Yarn needle

Tape measure

Scissors

1. Cast on 29 stitches.
2. Begin the foot pattern: knit 14, purl 1, knit 14 across.
3. Work the foot pattern until the piece measures 8".
4. Begin the toe pattern:

   Row 1: Knit 1, purl 1 across the row.

   Row 2: Purl 1, knit 1 across the row.

   Repeat these 2 rows.
5. Work the pattern 2 more.
6. Break off the yarn.
7. Using the yarn needle, thread the tail through the open stitches, and pull through.
8. Fasten securely.
9. With right sides together, sew the top seam from the toe toward the heel approximately 4".

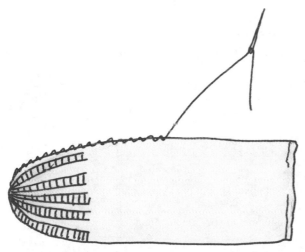

Turn the slipper inside out and sew the toe seam.

10. Fasten off, and weave in the ends.
11. With the slipper still right sides together, fold in half lengthwise.
12. Sew the cast on edge together to form the heel seam.

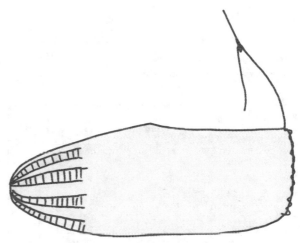

Turn the slipper inside out and sew the heel seam.

13. Fasten off, and weave in the ends.
14. Turn right side out.
15. Make 2.

You can decorate the top with a tassel or a pom-pom. Or if you want, you can make a 24" length of I-Cord, thread it through the stitches around the top edge, and tie it in a bow.

Fluffy Cuff Slippers

For some fun on your feet, crochet one or two rows of a fluffy yarn around the opening. Fun fur would work nicely.

Men's Slippers

Many men find slippers very comfortable to wear around the house. Slippers are a good project for a young knitter who wants a special present to give on Father's Day or his birthday.

You can guesstimate the size of men's slippers by measuring the length of his shoes or his foot if he'll stand still long enough. Refer to the following size chart for measurements if you don't have access to the man or the shoes.

> *Size:* Men's medium
>
> *Yarn:* 2 skeins Bollicine Victor bulky merino wool blend
>
> *Needles:* Size 11
>
> Yarn needle
>
> Tape measure
>
> Scissors

This variation is simple: just work the basic slipper pattern, but use size 11 needles.

Knit Tips

If the project is a gift, you can give the yarn label to the recipient, too. Then they'll have a record of how to wash and care for their present.

Chart of Common Foot Sizes

To be sure your slippers fit like … slippers, here are some common foot sizes.

Size	Foot Length (Inches)	Toe Length (Inches)
Women's		
6	8	1
7	8½	1
8	8½	1½
9	8¾	1½
10	9	1½
11	9½	1½
Men's		
8	8½	1½
9	9	1½
10	9½	1½
11	9½	1½
12	9¾	1½
13	10	1¾
14	10½	1¾

Once you've decided on the shoe size of the person who will wear the slippers, follow the basic pattern and knit to the dimensions stated. Be sure to use the gauge and needle size recommended with your yarn choice.

Knots!

You can make the slipper foot pattern longer, but remember that the top section will need to be adjusted as well. Measuring the fabric against the foot that will wear it is an excellent way to get the correct fit.

In This Chapter

◆ Get cozy with your tea or coffee pot

◆ Work fun cozy variations, like a Basket Weave Cozy, a Primitive Angel cozy, an English Cottage cozy, and more!

◆ Keep your cell phone cozy, too!

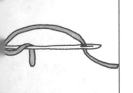 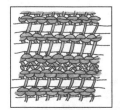    

Chapter 19

Tea and Cell Phone Cozies

When I sent an image of my completed tea cozy to a friend, he wrote back and said, "Nice hat." I e-mailed back, "It's not a hat. It's a tea cozy." "What do you do with that?" he asked.

True, we don't see tea cozies as much as we once did, but those Anglophiles among us who want to live like Brits know that it's imperative to insulate your teapot so the tea doesn't grow cold. I was recently surprised to learn that people also use coffeepot cozies for the same reason.

If you want to keep your tea or your coffee warm—or your cell phone clean and dry—an investment of a few hours can help you do it. Plain or extravagant, you can let your imagination run wild.

What You Need and Need to Know

The projects in this chapter work up quickly and won't challenge your newly acquired skills. The challenge is in the creativity you can bring to these simple objects. Go to a yarn store and touch every skein. Think about the textures and how they'll work for you. What would make a good roof for the English cottage tea cozy? Is there a yarn that shimmers and evokes fish scales?

Materials to complete all projects:

Yarn: 2 skeins worsted weight wool; 2 skeins Cascade Fun yarn; assorted scrap yarns in red, green, and gray

Needles: Size 7 straight

Large bead for fish eye

Small beads (One small container of assorted beads will give you a nice selection.)

Flower-shaped glass beads

Leaf-shaped glass beads

Tear drop–shaped glass beads

Metallic thread

Yarn needle

Fine yarn or thread

Measuring tape

Scissors

Stitches and techniques used in this chapter:

Garter stitch

Stockinette stitch

Seed stitch

Basketweave stitch

Duplicate stitch

French knot

I-Cord

Knit Tips

It's perfectly acceptable to make a plain cozy—and it's easy to do. Simply measure the circumference of your teapot and, following the directions for the basic hat in Chapter 2 and using about 2 skeins of worsted weight yarn, make a very large "hat" for your teapot. In this case, my pal Jon would have been absolutely correct in saying "Nice hat!"

Plain Rectangle Cozy

If you just want to make a cover for your teapot, a simple rectangle will do the job. You might look for an interesting and unexpected yarn such as a chenille. Or go wild and use a plain worsted weight with a carry along eyelash yarn. A fun fur might look like an animal crouched on the table, especially if you sew on plastic eyes.

1. Knit 2 garter stitch rectangles approximately 12" × 8", or to fit the general dimensions of your teapot.
2. Place the rectangles right sides together, and sew three sides together.
3. Weave in all ends.
4. Turn right side out.

You're done!

Basket Weave Stitch Cozy

You can make your cozy far more decorative simply by altering the stitch pattern. Basket weave is a traditional stitch that works up beautifully and is eye-catching as well. (See Chapter 13 for basket weave instructions.)

Basket weave is a simple stitch using knit and purl stitches.

Be sure to choose a yarn that's not so busy with color or texture that it detracts from the stitch pattern.

Primitive Angel Cozy

I love going to a country auction and seeing all the early American primitive items come up for sale. Some of these very wonderful objects can be expensive, so I've tinkered around with a scroll saw and made a few for myself. The primitive angel was originally a large weathervane that I decreased in size until I was able to fit one on my bookshelf. Here I've adapted it for the tea cozy. (It could just as easily go on a sweater.)

I would make the main color an off-white, even drifting into very light beige, to give an antique feel. A handspun natural yarn would lend itself very well to this variation. Shetland wools come in many natural earth-tone colors, so you might look into those.

You would do this in duplicate stitch in the colors of your choosing, perhaps yellow for her hair, light blue for her gown, dark blue for her shoes, white for her wings, and red for her horn. A gold metallic thread for the horn would be super. No facial features are really necessary.

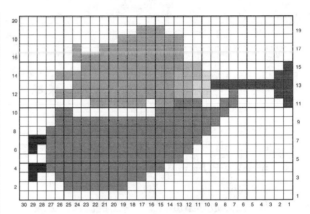

This angel motif will fit perfectly in any country décor.

English Cottage Cozy

Here I decided to go true Brit and design a country cottage for my teapot.

An English Cottage tea cozy for the Anglophile in each of us.

Yarn: Cascade Yarns' Superwash 220 worsted weight, 1 skein each of #824 and #828, and small amounts of scrap yarn in red, green, gray, and blue

Needles: Size 8 straight

Time to complete: 15 to 20 hours

Flower- and leaf-shape glass beads

Yarn needle

Measuring tape

Scissors

Basic Cozy Shape

1. With yellow yarn, cast on 60 stitches.
2. Work 4 rows in garter stitch. This creates the foundation and adds a bit of stability at the bottom.
3. Work in stockinette stitch until the piece measures 5½".
4. Break off the yellow, and attach sienna for the roof.
5. Begin seed stitch:

   Row 1: Knit 1, purl 1 across the row.

   Row 2: Purl 2, knit 2 across the row.

   Repeat Rows 1 and 2.

6. Also begin the roof shaping. At the beginning of every row, work 1 stitch in the established pattern and then knit 2 together. (This won't work out perfectly because you will always be knitting a purl stitch.) Continue in pattern immediately after the decrease.
7. Work in seed stitch for 3".
8. On the next right-side row, purl 1 row. This is the peak of the roof.
9. Continue in seed stitch, and shape the second side of the roof: at the beginning of every row, increase 1 stitch, keeping in the pattern.
10. Work in seed stitch for 3" from the purl ridge or to match the first side.
11. Break off the sienna, and attach the yellow.
12. Work in stockinette stitch until the length from the purl ridge is the same as the first side, including the last 4 rows in garter stitch.
13. Bind off, and weave in the ends.

The finished size will be approximately 12" × 8".

Knots!

Your first reaction might be to sew the cozy together, but wait until you've completed all your decorating. You need easy access to the wrong side.

Cottage Door

1. Using red scrap yarn, cast on 12 stitches.
2. Work 6 rows in garter stitch. The garter stitch runs vertically on the door. This made sense to me because a door is taller rather than wider, and I wanted the eye to travel upward.

Knit Tips

You may need to adjust your door if your teapot dimensions are different from the standard-size teapot I used to design my cozy. Eye the front of the cottage and decide how large the door should be. (No building inspector will be by to grade you on this.)

3. Sew the door to the middle of the front of the cottage.
4. Make a single French knot in brown yarn for the doorknob. (See Chapter 1 for a refresher on French knots.)

Plant

For the side of the house, I wanted a bush.

"Grow" your own plant or bush for your house.

1. Using green worsted weight yarn scraps, cast on 5 stitches.
2. Work as follows:

   Row 1 (right side row): Knit 2, yarn over, knit 1, yarn over, knit 2.

   Row 2 and all wrong side rows: Purl.

   Row 3: Knit 3, yarn over, knit 1, yarn over, knit 3.

   Row 5: Knit 4, yarn over, knit 1, yarn over, knit 4.

   Row 7: Knit 5, yarn over, knit 1, yarn over, knit 5.

   Row 9: Knit.

   Row 11: Knit.

   Row 13: Slip slip knit, knit 9, knit 2 together.

   Row 15: Slip slip knit, knit 7, knit 2 together.

   Row 17: Slip slip knit, knit 5, knit 2 together.

   Row 19: Slip slip knit, knit 3, knit 2 together.

   Row 21: Slip slip knit, knit 1, knit 2 together.

   Row 22: Slip 1, knit 2 together, pass over the slipped stitch.

3. Break off, and fasten yarn.
4. Weave in the ends.
5. Sew the bush to one side of the cottage.

Window and Window Box

Next I wanted a window and a window box. I found a single strand of Cascade Fun, cotton and viscose, a somewhat shiny blue yarn that I could persuade myself was glasslike. Without being overly concerned with the squareness of the small rectangle, I used the yarn needle to stitch an outline of the window. No, it's not "perfect," but that's what makes it quaint.

Make the window with thread and a yarn needle. It can be as large or as small as you'd like.

For the window box, I used the sienna yarn I used for the roof:

1. Cast on 4 stitches.
2. Make an I-Cord slightly longer than the window. (Window boxes are often longer than the window they're under.) Using short double point needles, cast on a small number of stitches, around 3 to 6.
3. Knit all the stitches.
4. Switch the needles in your hands so the needle with the stitches is in your left hand again.
5. Slide the stitches to the other end of the needle, and pull the yarn across the back of the stitches. Knit the row again.
6. Continue this way, sliding and knitting, until the cord is the length you want.
7. Give the cord a tug to make the little carry across the back disappear. There shouldn't be much of a carry if you're knitting on only 3 or 4 stitches.
8. Sew the window box in place.
9. Cut apart 2 sections of a green, textured yarn in the nearest approximation of ivy you can find, and sew them over the windows.

Flowers, Leaves, and Chimney

Use tear drop–shaped glass beads to decorate the top of the window as well as the uprights. Sew 3 flower-shaped glass beads evenly spaced in the window box. In the spaces between the flowers, attach green leaf beads.

Make the chimney with a gray chunky weight yarn:

1. Cast on enough stitches for the chimney to be approximately $1\frac{1}{2}$" tall.
2. Work in garter stitch for 6 rows.

3. Bind off. (Your mileage may vary with the scrap yarn you have.)
4. Turn the chimney so the rows run vertically, and sew it to the peak of the roof. You know where the peak is because that's the one purl row you made. It's also the fold line.

The Finishing Touches

To finish your cottage, turn it inside out and sew the side seams together. Then, weave in any remaining ends.

Gently wash the tea cozy in lukewarm water and a squirt of shampoo. Squeeze out the excess water and roll the cottage into a towel to press out still more water. Laying the cottage on a dry towel, block it into shape, making sure there are no buckles in either the front side or the backside. Pay special attention to the seam sides and the bottom so they remain straight. Wait approximately a day until the tea cozy is completely dry.

Red Barn

Using the same basic pattern as for the cottage, the cozy could easily be transformed into a barn by using a barn-red wool with a gray wool for the roof. No chimney would be necessary—a fire hazard in a barn, of course.

You could make a larger door in brown yarn so the tractor and horses and cows could get through, and include a window, too. Instead of the specimen plant, you could knit a cow and sew her in place.

A gray square in the roof could be the hay loft. Make a small tassel no larger than about $\frac{1}{2}$" yellow sock or sport weight yarn or heavy thread, and attach it to the loft to represent hay.

Cell Phone Cozies

If you have a cell phone, protecting it is a must. You can purchase a leatherette pouch like any business guy on the train and be done with it. But that's not why we learned to knit, so we could have the same things everyone else has. We knit because it's a means to express ourselves. Once you understand the basics of a cell phone cozy, you can begin to imagine your own design.

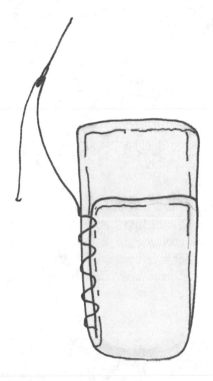

Knots!

When choosing yarn, be careful you don't get something too slippery. I once bought what I thought was a very pretty yarn, and by the time I threw it away, I was sure it had been made of shredded plastic bread bags. Even wooden needles wouldn't have helped because the knitting unraveled itself the moment I stopped holding it.

Measure your phone first to be sure it will fit this design. The basic cozy is a simple rectangle approximately 4"×11" when finished.

Yarn: 1 skein worsted weight yarn of your choice

Needles: Size 7 straight, or to obtain gauge

Gauge: 5 stitches per inch

Time to complete: 5 to 6 hours

Yarn needle

Measuring tape

Scissors

1. Cast on 20 stitches.
2. Work in seed stitch until the piece measures approximately 12".
3. Bind off loosely.
4. Fold, right sides together, so a flap of approximately 3" is at the top.
5. Sew the side seams, weave in the ends, and turn right side out.
6. Sew a bead on the cozy close to but not directly at the bottom edge of the flap.
7. Work the bead between two stitches in the flap. It will be tight at first, but with use, a "buttonhole" will develop.
8. Make an I-Cord strap, if desired, of whatever length suits you to serve as a handle.

Make several cell phone cozies to coordinate with your wardrobe!

Purl Pearls _____

Cotton and rayon yarns are especially good for cozies. For many yarns, they can be thrown into the wash without harm, and there's little or no chance of static.

Fish Cozy

A whimsical fish cell phone cozy is a terrific gift and a wonderful intermediate project. The only stitch used for the fish body is a stockinette stitch the head and tail are in garter stitch, and the shaping is pretty straightforward. If you absolutely hate sewing, you can glue the beads on with fabric glue.

This fish cell phone cozy is sure to be a hit with your favorite fisherman (or fisherwoman).

Yarn: 1 skein Cascade Fun yarn in green; 1 skein Fun yarn in blue
Needles: Size 5 straight
Time to complete: 3 to 4 hours
Large bead
Seed beads or silver beads
Thread
Metallic thread
Small amount of red yarn or red embroidery thread
Sewing needle
Yarn needle
Measuring tape
Scissors

1. To make the body, cast on 12 stitches in the green yarn.
2. Begin working in seed stitch and increase 1 stitch at the beginning of each row until there are 26 stitches.
3. Change to stockinette stitch.
4. Work even until the piece measures 5½".
5. Bind off.
6. Make 2.

Purl Pearls _____

There are several ways to increase 1 stitch. At the beginning of a row, I like to knit in the front and then the back of the stitch. It's very neat and almost undetectable.

7. To make the fins, cast on 12 stitches with the blue yarn.
8. Working in garter stitch, knit 1 row.

9. Begin shaping:

   Row 1: Knit 2 together at the beginning of the row.

   Row 2: Knit.

   Repeat Rows 1 and 2 until 1 stitch remains.

10. Fasten off.

11. Make 2.

12. To embellish, sew silver beads randomly about the stockinette/body section.

13. Sew the eye in place.

14. Then, with wrong sides together, insert the fins into the square end of the fish body. Pin in place.

15. Starting about 1" above the stockinette section, begin sewing the seams together. Sew the side and bottom seams firmly.

16. With blue yarn, knit an I-Cord strap 6 stitches wide and about 12" long. Fasten off. Sew to the inside of the fish where the side seam begins.

17. Using red yarn, overcast stitch for the lips.

Knit Tips

Once you make a cell phone cozy, you're only a short distance from a sunglass cozy. Make it a little longer, perhaps 12" and then another 2" or 3" for a flap, if you want one. Then just follow the directions for the basic cozy.

Fur Sure Cozy

Some of the fake fur yarns on the market today could fool anyone at the distance. For this fun cozy, knit the basic cozy with a dark mink brown yarn. Find trim at your local fabric store that is already sewn with beads and flourishes. You'll need only 12" to 18". Use this as your bejeweled strap.

Suede Cozy

Many faux-leather yarns are available. They're very realistic both to the touch and visually—and best yet, some are machine washable. Knit the basic cozy, and drip long strands of fringe from the lower edge.

In This Chapter

◆ Knit a tote

◆ Make fun variations like a Trinket Tote, a Silk Road Tote, and more

 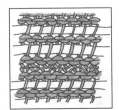 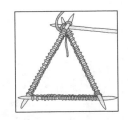 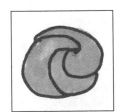  

Chapter 20

Tote Bags

Small and sweet. Large and showy. Delicate. Bold. Totes come in all sizes and shapes and uses. Plus, purses, totes, and bags are so very practical. There isn't a woman (and many a man, too) who doesn't need a way to carry around all the items required during the day.

But having the same few bags or purses is downright boring. Knitting one is an outstanding way to have something new and just the way you want it. You can pay a ton and not have the bag reflect the real you (which is exactly how some people prefer it), or you can make a bag that's all you.

What You Need and Need to Know

So many interesting yarn textures are available now, you're certain to find it hard to decide on just one. Pick a yarn with some heft and stability to it because a light, delicate yarn won't be able to take the strain of a big load. Years ago, one would have used a rug yarn, but no longer. The choices are wide and varied, and you're not relegated to wool. Linens and even stringlike yarns are perfect for these projects. A soft chenille makes a perfect evening purse. You could even use a metallic thread if you enjoy using very small needles.

Knots! —————

If your intention is to felt the item, don't purchase a machine-washable wool. (See more on felting in Chapter 1.)

Materials to complete all projects:

Yarn: 2 skeins space-dyed merino wool, 2 skeins recycled Himalayan silk, 2 or 3 skeins metallic yarn or worsted weight yarns of your choice (See individual patterns for specific amounts.)

Needles: Size 7 or appropriate to the yarn used that works to the size desired

Yarn needle

Measuring tape

Scissors

Mild soap

Towels

Stitches and techniques used in this chapter:

Garter stitch

Moss stitch

Seed stitch

Mitered square

I-Cord

Basic Tote Bag

This is a bag for when you have lots to tote. You'll probably be best off with a worsted weight or slightly heavier yarn. Use the needle size the yarn label calls for.

Size: Your choice

Yarn: Worsted weight yarn of your choice

Needles: To correspond to the yarn label

Gauge: As stated for the yarn

Time to complete: 8 to 12 hours

Yarn needle

Measuring tape

Scissors

---

1. Cast on stitches to measure 12".
2. Work in garter stitch, seed stitch, or moss stitch until the piece measures 40".
3. Fold in half to make a bag 12" × 20".
4. With right sides together, sew the side seams.
5. Cast on 3 to 6 stitches, and knit the I-Cord strap the length you desire.
6. Sew the strap firmly in place inside the bag at the top side seams.

You're done! Go tote something!

Felted Trinket Bag

I love the spirited, almost saucy look of this mitered square tote bag, perfect for when you have a few things to carry. You can leave it plain and let the yarn do all the talking, but adding fancy buttons, faux gemstones, or even small bells would make this adorable.

A trinket bag is perfect if you only need to carry a few things along on your adventure.

Knit Tips

Want to make a quick and simple pot-holder? Use one of the worsted weight cottons available almost everywhere. Make a mitered square just like for the small tote bag. This is a gift that will be most appreciated.

Size: Approximately 5"x5"

Yarn: 1 skein Madil Merino Wool Pierrot Print #322

Needles: Size 7 straight

Gauge: Don't worry too much, as the felting will take care of it

Time to complete: 3 to 6 hours

Yarn needle

Measuring tape

Scissors

1. Cast on 50 stitches.

2. Knit across the row, placing the marker after stitch 25. (This is a wrong-side row.)

3. Beginning on the next right-side row, knit to within 2 stitches of the marker, knit 2 stitches together, slip the marker, and slip 2 stitches one at a time and then knit them purl wise, knit to end of row.

4. *All wrong-side rows:* knit.

Purl Pearls

You will be decreasing 2 stitches on every other row and creating a square. This works because the stitches in garter stitch are as wide as they are tall.

5. Continue in garter stitch with decreases until 2 stitches remain.

6. Knit the remaining 2 stitches together.

7. Break off the yarn, and fasten off.

8. Make 2 squares.

9. To finish the bag, with right sides together, sew the squares together leaving 2 sides open.

10. Sew the bag together in a diamond fashion so the point is downward and the seaming is from approximately the 10 o'clock position to the 2 o'clock position. You don't want the bag to open fully, to keep your precious objects from falling out.

11. For the strap, cast on 3 to 6 stitches and knit a length of I-Cord as long as you'd like. I used 4 stitches and knit for approximately 24".

12. Sew the I-Cord to opposite inside edges of the bag.

13. To complete your bag, make tassels approximately 3" long and sew them to the 3 bottom corners of the bag. If you need the bag to stay shut reliably, sew a small square of Velcro to each of the top inside pieces.

Knit Tips

You can felt this bag, if you want to, but do that before you add the tassels. (See the felting instructions in Chapter 1.)

Silk Road Tote

Hardly a yarn today is more exotic than recycled Himalayan silk. It's made from the remnants of cloth destined to be saris in India and spun into yarn in Nepal. Although it's fairly pricey, it's possible to get it online at a price that won't make you gasp (too much!).

You'll need 1 or 2 skeins for this bag, depending on how large you make it. Using the standard tote bag pattern, make the rectangle larger or smaller, as your needs dictate. Make I-Cord for the strap or cast on 4 to 6 stitches and work in garter stitch for a strap about 24" to 36". Sew the cord or strap to the inside seams.

Go all out and sew gold beads randomly across the surface, attach tassels at the bottom corners, and stitch gold thread anywhere you like.

Evening Purse

For this fun bag, choose a metallic yarn like Berocco's Jewel FX. You'll probably need 2 or 3 balls. Knit a rectangle approximately 6"×14" in whatever stitch tickles your fancy. Fold right sides together so you have a 6"×12" rectangle with an approximately 2" flap at the top. Sew the side and bottom seams together, and turn right side out.

Find an elegant button for the front of your purse. Close the flap, and sew the button directly beneath the edge of the flap, not underneath the flap itself. Attach a short length of elasticized thread to the underside of the flap edge in the middle. The elasticized thread loop should be large enough to go around your button, but not so large that it won't stay closed.

In This Chapter

◆ Snuggle up with a throw

◆ Work such variations as a Nine Patch Throw, a
  Sampler Throw, and more

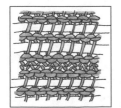

Chapter 21

Simple Throws

Sometimes you need something to keep you warm, but not a full-size blanket. A throw is just the thing. A throw is a terrific project if you're practicing your knitting or just want to knit without putting a lot of thought into it. The end result will be useful for yourself and suitable for a gift.

I'm sure you've seen some large and complicated afghans, but you shouldn't be intimidated by any of these. This project can be as simple or as complicated as you want it to be. It's up to you. The following are some suggestions. You can use them as a plan or inspiration.

What You Need and Need to Know

I always think any project begins at the yarn shop or website. I want to be inspired by the yarn available. Sometimes I know what I want to do and need to find yarn to match my plan, but sometimes I'll see a great yarn I didn't know existed and decide to scrap everything and go with that. Beautiful yarn just shouts out for you to grab it and take it home to snuggle with.

Wool gives you warmth; cotton gives you comfort. If you think the throw will be getting quite a bit of use and may require a lot of cleaning, choosing a machine-washable yarn will make your life much easier.

You can chose contrasting or complementary colors. You can even choose yarns with different textures, provided they're the same weight and will give you the same gauge. Remember, swatching is your friend. Be sure you're getting the size squares you need.

Compact but warm, a throw is as practical as it is comfortable.

Basic Striped Throw

The easiest design is to knit stripes in garter stitch the length of the throw and then sew them together. These instructions assume you want a throw 36" square.

Knit Tips _____

If you want to turn your throw into a bedcover, it needs to be quite a bit larger. Measure the width of the bed and add 20" to allow for 10" of drop on each side. Then, measure the length from the pillow to the foot and add 10" for drop at the end. This holds true for any mattress size.

> *Yarn:* 4 skeins worsted weight yarn in color A, 4 skeins in color B
>
> *Needles:* Size 7, or to obtain gauge specified
>
> *Gauge:* 5 stitches per inch
>
> *Time to complete:* Approximately 30 hours
>
> Yarn needle
>
> Measuring tape
>
> Scissors

> **Materials to complete all projects:**
>
> *Yarn:* Worsted weight yarn in main colors and contrasting colors in amounts noted in individual instructions
>
> *Needles:* Sizes 7 and 13 straight and/or circular, or to obtain specified gauge
>
> Marker
>
> Yarn needle
>
> Measuring tape
>
> Scissors
>
> **Stitches and techniques used in this chapter:**
>
> Garter stitch
>
> Stockinette stitch
>
> Crochet edging
>
> Duplicate stitch

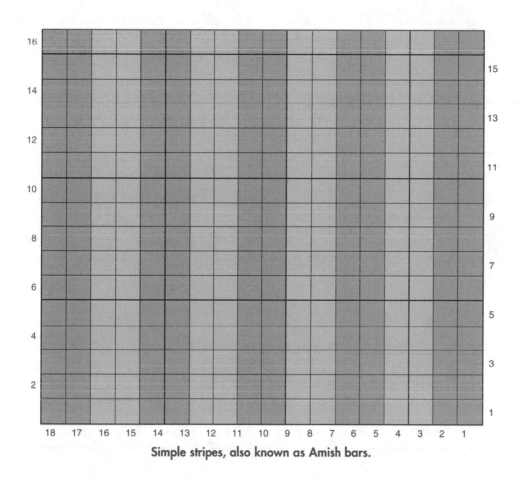

Simple stripes, also known as Amish bars.

1. To make the strips, cast on 20 stitches.
2. Working in garter stitch, knit every row until the piece measures 36".
3. Loosely bind off and weave in the ends.
4. Make 5 strips of color A and 4 strips of color B.
5. To finish, sew a strip of color A to one of color B, right sides together.
6. Continue to sew alternating strips together, being sure to keep one side as the right side, until 9 strips have been assembled, as in the diagram.
7. Weave in all ends.

If you'd like, you can crochet a border around the edges to finish the throw.

Quick Throw

If you're pressed for time, this may be the way to go: you use 2 strands of worsted weight throughout on size 13 circular needles.

Yarn: Approximately 4 skeins color A, 2 skeins color B, 2 skeins color C, 2 skeins color D, and 2 skeins color E

Needles: Size 13, 30" circular

Yarn needle

Measuring tape

Scissors

Knit Tips _____

Use a row counter and a piece of paper and pen if you need to keep track of what row you're on. You may think you'll remember, but if you're anything like me, once you put down the garment, you'll get complete amnesia. Make notations of where you've increased or decreased, too. Then you won't ever wonder.

1. With color A, cast on 90 stitches.
2. Begin the pattern as follows:

   Row 1: *Knit 15, purl 15*, repeat from * to * across.

Row 2: *Purl 15, knit 15*, repeat from * to * across.

Repeat Rows 1 and 2 for 15 total rows.

Row 16: *Purl 15, knit 15*, repeat from * to * across.

Row 17: *Knit 15, purl 15*, repeat from * to * across.

3. Repeat entire pattern 8 more times, for a total of 9 blocks.
4. Bind off loosely and weave in the ends.
5. With color B, cast on 16 stitches.
6. Work garter stitch until the strip measures 35".

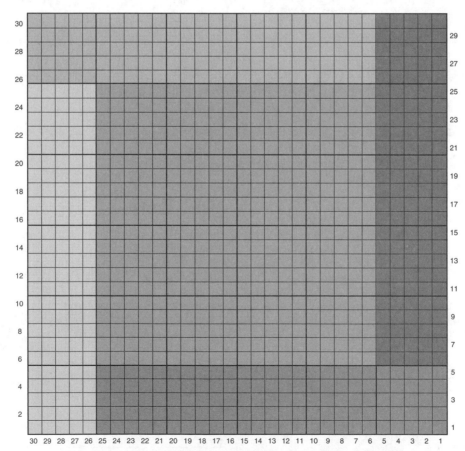

Use clips or pins to hold the pieces in place and then sew together.

7. Bind off loosely and weave in the ends.

8. With color C, cast on 16 stitches.

9. Work garter stitch until the strip measures 35".

10. Bind off loosely and weave in the ends.

11. With color D, cast on 16 stitches.

12. Work garter stitch until the strip measures 38".

13. Bind off loosely and weave in the ends.

14. With color E, cast on 16 stitches.

15. Work garter stitch until the strip measures 38".

16. Bind off loosely and weave in the ends.

17. To assemble, following the diagram, sew the strips right sides together.

Nine Patch Throw

This simple design lends itself well to travel, if you have to commute to work or want something to work on during your lunch break.

> *Yarn:* Approximately 4 skeins worsted weight yarn in color A, 4 skeins color B, and 5 skeins color C
>
> *Needles:* Size 7 or to obtain gauge
>
> *Gauge:* 5 stitches per inch on size
>
> Yarn needle
>
> Measuring tape
>
> Scissors

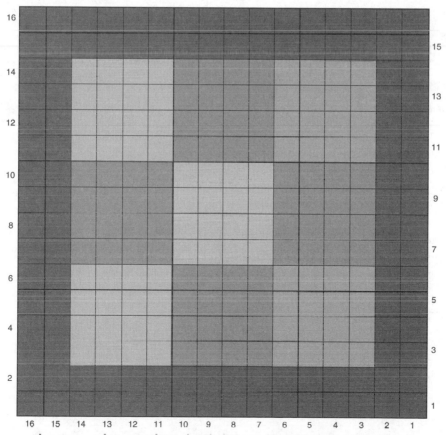

The nine patch is a traditional quilt design adapted here for the knitter.

1. For the throw, cast on 50 stitches.
2. Knit in garter stitch until the piece measures 10"×10".
3. Bind off loosely.
4. Make 5 squares of color A and 4 squares of color B.
5. Begin by sewing two squares together, right sides together, as in the diagram.
6. Sew all 9 squares together, as in the diagram.
7. For the border, cast on 25 stitches in color C.
8. Work in garter stitch until the piece measures 30". Repeat for a second strip.
9. Make 2 more strips 50" long.
10. With right sides together, sew the 30" strips to the top and bottom of the throw.
11. With right sides together, sew the 50" strips to the sides.
12. Weave in all ends.

Nine Patch Sampler

This is a good opportunity to practice different stitches. You can mix and match 2 or 3, or use 9 different stitches from the book. You might choose basketweave stitch for one block, raspberry stitch for another, seed stitch for another, and so on. Or you can take any of the duplicate stitch designs and use them against a stockinette background. If you get confused or need help with assembly, refer to the preceding figure.

Knit Tips

All those swatches will come in handy one day. Keep your sample swatches in a binder so you can refer to them in the future. A notebook is also a good place to keep the labels from the yarn you've used. At some point in your knitting career, you'll have made so many sample swatches, you can sew them together to make a throw.

Amish Bars

Amish Bars is a quilt pattern that lends itself well to a knitted throw. Traditional colors are bright, saturated jewel tones, such as amethyst, emerald, ruby, and sapphire, but choose whatever colors please you most. This is another throw knit in sections, so it's portable if you need a project to pass the time waiting in the doctor's office or at the airport.

> *Yarn:* Approximately 4 skeins of worsted weight yarn in color A, 3 skeins of color B, 4 skeins of color C, and 3 skeins of color D
>
> *Needles:* Size 7, or to obtain gauge
>
> *Gauge:* 5 stitches per inch on size
>
> *Time to complete:* Approximately 75 hours
>
> Yarn needle
>
> Measuring tape
>
> Scissors

Here are the bars and blocks you need to assemble this throw:

Color A:

2 strips 4" wide, 24" long

2 strips 6" wide, 24" long

Color B:

3 strips 4" wide, 24" long

4 squares 4"×4"

Color C:

2 strips 4" wide, 24" long

2 strips 4" wide, 32" long

Color D:

2 strips 4" wide, 32" long

4 squares 4"×4"

1. With color A, cast on 20 stitches and work in garter stitch until the piece measures 24".

2. Bind off loosely.

3. Make 2.

4. Cast on 30 stitches and work in garter stitch until the piece measures 24".

5. Bind off loosely.

6. Make 2.

7. With color B, cast on 20 stitches and work in garter stitch until the piece measures 24".

8. Bind off loosely.

9. Make 3.

10. Cast on 20 stitches and work in garter stitch until the piece measures 4".

11. Bind off loosely.

12. Make 4.

13. With color C, cast on 20 stitches and work in garter stitch until the piece measures 24".

14. Bind off loosely.

15. Make 2.

16. Cast on 20 stitches and work in garter stitch until the piece measures 32".

17. Bind off loosely.

18. Make 2.

19. With color D, cast on 20 stitches and work in garter stitch until the piece measures 32".

20. Bind off loosely.

21. Make 2.

22. Cast on 20 stitches and work in garter stitch until the piece measures 4".

23. Bind off loosely.

24. Make 2.

25. To assemble, following the diagram, pin or clip, sew the strips right sides together.

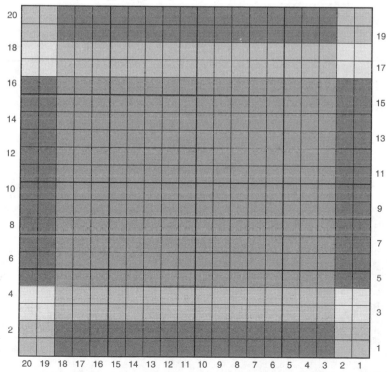

Working from the middle outward is best. Pin or clip the pieces in place and then sew.

In This Chapter

◆ Rest your head on a fun Moose Pillow

◆ Not in the mood for moose? Try some fun variations: a Nine Patch Pillow, a Sunflower Pillow, a
Ribbon Pillow, and more

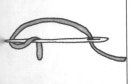 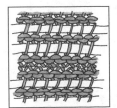    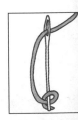

Chapter 22

Decorative Pillows

Decorative pillows are a quick and simple project, easily within the range of all knitters. Two pieces of knit fabric cover a pillow form—how hard is that? Of course, you can keep it very simple or make it more complicated with stitches or decoration.

Cheaper than repainting and much less muss and fuss than wallpaper, a pillow—or several—is a way to brighten a room in next to no time. Whether you want to complement the room's existing colors, contrast them, or both, it's all up to you. Go bold or go subtle. If it doesn't work as you intended, you can always give the pillow away!

What You Need and Need to Know

There's no reason to go to a store and buy a pricey decorator pillow when it's easy to make one for yourself just the way you want it. Texture, color, and size are all at your creative fancy. In this chapter, I give you but a few suggestions to get you started.

You need a pillow form. These are available in a range of sizes at craft stores and fabric stores, mostly priced under $10, so you can splurge on your yarn choice. Whatever the size of the pillow form, you need to make the cover approximately 2" larger to accommodate the roundness, as the insert isn't flat.

Materials to complete all projects:

Yarn: 2 skeins dark green worsted weight yarn; 1 skein brown worsted weight wool; 2 skeins recycled Himalayan silk; approximately 8 ounces worsted weight yarn in assorted colors for decorations; 2 or more skeins ribbon yarn, depending on size of skein; and red, white, and blue worsted weight yarn (See individual patterns for specific information.)

Needles: Size 7 straight or to obtain gauge

Novelty star buttons

Pillow form(s)

Fiberfill

Yellow felt

Small brown pom-poms

Bead(s)

Fabric glue

Yarn needle

Measuring tape

Thread or fine yarn

Scissors

Stitches used in this chapter:

Garter stitch

Stockinette stitch

Moss stitch

Duplicate stitch

Double wrap drop stitch

Adirondack Moose Pillow

This pillow would be good for a weekend retreat in the mountains or a den in the city.

A moose pillow is the perfect accompaniment for a wooden Adirondack chair.

Size: 14"×14"

Yarn: Cascade Yarns' Superwash 220 worsted weight, 2 skeins dark green and 1 skein brown

Needles: Size 7 straight or to obtain gauge

Gauge: 5 stitches per inch

Time to complete: 8 to 10 hours

Bead or small button for eye

Needle

Thread

Yarn needle

Measuring tape

Scissors

1. For the pillow backs, cast on 70 stitches in the dark green yarn.
2. Knit every row until the piece measures 11".
3. Make 2.
4. For the pillow front, cast on 70 stitches in the dark green yarn.
5. Work in stockinette stitch until the piece measures 14".
6. Following the moose chart, center him on the pillow front.
7. Duplicate stitch the moose in brown yarn.
8. Sew the eye in place.
9. To finish, with right sides together, overlap the back sections so they form a square 14"×14".
10. Place the overlapped sections on the pillow front, right sides together, and pin to secure.
11. Sew all four sides together through all thicknesses.
12. Weave in the ends, and turn the pillow right side out through the opening.
13. Insert the pillow form.

Purl Pearls

This type of pillow is called a French pocket. It enables you to remove the form and wash the cover, if necessary.

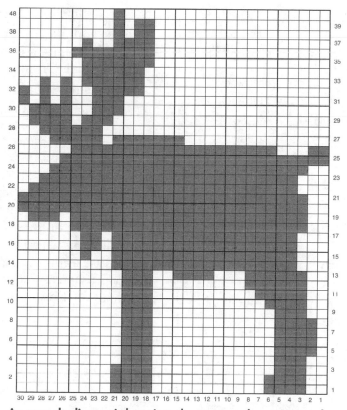

An easy duplicate stitch project, the moose only uses two colors.

Sew It Up Tight

You don't have to make a French pocket so the form can be removed. You can make two squares the same size, sew three seams together, insert the form into the cover, and neatly sew the remaining seam.

Sampler Square

If you'd like to try out a stitch you've never worked before, a pillow is the perfect opportunity. You might also be able to use some of those swatches you made for all your other projects. Simply sew them together into a square. Make a back piece the same size either plain, in a special stitch pattern, or with more swatches.

Nine Patch

One of the most recognizable traditional quilt designs is the nine patch. To make this, use whatever colors please you. If your pillow form is 14", your completed pillow front and back need to measure approximately 16" square each.

1. Make 1 back section 16" square in garter, seed, or moss stitch.
2. Make nine 4" squares in the same stitch you used for the back.
3. Make two strips, each 2" wide and 16" long.
4. Make two strips, each 2" wide and 12" long.
5. Refer to the illustration for placement of the squares and borders.

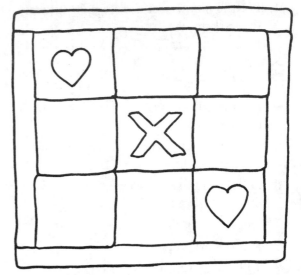

Whether you using jewel tones, bold colors, or muted colors, the traditional nine patch square is always eye-catching.

6. Sew all the pieces together.
7. Place both the front and back right sides together, and sew around three sides through all thicknesses.
8. Turn pillow right side out and insert form.
9. Stitch the opening closed.

Sunflower

This is one of the quickest pillows you've ever make. Using a warm orange background, make a pillow top in a textured stitch. Cut petals from yellow felt using the template provided. Sew these in place as in the illustration. Attach small pom-poms to the center of the sunflower. If you really want to be fast, use fabric glue.

The simple leaf template can be used in many ways.
The sunflower is just one.

Purl Pearls _____

You can find pom-poms and felt at your local fabric or craft store. Both come in a wide range of colors.

Make a back section in either the French pocket or plain styles, and complete as directed in the appropriate instructions.

Silk Road Caravan Pillow

When I first saw this recycled Himalayan silk yarn, I immediately thought it would make a wonderful pillow. Because this yarn is of the thick and thin style and contains so many colors, you don't need to do anything to improve upon it. A simple stockinette or garter stitch lends itself well to making the front and back. The yarn makes such a thick fabric that the plain back is better here.

Make a front and a back 2" larger than your form, sew around the three sides with right sides together, insert your form, and sew the remaining seam closed. Make 4 tassels, 1 for each corner.

Purl Pearls _____

Himalayan silk yarn is made of remnants of silk from the manufacture of silk saris in India.

Ribbon Pillow

This pillow can be as complicated or as simple as you would like to make it. You could knit with yellow and use blue ribbon for a pillow on a sun porch. Or try using several colors, giving the pillow an almost plaid effect by using a chain stitch finish, going in a crosswise direction across the top.

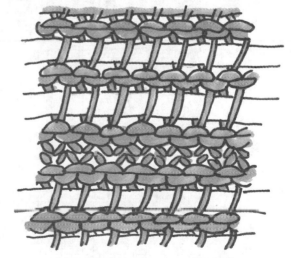

Weave the ribbon between the stitches.

Size: Your choice

Yarn: 1 skein worsted weight yarn of your choice

Needles: To correspond to yarn label

Gauge: As stated for yarn

Time to complete: 6 to 10 hours

Ribbons or ribbon tape yarn

Yarn needle

Measuring tape

Scissors

3. Fasten securely at each end.
4. Sew the back and front together as directed in previous instructions.

Patriotic Pillow

Knit a rectangle of dark blue and stripes of red and white. Position them as in the illustration. Sew star buttons onto the blue field.

1. Using double wrap drop stitch, make a pillow top to correspond to the size form you have.
2. Weave the ribbon or ribbon yarn over and under the double wrap drop stitches.

Knit Tips _____

Because pillow forms come in a limited number of sizes and shapes, you might want a pillow that's smaller or a different shape. You can use a polyester fiberfill to stuff the pillow, but make certain your stitches are quite close and firm so the filling won't work through.

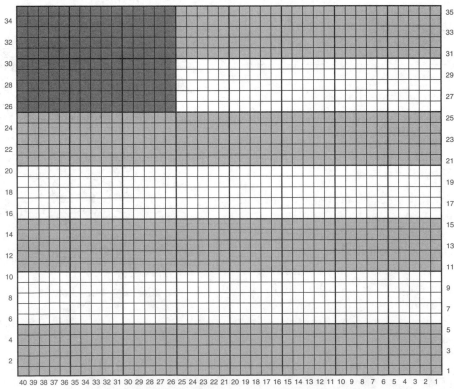

You can enlarge the flag if necessary; just maintain the same ratios.

Triangle Pillow

This is a one-piece pillow; the shaping coming simply from folding a square into a triangle. A textured stitch will be more substantial and add visual appeal to the unexpected shape. Depending on the size of the pillow, you might be able to make this with 1 skein of yarn, so you could splurge and get an interesting or luxurious fiber.

1. Using a firm stitch pattern such as a moss or seed stitch; and knit a square or stripes, or keep it plain, changing yarns or not.

2. Bind off loosely.

3. Fold in half diagonally into a triangle with right sides together.

4. Sew the edges together, leaving an opening for the stuffing.

5. Stuff the pillow with fiberfill.

6. Stitch the opening closed.

7. Add tassels to the corners, if you'd like.

In This Chapter

◆ Surround yourself with sweet-smelling sachets

◆ Get fruity with an Apple Sachet, Orange Sachet, and Strawberry Sachet

◆ Learn about essential oils

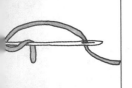
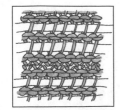

Chapter 23

Scent-uous Sachets

Sachets can be very simple, or they can be more complicated. Among the projects that follow will be one you can handle, whether you're a novice knitter or more accomplished. Plus, sachets require very little yarn, so more than likely, you have plenty of leftover yarn in your stash to complete one.

If you need a quick present, a sachet is something you can make easily in an afternoon or an evening while watching television. A grab bag gift, a memento for someone in the office, or a present for a teacher—you can hardly go wrong with a small sachet. Whereas you might get the size of a garment or someone's favorite color wrong, nearly everyone will pop a sachet into their lingerie drawer or linen closet. Each time the drawer is opened, the scent will remind the recipient of you.

A scented strawberry sachet can brighten a closet or lingerie drawer and makes a wonderful little gift.

What You Need and Need to Know

So many yarn choices exist. You can use a solid color or a variegated one. You could use a textured yarn for an interesting effect. Feel free to experiment with yarn and stitches. This isn't a big investment in time or yarn.

Materials to complete all projects:

Yarns: Worsted weight yarn in a variety of colors, wool or cotton or blends; use your scrap yarn

Needles: Sizes 7 and 9 circular or straight

Yarn needle

Seed beads

Green felt

Lavender buds (1 ounce)

Juniper berries (1 ounce)

Potpourri

Fiberfill

Fragrance oils

Measuring tape

Thread or fine yarn

Scissors

Stitches and techniques used in this chapter:

Garter stitch

Stockinette stitch

Felting

Basic Mitered Square Sleep Sachet

These sleep sachets are ridiculously overpriced at the boutique shops in the mall, and you can create them for next to nothing. You'll probably need to make a quick trip to your local health-food store or garden emporium for dried lavender blossoms and juniper berries.

> *Yarn:* 1 ounce purple or lavender solid or hand-dyed yarn
>
> *Needles:* Size 7 (Try using short bamboo needles for a small project like this.)
>
> *Time to complete:* 4 to 6 hours
>
> Yarn needle
>
> Measuring tape
>
> Scissors

1. Cast on 26 stitches.
2. Knit across the row, placing a marker between the 2 center stitches. (This is a wrong-side row.)
3. *On every right-side row:* Knit to within 2 stitches of the marker, knit 2 stitches together, slip marker, slip 2 stitches one at a time and then knit them purl wise, and knit to the end of the row.
4. *Wrong side rows:* Knit.
5. Continue as established until 2 stitches remain.
6. Knit 2 stitches together.
7. Break off the yarn.
8. Weave in the ends.
9. Make 2.
10. To assemble the sachet, sew 3 sides of the squares, right sides together.
11. Turn right side out and, using the tip of a knitting needle, press the corners out, if necessary. Try to keep the sachet as square as possible.
12. Fill with a mixture of lavender and juniper berries.
13. Carefully sew the opening closed.

You can place this under your pillow, and just before you go to sleep, give it a little squeeze to release some of the fragrance. Lavender and juniper are very relaxing, and you should be asleep in no time.

Apple Slice Sachet

Because this sachet requires you knit only one piece, it's a quick project easily completed in an afternoon. It doesn't require much yarn either, so you might have enough left over from another project. Wool is fine, but you may also find that a worsted weight cotton the type used for craft projects will work perfectly well. You'll have enough left over for a potholder, too!

> *Yarn:* 1 ounce Red worsted weight
>
> *Needles:* Size 7 (Try using short bamboo needles for a small project like this.)
>
> *Time to complete:* 4 to 6 hours
>
> Green felt for leaves
>
> Apple spice fragrance oil
>
> Small amount of fiberfill
>
> Yarn needle
>
> Measuring tape
>
> Scissors

1. Cast on 12 stitches.
2. Knit 2 rows.
3. Continue working in garter stitch; increase 1 stitch at the beginning of each row to 24 stitches.
4. Work even for approximately $1\frac{3}{4}$".
5. Begin decreasing 1 stitch at the beginning of each row until there are 12 stitches on the needles.
5. Bind off loosely.
6. Break off yarn.
7. Weave in the ends.
8. To assemble the sachet, with right sides together, fold in half lengthways and sew the edges together, leaving an opening for turning and stuffing.
9. Turn right side out.

10. Fill with scented fiberfill.

11. Stitch the opening closed.

12. Cut 1 or 2 leaf shapes from the green felt.

13. Stitch the leaves to the top of the apple.

Purl Pearls

A fishing tackle box makes a great carrier for your scissors, tape measure, needle gauge, yarn needles, crochet hooks, and whatever else you might need. You can also find large plastic pencil boxes or boxes designed to hold crafting equipment.

Orange Slice Sachet

Citrus is very refreshing in the hot weather. You can carry this with you in your purse or put it on your desk for a quick pick-up during the day—that is, if you don't hide it in with the towels for a sweet orangey surprise when you get out of the shower. Don't forget to use unscented fabric softener!

> *Yarn:* 1 ounce Orange worsted weight
>
> *Needles:* Size 7 (Try using short bamboo needles for a small project like this.)
>
> *Time to complete:* 4 to 6 hours
>
> Orange fragrance oil
>
> Small amount of fiberfill
>
> Yarn needle
>
> Measuring tape
>
> Scissors

1. Cast on 12 stitches.

2. Knit 2 rows.

3. Continue working in garter stitch; increase 1 stitch at the beginning of each row to 24 stitches.

4. Work even for approximately $1\frac{3}{4}$".

5. Begin decreasing 1 stitch at the beginning of each row until there are 12 stitches on the needles.

6. Bind off loosely.

7. Break off the yarn.

8. Weave in the ends.

9. To assemble the sachet, with right sides together, fold in half lengthways and sew the edges together, leaving an opening for turning and stuffing.

10. Turn right side out.

11. Fill with scented fiberfill.

12. Stitch the opening closed.

13. Cut 1 or 2 leaf shapes from the green felt.

14. Stitch the leaves to the top of the apple.

Strawberry Sachet

Monette Satterfield created this delightful little treat to hang in your closet or keep in your drawer. There's no reason why you couldn't put one in the car or anywhere you need a soft scent to create a sweet ambience.

> *Yarn:* Approximately 2 ounces red and 1 ounce green worsted weight
>
> *Needles:* Size 9 (Try using short bamboo needles for a small project like this.)
>
> *Time to complete:* 4 to 6 hours
>
> Seed beads (size 6)
>
> Small amount of fiberfill
>
> Yarn needle
>
> Measuring tape
>
> Scissors

1. Cast on 3 stitches.
2. *Row 1:* Knit.
3. *Row 2* and all wrong-side rows: Purl.
4. *Row 3:* Increase 1 stitch at the beginning and end of the row.
5. *Row 5:* Increase 1 stitch in 1st, 3rd, and 5th stitches.
6. *Rows 7 and 9:* Increase in 1st and every other stitch across.
7. *Row 11:* Increase 1 stitch at the beginning and end of the row.
8. *Rows 13, 15, and 17:* Work even, ending with a wrong-side row.
9. Bind off.
10. Gather top to a 1" opening, and stitch to secure.
11. Stuff firmly.
12. To make the leaves, cast on 20 stitches.
13. *Row 1:* Knit.
14. *Row 2:* *Knit 2, yarn over, knit 1, yarn over, knit 2, repeat from * 4 times.
15. *Row 3:* Knit.
16. *Row 4:* *Knit 3, yarn over, knit 1, yarn over, knit 3, repeat from * 4 times.
17. Bind off.
18. Sew the short ends together.
19. Gather the cast on edge, and pull up to close the opening.
20. To assemble the sachet, sew the leaves to the top of the berry.
21. Sew beads randomly on the berry to represent seeds.
22. Attach a tassel to the bottom of the berry.

Felted Sachet

If you've used wool, you can felt the sachet before filling it. Dunk the knit sections in warm water with a bit of shampoo or mild soap. Agitate firmly and rinse. Repeat these steps until the sachet is the size you want. Squeeze out excess water and roll in a towel. Remove and place on a dry towel and let dry thoroughly.

A Note About Fragrance Oils

You can purchase fragrance oils in craft shops or online. Choose the ones used for soap making instead of those for candle making because they will be less likely to cause a problem if you get some on your skin. The oils come in hundreds of scents, florals, spices, and copycats. Check the resources appendix for more.

In This Chapter

◆ Dress up a basic knitted T-shirt

◆ Get whimsical with some fun T variations

◆ Tips on changing colors

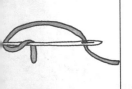
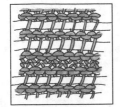

Chapter 24

Suits-You-to-a-T-Shirt

What makes a T-shirt such a great fashion statement? It's as timeless as blue jeans. The guy who comes to fix your sink wears a common white cotton T-shirt, and it's work clothes. When Harrison Ford wears one, suddenly he's on the cover of *People* magazine being touted as the sexiest man in America. From a plain cotton T you pick up at the discount store to a little shirt a supermodel pays hundreds of dollars for, T-shirts—like blue jeans—never go out of style.

You'll find this T-shirt a necessity in your summer wardrobe.

Let's take it up a notch by using a worsted weight cotton instead of trying to duplicate the lightweight jersey we're accustomed to. But don't stop there—you can take it up another couple notches before the day is done.

What You Need and Need to Know

Cotton is a wonderful fiber to work with, but it does shrink over repeated washings and wearings. If you like your T-shirt on the roomy side, consider making the next size up.

> **Knit Tips** _____
>
> Purchase enough yarn to complete your project. If you have a full skein left over and you don't want to keep it, most yarn shops accept returns.

Materials needed to complete all projects:

Yarn: 1,000 to 1,275 yards worsted weight cotton

Needles: Sizes 5 and 7, straight or circular or to obtain gauge, and either double points or a circular needle in the smaller size

Gauge: 5 stitches per inch

Time to complete: 15 to 20 hours

Long pins

Yarn needle

Tape measure

Scissors

Stitches used in this chapter:

Stockinette stitch

Knit 1, purl 1 ribbing

Basic T

A T-shirt is a blank canvas. There are so many directions you can go in, don't restrict yourself!

Small T

Yarn: 1,000 yards worsted weight cotton

Needles: Size 5 and 7, straight or circular or to obtain gauge and either double points or circular in the smaller size.

Gauge: 5 stitches per inch

Time to complete: 15 to 20 hours

Knots!

Cotton is often handled quite differently from wool. Check the yarn label for washing and drying directions. Some cottons need to be machine dried or become hopelessly out of shape.

1. For the back, cast on 102 stitches using the smaller needles.

2. Work knit 1, purl 1 for 1".

3. Switch to larger needles, and work even stockinette until the piece measures 15". Bind off 5 stitches at the beginning of the next 2 rows.

4. Work even until the piece measures 24½" at 142 rows.

5. Bind off 30 shoulder stitches. Bind off 32 neck stitches. Bind off 30 shoulder stitches.

6. For the front, work as for the back, including all shaping.

7. When the piece measures 21½" begin neck shaping.

8. Work to center 16 stitches, attach another ball of yarn, bind off center 16 stitches, and complete the row.

9. Work both sides at once.

10. Decrease 1 stitch at each neck edge, every other row 8 times.

11. Work even until piece measures 24½" (Row 142).

12. Work the shoulder as for the back.

13. Turn inside out.

14. Seam each shoulder (30 stitches).

15. To finish the neck, using smaller circular or double point needles, pick up 90 stitches around the neck edge. Increase or decrease as necessary on the first row, to balance the pattern.

16. Work in rib for 1".

17. Bind off loosely.

18. For the sleeves, cast on 96 stitches on ribbing needles.

19. Work same as body rib for 7 rows (1").

20. Switch to larger needles. Work in stockinette stitch until piece measures 6" (Row 30).

21. Loosely bind off.

22. With T-shirt flat, pin the sleeves to the body.

23. Turn inside out.

24. Sew armhole seams.

25. Sew side and sleeve seams.

26. Weave in all ends.

Medium T

Yarn: 1,150 yards worsted weight cotton

Needles: Sizes 5 and 7, or to obtain gauge and either double points or circular in the smaller size

Gauge: 5 stitches per inch

Time to complete: 15 to 20 hours

1. For the back, cast on 112 stitches on smaller needles.

2. Work knit 1, purl 1 for 1".

3. Switch to larger needles. Work even stockinette until piece measures 15½". Bind off 7 stitches at the beginning of the next 2 rows.

4. Work even until the piece measures 26".

5. Bind off 31 shoulder stitches. Bind off 36 neck stitches. Bind off 31 shoulder stitches.

6. For the front, work as for the back, including all shaping,

7. When the piece measures 23" (Row 110), begin shaping the neck.

8. Work to center 18 stitches, attach another ball of yarn, bind off center 18 stitches, and complete the row.

9. Work both sides at once.

10. Decrease 1 stitch at each neck edge, every other row 9 times.

11. Work even until the piece measures 26" (Row 126).

12. Work the shoulder as for the back.

13. Turn inside out.

14. Seam each shoulder.

15. To finish the neck, using smaller circular needles or double points, pick up 96 stitches around the neck edge. Increase or decrease as necessary on the first row to balance the pattern.

16. Work in rib for 1".

17. Bind off loosely.

18. For the sleeves, cast on 106 stitches on smaller needles.

19. Work same as body rib for 7 rows (1").

20. Switch to larger needles. Work in stockinette st until the piece measures 6" (Row 30).

21. Loosely bind off.

22. With the T-shirt flat, pin the sleeves to the body.

23. Turn the T-shirt inside out.

24. Sew the armhole seams.

25. Sew the side and sleeve seams.

26. Weave in all the ends.

Large T

> *Yarn:* 1,275 yards worsted weight cotton
>
> *Needles:* Sizes 5 and 7, or to obtain gauge and either double points or circular in the smaller size
>
> *Gauge:* 5 stitches per inch
>
> *Time to complete:* 15 to 20 hours

1. For the back, cast on 122 stitches on ribbing needles.

2. Work knit 1, purl 1 for 1".

3. Switch to larger needles. Work even stockinette until the piece measures 16" (Row 84). Bind off 7 stitches at the beginning of the next 2 rows.

4. Work even until the piece measures 27" (Row 130).

5. Bind off 35 shoulder stitches. Bind off 38 neck stitches. Bind off 35 shoulder stitches.

6. For the front, work as for the back, including all shaping,

7. When the piece measures 23½" (Row 112), begin shaping the neck.

8. Work to center 20 stitches, attach another ball of yarn, bind off center 20 stitches, and complete the row.

9. Work both sides at once.

10. Decrease 1 stitch at each neck edge, every other row 9 times.

11. Work even until the piece measures 27" (Row 130).

12. Work the shoulder as for the back.

13. Turn inside out.

14. Seam each shoulder (42 stitches).

15. To finish the neck, on smaller circular needles, pick up 104 stitches around the neck edge. Increase or decrease as necessary on the first row, to balance the pattern.

16. Work in rib for 1".

17. Bind off loosely.

18. For the sleeves, cast on 110 stitches on ribbing needles.

19. Work same as body rib for 7 rows (1").

20. Switch to larger needles. Work in stockinette stitch until piece measures 6" (Row 30).

21. Loosely bind off.

22. With the T-shirt flat, the pin sleeves to body.

23. Turn inside out.

24. Sew armhole seams.

25. Sew side and sleeve seams.

26. Weave in all ends.

Whimsical T

Here's where you can add on whatever you'd like to make this T-shirt your own. Colorful beads or novelty buttons are easy to sew. If you had a dark blue T-shirt and you sewed gold or silver beads randomly above the armhole, it would appear to be the night sky.

Throughout this book, I've given you a number of patterns you can use for duplicate stitch. Use the apple graph here for a country style. Maybe you want to do several along the bottom edge, both front and back. Maybe you want to make just one apple or several, it's up to you.

School Tees

Do you have school spirit? Maybe you'd like to knit a striped T-shirt in your school colors. Buy half the requirement in one color and half in

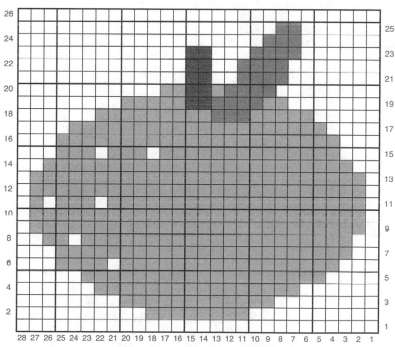

A bright red apple on a white sweater is a striking contrast. Choose your own favorite colors to suit your tastes.

the other. Knit 10 rows of color A and 10 rows of color B, remaining in the pattern and changing colors when needed.

Business T

Unless you work in a very unusual office, you'll probably want a design that attests to your professionalism, in that it's attractive but not overstated. A cream color goes with everything. To dress it up, you might find an attractive art glass button to sew on the neckline, as if it were a pendant. If you intend to wear this T-shirt with a jacket, you might make the body of the shirt in a contrasting color and the crew neck in the same color as the jacket.

Evening on the Town T

Who says a T-shirt isn't evening wear? You can choose a solid color and, to add sparkle, use a metallic carry-along fiber that won't change the gauge.

Knit Tips

Remember, if you're buying a carry-along yarn, check the yardage requirements and buy enough to finish your shirt.

A dark blue yarn with a silver carry along would be fantastic. I'd try to find a sparkly star pin or extravagant fashion button to attach to the shoulder, if needed, for the evening.

Purple and gold are always eye-catching, but nothing prevents you from teaming purple yarn with a scarlet carry along. This is your decision to make!

If you're going clubbing, you probably want to go as wild as the music. If you're going to a sophisticated restaurant, white and gold will probably achieve the results you want.

Weekend Away T

To wear on a weekend escape, I would want to make something light, something that reminded me of standing on the beach with the sun and the sand and the ocean breeze. I'd use the colors of summer, lemonade, berries, and blue sky.

A Note on Changing Colors

When changing colors, do not tie your yarn together. Instead, simply lay the new yarn against the old, knit several stitches, drop the old color, and continue on with the new, as shown in the following figures.

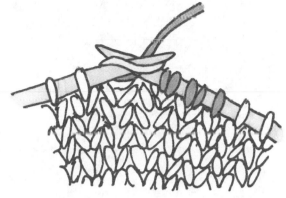

Then go back and weave in the ends so no bumps are visible from the outside.

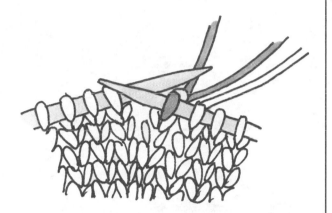

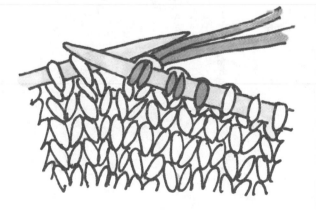

Resources

You will be able to find many fine retailers of fibers and supplies both in the real world as well as online. If you're new to knitting, visiting your local yarn shop (*LYS*, as it's known in the blogosphere) can be a learning experience. Most shop owners are all too pleased to pass on knowledge and will happily show you techniques or help you purchase the correct yarn for a certain project. When you have more confidence, surfing the Net for the myriad choices available can awaken the sleeping fiber artist in you.

Here is a small sampling of sites and businesses to get your adventure started.

Artyarns
www.artyarns.com
Space-dyed merino and silk ribbon yarns. Available in stores.

Cascade Yarns
www.cascadeyarns.com
An extensive range of worsted weight and novelty yarns. Available in stores.

KnitPicks
1-800-574-1323
www.knitpicks.com
Imported yarns at wholesale prices. Call for catalog or go online.

Jimmy Beans Wool
5000 Smithridge Drive, #A11
Reno, NV 89502
1-877-532-3891
www.jimmybeanswool.com
Yarns and accessories with a smile.

Malabrigo Yarn
www.handpaintedyarns.com
Kettle-dyed handspun merino direct from
Uruguay. Available online and in stores.

Patternworks
Route 2, PO Box 1618
Center Harbor, NH 03226-1618
1-800-438-5464
www.patternworks.com
Needles, yarns, and more. Available online and
at their retail location.

PRO Chemical
PO Box 14
Somerset, MA 02726
1-800-228-9393
www.prochemical.com
Many choices of dyes, if you want to experiment
with dyeing your fiber.

Sweetcakes Fragrance Oils
www.sweetcakes.com
Sweetcakes carries an extensive offering of fragrance oils appropriate for soap making, candle
making, beauty products, and potpourri.

WEBS
www.yarn.com
Skein and cone yarn at discount prices. Online
and at their retail location.

Wool2Dye4
www.wool2dye4.com
Dye it yourself, with many fine choices in
weights and fibers below retail cost.

Wool Works
www.woolworks.org
This is a not-for-profit site with amazing
amounts of information regarding knitting and
fibers. There's also a listing of yarn shops by
state which is updated periodically.

Yarndex
www.yarndex.com
A wonderful database of yarns, with plenty of
information.

Index